TRANSFORMING TEACHER EDUCATION

TRANSFORMING TEACHER EDUCATION

What Went Wrong With Teacher Training, and How We Can Fix It

Edited by Valerie Hill-Jackson and Chance W. Lewis

Foreword by Peter McLaren

STERLING, VIRGINIA

Sty/us

Published by Stylus Publishing, LLC
22883 Quicksilver Drive
Sterling, Virginia 20166-2102

Library of Congress Cataloging-in-Publication Data
Transforming teacher education: What went wrong with
teacher training, and how we can fix it / edited by Valerie
Hill-Jackson and Chance Lewis ; foreword by Peter
McLaren.
    p.   cm.
Includes bibliographical references and index.
ISBN 978-1-57922-436-3 (cloth : alk. paper)
ISBN 978-1-57922-437-0 (pbk. : alk. paper)
 1. Teachers—Training of—United States.   2. Educational
change—United States.   I. Hill-Jackson, Valerie, date-
II. Lewis, Chance W. (Chance Wayne), [date-]
LB1715.T6745   2010
370.71′1—dc22   2010005860

13-digit ISBN: 978-1-57922-436-3 (cloth)
13-digit ISBN: 978-1-57922-437-0 (paper)

Bulk Purchases

Quantity discounts are available for use in workshops
and for staff development. Call 1-800-232-0223

First Edition, 2010

10 9 8 7 6 5 4 3 2 1

*Because educational equity for all of America's children
remains one of the last unresolved Civil Rights issues,
this book is dedicated to those
whose voice should matter most in teacher education:
teachers and students in dispossessed school districts.
Hold on—we can see transformation on the horizon.*

CONTENTS

PART THREE: ACCOUNTABILITY AND EVALUATION

PART FOUR: TRANSFORMING TEACHER EDUCATION

ACKNOWLEDGMENTS

Unconsciously, I began co-editing this book as a novice and naïve middle school science teacher in Camden City, New Jersey, at the dawn of the 21st century. Unlearned, I recognized "something was profoundly flawed" in the field of teacher education in general, and in my school district in particular. What was worse, on some level, my students who sought an education in third-world conditions knew it too. Several years later, some of the best minds in education have assembled to help me articulate that "something" for America. So, to the children of Camden, I thank you for the daily, haunting reminders that you need and deserve dynamic teachers and schools.

I am appreciative of the contributors' time, energy, and scholarly talents in this volume. Your work leaves an indelible mark on teacher education and my newly constructed ideas on mentoring and collegiality. We all stand united in the common mission to advance the field—for the educator and the educated.

To the future teachers of America's children I am grateful for the many of you who will go into the classroom for 180 school bells a year and give your all. I hope you comprehend that teacher work stands between full democracy and oppression, self-actualization and self-pity, as well as life and death. You are my sisters and brothers in this fight for full parity for every student.

And to my husband Bowen, an unwavering supporter of my craft—I know you share my commitment for helping underserved learners. I am proud to call your love and encouragement my greatest earthly gifts.

—VALERIE HILL-JACKSON

First, I would like to thank my Lord and Savior Jesus Christ. I want to thank You for the opportunity to co-edit this much-needed book and allow me to make a lasting contribution to the field of education. It is only because of You that I can now write/edit books after being told early in my educational journey that writing was not my gift. It is amazing how perceived weaknesses actually have become a strength.

I would also like to thank my wife, Mechael B. Lewis, and my daughters, Myra Nicole Lewis and Sydney Camille Lewis, for allocating the room and space for me to complete this monumental project. It is for each of you that I continue to labor on the educational battlefield so that you may have a brighter future. I love you very much!

Also, I would like to acknowledge my mother, Mrs. Brenda C. Davis, a master educator, who taught me the essential skills needed to become a major contributor to the field of education. Thank you for all of your sacrifices!

Finally, I would like to thank all of my students—past and present—who have allowed me to share a portion of my life with them. It is my hope that you take the seed of greatness that I have planted in you and do great things in your life.

—CHANCE W. LEWIS

FOREWORD

Peter McLaren
University of California, Los Angeles

For decades, teacher education has weathered strategic assaults of reform from both the educational left and the right. Often the moral character of the country is reflected in the nature of the battles over public education and the education of its teachers. Teacher training has pointed to dispossessed children and society as its reasons for stunted growth, while society and families direct their dissatisfaction back on America's teachers. The casual observer would mistakenly diagnose these outlets as the sources of our educational maladies. But the critical observer understands "what went wrong in teacher training" has long roots; teacher education's demise is inextricably tied to the birth and purposes of public education. The continued corporate infiltration of education has negatively affected teacher education, and we are now facing a crisis of educational democracy.

Yet in the wake of our efforts to revitalize the sphere of teacher education, it is important to recognize that teacher education is never static; it is always in the process of changing. The question is, of course, in what direction is it moving? And just as important are the questions of who is suffering and who is benefiting? What is the role of teacher education in the name of democracy, to what end, and in whose interest?

There are two dangerous perspectives on student underachievement that divert our attention away from the collapse of teacher education. The first perspective points to the egregious achievement gap in school outcomes among ethnic groups and social classes. Traditionalists propose that students' failure is the result of their inability to be assimilated into the values of the dominant culture. For them, it is often a question of socialization (knowing the rules and the "right" behavior), symbolic embeddedness into society (respecting one's ascribed "place" in the existing social hierarchy), community (becoming a good citizen), and the family (marriage can be legitimate only if it is between a man and a woman). The dominant culture (especially

xi

those elite denizens from the "ruling class" whose views permeate the commercial media) has long told us that school failure occurs because of a *deficit* of *culture* (i.e., poor people of color don't have enough magazines in their homes and don't take their children regularly to museums). In this view, school failure occurs not because of material or economic inequalities or differences but because of a lack of a fully accepted and moralistic *absolutist* culture (i.e., poor people of color haven't allowed themselves to be "mainstreamed" enough in the United States melting pot).

The second perspective is also a deficit model, but it is a deficit model from the left: The achievement gap is an artifact of a lack of material goods linked to hierarchies of exploitation within capitalist society. The achievement gap in this view is a result of absolute deprivation: Students fail because they are not included in the economy. In other words, they fail because society has permitted poverty to exist. Of course, school failure is not simply a case of *absolute* deprivation (although where you sit in the system of class exploitation has a lot to do with it) but *relative* deprivation. Put less academically, students who are poor have more obstacles to face than do their middle-class and ruling class counterparts, but some students are more successful at overcoming these obstacles than are others. Here we need to include the subjective experience of inequality and unfairness that is related to meritocracy, not merely the poverty index of the neighborhoods into which students are born. Also, we need to consider how the students feel about living in poor neighborhoods and facing more violence than do those students who live in more affluent neighborhoods.

True, we live in a social universe saturated with capitalism and dripping with the logic of consumption. But just as crime is not a result of absolute deprivation but of cultural and social pressures (linked, of course, to the logic of capital) stemming from the heart of capitalist society (pressures to have more than your neighbors, to consume more, and to accumulate more high-status commodities), so too is the academic achievement gap the result of both structural and cultural dimensions of social life (a gap, by the way, that is still pronounced after 20 years of standards-based reform). Clearly, the academic achievement gap is linked to the social division of labor (the children of those who clean the streets are generally less prepared for college after high school than are the children of those who run the corporate executive offices). But this very entangling process is difficult to understand because, well, we aren't *supposed* to understand it. Many progressive educators, including me, have come to view the achievement gap as a crime against humanity that occurs when there is *both cultural inclusion and structural exclusion* (Young, 1999b). African Americans, Asians, and Latinos are now welcomed into the multicultural family known as America, but about the only real equality they find is in the equalitarian propaganda—in other words, the message that there exists real equality in the United States and that it is distributed evenly to the rich and the poor alike.

But the substance of such equality does not exist. When students from various ethnic groups and social classes are told that they are all equal members of our society, when they are invited into the schools and promised that their economic and social rewards will be in proportion to their individual effort, they face a rude awakening when they brush up against a very complex society that structurally excludes all but a few from their neighborhoods (unless they are from an affluent neighborhood, in which case their social class location is one of the best predictors of their impending academic success). In other words, most poor students face a reality check when they realize that they are, to a certain extent, structurally excluded from being able to enjoy the advantages of their more materially and racially advantaged counterparts.

When students feel that the game of school success is rigged from the start, they tune out, sometimes lash out, or are more frequently pushed out (structural constraints include everything from unearned male advantage and conferred dominance to unsafe neighborhoods with gang violence, poverty, lack of study space, disparities in per-pupil expenditures between states and within states due to local tax bases, homelessness, a legal system that privileges the law for privileged people of property, schools with high teacher attrition and low teacher retention rates, decaying buildings and lack of equipment, and the naturalization of White privilege within the dominant culture). Inside the dominant culture of consumption and possessive individualism, an emphasis on social justice initiatives leads many students to ask: Why should I care about making the world a better place when the world doesn't care much about me? If we live in a true meritocracy, why do more than 1 in 100 adults live behind bars? Why is there a greater proportion of African Americans and Latinos behind bars than Whites? Why does the richest 20% of Americans own 84% of the wealth of the country? For those remaining who own 16% of the wealth, what conditions do they live in? Why can't the poor get the same health care as the rich? Why can't they (well, those who are African American) even get rescued from a hurricane?

The average dropout rate in the 50 largest cities in the United States is 58%, with an overrepresentation of Native Americans, Latinos, and African Americans relative to their proportion of the total school-age population (see

Richardson, this volume). Such a response to our educational system is far from unnatural in a world in which everyone is exploited under capitalism and certain groups are differentially disadvantaged within the capitalist system on the basis of race and gender. I don't use the term *socioeconomic status* because such a term naturalizes capitalist exploitation, suggesting that class is merely a matter of "status" within a legitimate system. Class, of course, is a relation of owning, in which those who own the labor of others and make profits from it can be considered the ruling capitalist class, and those who only own their labor-power and sell it for wages, which they pay back to the owners of labor, can be considered the working class (Ebert & Zavarzadeh, 2008). To perpetuate the belief in the rewards of hard work in our so-called meritocratic society as an *ex post facto* cure for a social order that is failing our children through class exploitation is a swindle of belief. If a student is failed by the educational system, he is told by the guardians of the dominant culture that he just hasn't tried hard enough to succeed because hard work has been accorded as the single regulative ideal that will assure him that the fruits of his efforts will be just and fair. I would argue that we need to struggle for an egalitarian society, one that includes students culturally and at the same time creates an inclusive, participatory democracy in which social structures are enabling rather than constraining of personhood, livelihood, and academic achievement.

It's long been the case that education is used as a vehicle primarily to generate and promote the value of capitalist society. This is fine for those who benefit from such a system. But the vast majority of students don't benefit. When we understand why this is the case and why alternatives to the logic of capitalism are not being taught in schools across the country, we are one step closer to knowing what steps need to be taken to transform our schools. As they currently stand, schools have become bulimic: They have been changed into corporations in themselves, dedicated to engorging students, assimilating them into the culture of consumption, and then vomiting them out—some of the students, of course, are in a better position to consume (knowledge, material goods, life itself) than others are (Young, 1999a). Schools are producing students who are less likely to want to create meaningful knowledge and interactions in themselves and more likely to create the kind of knowledge that will help them succeed on standardized tests and to navigate successfully through the system until graduation. Unfortunately, this can lead to a condition that Freire describes as "semi-intransitive consciousness" (a form of "false consciousness" historically conditioned by social structures that do not enable the subject to objectify reality sufficiently enough to know it in a critical way) as students forgo critique and critical self-reflexivity in pursuit of manipulating the system for advantages for themselves in the unequal playing field of neoliberal capitalism. This is accompanied by forms of corporatist, bottom-line or means-ends thinking—a thinking that advances singular advantage as opposed to collective well-being, that offers a means to achieve an individual end and not a collective measure to advance solidarity and moral cohesion around the imperatives of creating a just and equitable society.

It is all about manipulating the rules to maximize individual advantage. This is part of a late-modern sensibility that Zygmunt Bauman (1995) terms *adiaphorization*—"the stripping of human relationships of their moral significance, exempting them from moral evaluation, rendering them 'morally irrelevant'" (p. 133). The underlying message our students are being taught is as follows: If knowledge can't advance students into the world of consumption and pleasure, then it isn't worth engaging. Consequently, students consume facts in the classroom in a way that is severed from understanding how such knowledge is produced.

What occurs in many of our classrooms is the *transmission of information*, not the *production of knowledge*, and still less the *production of meaningful knowledge*. Students often resist those types of knowledge that demand argumentation and critical discussion because they distract them from the kind of means-ends rationality that will get them ahead in the high-stakes testing system, and, similarly, teachers often resist teaching meaningful knowledge because they are pressured to teach to the multiple-choice tests in this self-same predatory world of teaching. This is not to suggest, of course, that students don't resist incorporation via schooling into mainstream society with its specific means of producing normativity and common sense through strict rules of conduct, zero tolerance, and curricula that lack cultural and historical relevance for Latino, African American, and other minority populations. They do resist in many ways the teaching of destructive worldviews and practices. But often their very means of resistance becomes co-opted by larger narratives of inclusion and exclusion linked to the social relations of capitalist production. The inertia embodied in dominant educational priorities and practices produced by blue-chip think tank jockeys, often CEOs of major corporations and appointed by the state to serve on national curriculum committees, glaringly demonstrates a studied amnesia that supports the role capitalism plays in our educational system.

Additionally, among the public-at-large is a mania for testing and standardization, with politicians serving as the most enthusiastic cheerleaders.

National and state agencies fervently promote incongruous policies and practices that have largely been responsible for the "moral panic" surrounding
teacher education and that have changed teachers, for the most part, into
glorified clerks and managers of the empire who are exhorted to engage in
shopworn audio-lingual methodologies that were dominant in the 1950s,
known as "drill and kill," and to participate unwittingly in the creation of
hypersegregated inner-city schools where the proportion of Black students in
majority White schools is in drastic decline. Programs that promote school
integration are declining, as well, in numerous parts of the country (Kozol,
2005). The policies that drive classroom teaching—such as the No Child
Left Behind Act—thoughtful and responsible members of the public under-
standably treat as a vaudeville act or burlesque theater. NCLB is a combination of *Lean on Me, Stand and Deliver, Freedom Writers,* and *Dangerous
Minds* re-scripted by Jim Carrey in his Ace Ventura role and Red Skelton as
Clem Kadiddlehopper, and guest starring the Three Stooges who are forced
to take tests in a mosh pit at a Black Sabbath concert.

To "fix" what's going wrong in education, teachers need to engage in a
critical pedagogy that includes an in-depth critique of structural exclusion.
An historical materialist critique of the dominant knowledges produced in
our schools and workplaces is socially necessary for the abolition of educational capitalism and the creation of a new postcapitalist democracy. Teacher
education faces a Faustian predicament and knowledge of the education
system—even how schools are situated within the larger social totality of
transnational capitalism so as to reproduce labor-power quality—cannot
spare you, the educator, in this complicity. Our potential as teachers to our
students is both empty (waiting to be fulfilled) and infinite (always exceeding
that which can possibly be filled).

How to meet that promise and become better professionals and social
agents of change is the topic of this wonderful new volume, *Transforming
Teacher Education,* edited by Valerie Hill-Jackson and Chance Lewis. The
contributors of this book understand that being a teacher requires a partner-
ship in a living present, an emotional engagement that is the first step toward
commitment to a being-for-the-other in which normatively engendered rules
and routines are bracketed, enabling an openness toward the future unteth-
ered by the de facto penetration of capitalist interests. We need the best
research, theories, and practices to make the kind of changes needed in the
field of teacher education. This volume helps us take a major step in this
direction. Breaking down the barriers to interdistrict integration and reducing residential segregation, strengthening social justice education through

critical pedagogy, developing teacher accountability policies and ways that will make teacher education programs more accountable, improving teacher candidate recruitment and induction, working through the contradictions of high-stakes accountability and teacher quality—all tasks designed to improve the skills of teachers and policymakers and improve the lives of students—are just some of the topics covered in this volume. Teachers, prospective teachers, educational planners, and policymakers will all benefit from engaging this book. Hopefully, they will engage the chapters with open minds and begin to challenge and transform "business as usual" approaches.

References

Bauman, Z. (1995). *Life in fragments.* Oxford: Blackwell.

Ebert, T., & Zavarzadeh, M. (2008). *Class in culture.* Boulder, CO: Paradigm Publishers.

Kozol, J. (2005). *The shame of the nation: The restoration of apartheid schooling in America.* New York: Crown Publishers.

Young, J. (1999a). Cannibalism and bulimia: Patterns of social control in late modernity. *Theoretical Criminology, 3*(4), 387–407.

Young, J. (1999b). *The exclusive society: Social exclusion, crime and difference in late modernity.* London: Sage.

TWO RATIONALES
FOR TRANSFORMING
TEACHER EDUCATION

Valerie Hill-Jackson and Chance W. Lewis

America's K–12 educational system is broken.

There is no need to cite seminal articles, federal reports, or share media sound bites from newly elected President Barack H. Obama or Secretary of Education Arne Duncan. For everyday examples of school failure among all of America's learners, we need only look to our communities, with marginalized groups disproportionately underperforming in many core academic subjects. As researchers, policymakers, educators, and private citizens, we shake our collective head and wonder why our K–12 educational system continues to push an open-ended, automated, misdirected, and destructive change agenda. It has long been established that the most important factor in determining learners' success or failure is well-trained teachers in a coherent educational system (Darling-Hammond, 2006b). Sarason (1993) in *The Case for Change: Rethinking the Preparation of Educators* explains this simple, primary prevention dialectic; identify and nurture great teachers in a dynamic and supportive environment who, in turn, can encourage self-actualized and successful learners.

Knowing this, *How is it possible that the field of teacher education continues to regurgitate the same inert policies and uncontested teacher preparation programs while expecting different results for underserved learners?* This question is more than a rhetorical quip; it forms the impetus for this edited work. *Transforming Teacher Education: What Went Wrong With Teacher Training, and How We Can Fix It* is an argument for the end of inconsequential tweaks and changes in teacher education. Change is easy to garner, but transformation requires courage to lead and must support our most valuable intellectual resource—teachers (Caldwell & Spinks, 2007). The contributors of *Transforming Teacher Education* endorse revolutionary and authentic alterations in the vision, implementation, methods of accountability, and reinvention of teacher education.

Since *A Nation at Risk* (National Commission on Excellence in Education, 1983) admonished America's teaching force for producing ill-prepared students who cannot compete globally, the enterprise of education has been compelled to reevaluate teacher training in America's colleges and universities as a complex and intellectually demanding professional undertaking. *Change-ism*, ineffective and irrelevant systemic reform or educational change for the sake of change, is educational restructuring spawned by frantic, reactionary, and politically charged discussions on teaching. Although the educational change movement ostensibly began after World War II, *A Nation at Risk* "officially" initiated the tweak and change movement and encouraged packaged K–12 curricula, generic large-scale professional development initiatives for teachers, and a shared narrative of success that was numbers centric as opposed to learners centric. It is not by happenstance that textbook publishers and professional teacher consulting agencies experienced a surge in district-level partnerships (Marshall, Sears, Allen, Roberts, & Schubert, 2007). As the late 1980s and 1990s approached, America's political and educational leaders cemented the course for systemic reform with national legislation that included Goals 2000, reauthorization of the Elementary and Secondary Education Act (Improving America's Schools Act), and the Schools to Work Opportunity Act. Many questioned what level of capacity building, if any, was accruing for teachers (Floden, Goertz, & O'Day, 1995).

By the late 1990s, the change pendulum, still driven by laissez-faire systemic reform and a new research movement in teaching (Cochran-Smith & Lytle, 1999), received formidable push backs from those who repeatedly questioned the ubiquitous assumptions and hegemonic model of teacher education. During this time, persistent researchers and practitioners shared a counterapproach to teacher education. Researchers critically investigated the knowledge base and thinking processes of teaching. Conceptual seeds of collaboration, social justice, reflection, culture, voice, context, and inquiry—once thrown to the wind—began to germinate in teacher education. This new generation of scholars and teacher educators, deeply committed to understanding inequities in education, was firmly established. Their efforts were inspired by postmodern ideas, formulated decades before and reinvigorated by the civil rights movement; but these champions of transformation heralded a drowning campaign. A critical engagement to empower teachers and students was never fully sought in public school reforms (Anyon, 2005); instead, they were silenced by the reverberating effects of the structuralist urgency created by *A Nation at Risk* (National Commission on Excellence in Education, 1983). Undaunted, many transformative minds continue to press on against the one-size-fits-all change agenda that was largely framed and enacted in an oppressive accountability-quantitative milieu.

Public Law 107–110, commonly known as the No Child Left Behind Act of 2001 (NCLB), represents the latest wellspring of reform in the 21st century—the prevailing force in the change agenda (No Child Left Behind Act of 2001, 2002). Directed research efforts of NCLB for teacher education try to provide direction and guidance on how educational institutions might work together to develop higher standards and expectations in the art of pedagogy. Some new teacher education propositions seem helpful (Darling-Hammond, 2006a). But most plans are citing clinical investigations and research shrouded in highly lauded literature reviews following an "aim, fire, fire" edict as opposed to an effective and well-articulated "ready, aim, fire" plan. Pseudo innovation is exploding in areas of school choice (Woods, Bagley, & Glatter, 1998) and for teacher training programs, which are nonreplicable and benefitting a select few (U.S. Department of Education, 2004). These proposals, upon closer scrutiny, offer more pre and post *A Nation at Risk* models, merely reformulated in 21st-century jargon, consequently securing the fruitless change agenda in teacher education.

Fascia alterations made in teacher education and training over the last two and a half decades have only goaded teachers of worth to leave the field while new generations are forgoing the profession altogether. Haberman (2005) identifies several causes for the shortage of quality educators, which include lack of lifelong career satisfaction, high number of teacher graduates who don't take teaching jobs, beginners who take jobs in urban schools but fail or leave, shortage of special education teachers, greater number of entry-level opportunities outside of teaching, and increased opportunities for persons of color outside of education (pp. 3–5). Moreover, the field of education has historically blamed families and students from underserved communities for school failure but now must accept culpability as a result of glaring teacher gap issues (Haycock, Lankford, & Olson, 2004) because unprepared and underprepared pre- and in-service teachers are not receiving the proper education and training to support the needs of our diverse learners in an evolving society (Lu, Shen, & Poppink, 2007).

These challenges caused by the *change-ism* phenomenon are exemplars of the bifurcated and damaged schema in teacher education, which has developed on two planes: The district and local levels compete with state and federal reform directives. At the local or micro level, teaching becomes actualized and entire school districts are confronted with: (a) unintelligible selection mechanisms for quality teachers, (b) ineffective recruiting of quality teachers and quality minority teachers, (c) inadequate teacher induction, (d) pitiable mentoring, (e) haphazard professional development experiences, and (f) poor retention rates. On the macro level, sweeping state and federal policy efforts, such as NCLB, are overly concerned with testing mandates that miss the mark for increasing student achievement in underserved communities and are mismatched to teacher preparedness and learners' needs.

This introduction to *Transforming Teacher Education* is not an exegesis on the ineffectiveness of NCLB; that argument has already been substantiated (Apple, 2007; Meier & Wood, 2004; Selwyn, 2007). A broader analysis adds that NCLB fails to: (a) provide a vision for valuing teachers' work and professionalism, (b) create a coordinated intra- and interstate system for quality, (c) submit an accountability system that can be adjusted to address specialized district needs to meet the contextual challenges at the local level, and (d) offer a serviceable education plan to equip teachers properly. The outcome is a schizophrenic teacher education model in which the interests of teachers and learners at the local level are forced to vie with uncoordinated and disconnected national policy mandates.

To address these concerns, each chapter in this volume uses nontraditional, radical, and grounded research sheathed within two schools of thought. First, transformative theory is employed to acknowledge the challenges teacher education faces in responding to marginalized groups who are not experiencing success in schools. Without being named in the chapters that follow, transformative theory takes a central and important role in this book and is used consciously and unconsciously by many of the contributors. With the important purpose of raising consciousness (Cranton, 2005) and rethinking knowledge construction to help people improve themselves and society (Mezirow, 1991), these transformative scholars assume that knowledge is not neutral but is influenced by human interests and that all knowledge reflects the power and social relationships within society. We propose a transformative model of teacher education that can address the tension between the traditional canons of teacher education and a new generation of knowledge that can move the field forward. The second school of thought is connected to the many conventions of critical theory. The development of critical thinking in education is a social critique for moving rhetoric about marginalized educators, learners, and communities to authentic change rooted in their lived realities. Additionally, critical theory is a discourse of possibility (Giroux, 1988) and challenges assimilation of knowledge. For those interested in the answer to the proverbial question "But how do you do it?" this volume offers a practice-driven retort that may lead to legitimate change in teacher education.

There are four sections in this book. As teacher education undergoes incremental and futile shifts, it is time to reflect on the history and philosophy in teacher education (Part I), with the hope of reconceptualizing implementation (Part II) and accountability efforts of teacher education reform (Part III) so that we can move forward productively and creatively to benefit the future of teacher education (Part IV).

Part I emphasizes the history and philosophy of teacher education. In chapter 1, Jennifer Milam chronicles the history of teacher education and explores missed opportunities in the field. Excavating education's past as a critical archaeologist, Milam encourages us to revisit the history of teacher education so that we might unearth new opportunities for advancing the field and chart a brighter future. In chapter 2, Nathalia E. Jaramillo asks us to reflect on ontology and the teaching encounter, proposing a move from "doing" educators to "thinking" artisans.

Part II is a collection of value-added research and ideas on the selection, training, and development of teachers. This part begins with chapter 3, an assertion that the category of teacher dispositions is an overlooked and crucial criterion in assessing 21st-century teachers, an imperative to consider if we are to develop teachers for social justice. Chapter 4 follows suit: F. Blake Tenore, Alfred C. Dunn, Judson C. Laughter, and H. Richard Milner establish a strong need for continued research and originality across the components of selection, recruitment, and induction in teacher education.

Part III focuses on accountability and evaluation and begins in chapter 5 with Martin Haberman offering disturbingly simple, yet genius ideas for holding teacher education accountable—on the university and school district levels. Jennifer King Rice, in chapter 6, reminds us that a qualified teacher does not equate to a quality teacher. Kris Sloan closes this section with chapter 7, which illustrates that teacher education programs are not adequately preparing pre-service teachers for the realities and rigors, both personally and professionally, of teaching in an era of intensified test-centric accountability and offers an alternate assessment literacy for novice teachers.

In Part IV, we delve deeper into our discourse of possibility with Jeanita W. Richardson (chapter 8) explaining how teachers and administrators are forced to conform their practices to legislation and asking educators to know the "political game," how to play it, and how to become the leaders in a field in which their voice is suppressed. In chapter 9, Linda Darling-Hammond posits that the realm of teacher education already holds the road map to creating effective teacher education programs and outlines the three critical avenues for getting there. The epilogue concludes this volume with a reflection on *the four moments in teacher education*, which include a transformed future.

Written by researchers, philosophers, teacher educators, and policy-thinkers, the chapters in this volume provide new ideological and methodological approaches to teacher preparation. All of the contributions in *Transforming Teacher Education* share a language of critique and advocate changing the very context of the teaching profession (Fullan, 2003). Buttressed by synthesized ideas and recommendations, we jointly try to answer the question, *How is it possible that the field of teacher education continues to regurgitate the same inert policies and uncontested teacher preparation programs while expecting different results for underserved learners?* Toward this end, it is the beneficial education of teachers and the improvement of the life chances of learners in underserved communities which serve as our most salient motivations for transforming teacher education.

References

Anyon, J. (2005). *Radical possibilities: Public policy, urban education, and a new social movement.* New York: Routledge.

Apple, M. (2007). Ideological success, educational failure? On the politics of NCLB. *Journal of Teacher Education, 58*(2), 108–116.

Caldwell, B. J., & Spinks, J. M. (2007). *Raising the stakes: From improvement to transformation in the reform of schools.* New York: Routledge.

Cochran-Smith, M., & Lytle, S. L. (1999). The teacher research movement: A decade later. *Educational Researcher, 28*(7), 15–25.

Cranton, P. (2005). *Understanding and promoting transformative learning.* San Francisco: Jossey-Bass.

Darling-Hammond, L. (2006a). *Powerful teacher education: Lessons from exemplary programs.* New York: Teachers College Record.

Darling-Hammond, L. (2006b). Securing the right to learn: Policy and practice for powerful teaching and learning. *Educational Researcher, 35*(7), 13–24.

Finn, C., Manno, B., & Vanourek, G. (2001). *Charter schools in action: Renewing public education.* New York: Princeton University Press.

Floden, R. E., Goertz, M. E., & O'Day, J. (1995). Capacity building in systemic reform. *Phi Delta Kappan, 77*(1), 19–21.

Fullan, M. (2003). *Change forces with a vengeance.* New York: Routledge.

Giroux, H. A. (1988). *Teachers as intellectuals: Toward a critical pedagogy of learning.* Westport, CT: Bergin & Garvey.

Haberman, M. (2005). *Star teachers: The ideology and best practice of effective teachers of diverse children and youth in poverty.* Houston, TX: Haberman Educational Foundation.

Haycock, K., Lankford, H., & Olson, L. (2004). *The elephant in the living room.* Washington, DC: Brookings Institute Press.

Lu, X., Shen, J., & Poppink, S. (2007). Are teachers highly qualified? A national study of secondary public schools teachers using SASS 1999–2000. *Leadership and Public Policy in Schools, 6*(2), 129–152.

Marshall, J. D., Sears, J. T., Allen, L. A., Roberts, P. A., & Schubert, W. H. (2007). *Turning points in curriculum: A contemporary American memoir* (2nd ed.). Boston: Allyn & Bacon.

Meier, D., & Wood, G. (Eds.). (2004). *Many children left behind: How the NCLB Act is damaging our children and our schools.* Boston: Beacon.

Mezirow, J. (1991). *Transformative dimensions of adult learning.* San Francisco, CA: Jossey-Bass.

National Commission on Excellence in Education. (1983). *A nation at risk: The imperative for educational reform.* Washington, DC: U.S. Department of Education.

No Child Left Behind Act of 2001, PL 107–110, 107th Congress. (2002). Retrieved February 21, 2009, from http://www.ed.gov/policy/elsec/leg/esea02/index.html

Sarason, S. B. (1993). *The case for change: Rethinking the preparation of educators.* San Francisco: Jossey-Bass.

Selwyn, D. (2007). Highly quantified teachers: NCLB and teacher education. *Journal of Teacher Education, 58*(2), 124–137.

U.S. Department of Education. (2004). *Innovation in education: Alternative routes to teacher education.* Washington, DC: Office of Innovation in Education, Author.

Woods, P. A., Bagley, C., & Glatter, R. (1998). *School choice and competition: Markets in the public interest?* New York: Routledge.

PART ONE

HISTORY AND PHILOSOPHY
IN TEACHER EDUCATION

(RE)ENVISIONING TEACHER EDUCATION

A Critical Exploration of Missed Historical Moments and Promising Possibilities

Jennifer Milam

Those who cannot remember the past are con-
demned to repeat it.

Santayana, *Life of Reason*

While they may not work in an established political "war zone," public school teachers should
know that the history of schooling reveals
heated debates over curriculum and over policies that continue to shape our classrooms.

Kincheloe, Slattery, & Steinburg,
Contextualizing Teaching

Teacher education (if it remains at all) must be
reconceived from a skills-identified induction
into the school bureaucracy to the interdisciplinary, theoretical, and autobiographical study of
education experience in which curriculum and
teaching are understood as complicated conversations toward the construction of a democratic public sphere.

Pinar, *What Is Curriculum Theory?*

The inseparable histories of discrimination, ideological jockeying, schooling, and teaching account for the failure of teacher education—past and present. "It becomes apparent," analyzes Bernard (1972), "when one thinks of education not only as pedagogy but as the entire process by which a culture transmits itself across generations" (p. 14). Leaders at the infancy of the American educational system promoted the use of education as a means to sort the classes (Cubberly, 1919), thereby ensuring that schools would become the factories producing humans suitable for society (Cremin, 1961). The public school as an organization was never designed to teach poor and diverse children (Lezotte, 1994) or herald women as engaged professional/educational figures (Spring, 1997).

Hofstadter (1963) notes, "The figure of the school teacher may well be taken as a central symbol in any modern society" (p. 309). However, the identities, purposes, and true nature(s) of teaching, or what it means to be a teacher, are often much more elusive—as have been (and remains) the education and preparation for the profession. The roles and societal prescription of what it means to become and be a teacher have changed as public demands and political agendas have changed throughout history since the very inception of teaching and schooling. Speaking directly of this power and influence, Sarason, Davidson, and Blatt (1986) explain, the "events and conditions outside physical boundaries of the school profoundly affect the processes, goals and quality of education" therein—perhaps, most important, the education of its teachers (pp. 1–2). These conditions and politics, and the policies trickling down, have affected and continue to affect and reflect the multiple routes, pathways, and programs designed to prepare teachers.

In 1962, the first edition of *The Preparation of Teachers* sought to more clearly understand and connect the relevance of teacher training to the day-to-day workings of the teacher in the classroom. Sarason (1962) noted that the importance of such work could be denied by nobody; however, systematic studies of teacher education were rare—it was for them "an unstudied problem in education." Two decades later, Goodlad (1984) warned us that we would quickly arrive at "full-blown" educational maladies in teacher education, by the year 2001, with little clue as to how we got there. He urged us—policymakers, teachers, professors of education, politicians, parents, and community members—to (re)consider how "decisions made and not made will shape the schools of tomorrow" (p. 321). As we marched into the 21st century, debates raged about curriculum and the most effective way to prepare teachers. The American Educational Research Association (AERA)

Panel on Research and Teacher Education produced an exhaustive (and very lengthy) report confirming, once again, that "teachers are among the most, if not the most, significant factors in children's learning and the linchpins in educational reforms of all kinds" and proposed a new research agenda for teacher education (p. 1). Proposal after report, commentary and critique have all set out to define, (re)articulate, and (re)form teacher education and schooling; however, few, if any, studies have taken seriously the historical situation and evolution of teacher education and its relationship to the present—a critically important undertaking if we are to fully grasp and understand the complexities of the educational issues that exist today (Fraser, 2007).

This chapter offers a critical and historical overview of the curricula and programs in teacher education in the United States from the beginnings of public schooling in the early 17th century to present day. Conceived broadly as those programs that "prepare" and "train" teachers, careful attention to various aspects of teacher education that includes the selection of prospective teacher candidates, curriculum and standards (or lack thereof), and overarching purposes of teacher education and schooling in the context of an ever changing, increasingly diverse society is warranted. More important, this chapter shows that the often narrowly defined goals of teacher education and schooling, as well as the significant lack of inclusivity, of all students and citizens with regard to race, culture, faith, and socioeconomic status throughout this nation's history is a problem. Finally, the chapter concludes with several recommendations for transforming our philosophies and ideologies of teacher education so that we can learn the lessons of missed historical moments and realize the promises and possibilities of the future of teacher education.

Let us begin with those we serve.

The American School Student

It is indeed true that the profile of the original American school student looks strikingly different from that of the young people bustling through the corridors of our school buildings today. Schools, first conceived as institutions to socialize and prepare young citizens for participation in the colonial democracy, included catechisms in religious orthodoxy and lessons on service to the public. It was thought that education and schooling might offer protection against dissent and encourage subservience in the new nation.

Whether in grammar schools or petty schools, academies or missionary schools, the message was clear: Learn the Bible, learn English, and learn loyalty and patriotism to the republic. It was not until much later that the school and what happened therein were considered by some as means by which to bring about social change, opportunity, and equality for all.

Among the first students in American schools, few were female and even fewer were racial and ethnic minorities. In fact, it was rare that any young person who was not of European descent, upper-class status, male, and of the Protestant faith had access to any type of formal schooling and education. Young women were "educated" in ways of the home and domesticity (Kincheloe, Slattery, & Steinberg, 2000) and at most were taught to read the Bible. Moreover, any education for non-White people, specifically slaves, Native Americans, and new immigrants, was very often limited to church services on Sundays (Woodson, 1919) or was imparted in "mission schools" that aimed to convert the "heathens" to civilized living (Button & Provenzo, 1989). This trend of limited access to quality public schooling continued for decades, even centuries, and, as some would argue, persists still today.

The most recent data available from the National Center for Educational Statistics (NCES, n.d.) shows that the public school population in the United States is more diverse than ever before in its history. The American public school system currently serves approximately 48.8 million students. Of that, just more than half are White, non-Hispanic students (56.9%). The next largest demographic groups are Hispanic students (18.8%) and African American students (17%). Making up a smaller but still significant part of the school-aged population in the United States are Asian/Pacific Islander students (4.3%) and American Indian/Alaskan Native students (1%). Perhaps now more than ever before in our history it is important to critically (re)consider public education and teacher preparation if we are to (re)conceptualize quality schooling experiences for an increasingly diverse population of students. If we are to (re)envision teacher education, we must do so while holding central to our focus the reality that our students have changed—culturally, linguistically, racially, ethnically, and socioeconomically—and that the teacher education of yesteryear in which our conception of the student was much more narrow (read: White, middle/upper class, and male) is no longer sufficient or appropriate.

A Brief History of American Teacher Education

Although the importance of teachers and their role in student learning has been articulated in both educational research and anecdotal stories of parents

and families of school-aged children, the role and purpose of teacher education are matters of much greater contention (Darling-Hammond, 2006).
More specifically, ideological and philosophical differences with regard to
the types of programs offered, the duration of such programs, the curriculum
promoted therein, and the selection of those deemed qualified to enter and
become certified by such programs have made the venture of teacher education complicated, convoluted, and extremely divergent in its conception(s)
and implementation.

In the most recent and thorough study of American teacher education,
Fraser (2007) explains, as have others (Goodlad, 1990; Sarason et al., 1986),
that teachers and their education have to date been largely understudied. In
his introduction, Fraser further contends that throughout most of the history
of the United States, "teacher preparation was a haphazard affair" (p. 3).
Although many teachers entered classrooms to teach with little or no professional training (and were not required such), programs at normal schools,
teacher institutes, and later colleges and academies began to develop specialized preparation for teachers. The often disorganized and seemingly unfo-
cused nature of development to which Fraser (2007) refers is reflected in the
variety, inconsistency, and inequity with which programs were designed,
implemented, and funded.[1] Using this landmark study of teacher education
as a foundation, this chapter offers a brief glimpse into the historical aspects
of teacher education and comments on what might be seen as missed historical moments to grow teacher education as well as education writ large into a
more democratic enterprise for all citizens.

Schooling in the Colonies (1600–1750)

In the very infancy of what would later be called the "New Nation," the
earliest structures of schooling were strictly regulated and were begun by the
Puritans in early 17th-century New England. In these early educational
efforts, the church and state were inextricably linked and the Puritan ideology guided daily living and sociopolitical agendas. Initially hostile toward
any notion of democracy, these schools were only accessible to "church
members, freemen, and property owners." Notably, voting privileges were
held only by this select population as well. Because in the Puritan ideology
man was created in the image of God, he occupied the top position in the
social hierarchy whereas women remained the property of their family or
husband. Children were subordinate to all adults. Education during this
time held central the home and the church. Teachers within this authoritarian social order were quite typically ministers, parents, or members of the

clergy who were almost exclusively male and focused on teaching students to read the Bible and know God (Kincheloe et al., 2000).

Through attendance at either "petty" or grammar schools, young, upper-class boys were taught reading, writing, and arithmetic, and the goal was explicit: They were to become clergymen and community leaders. The purpose of education was the maintenance of social order and control. In fact, by the mid-17th century, Massachusetts law required that teachers be hired and schools established where there were critical masses of households and people. These schools were to train men to attend the recently established Harvard College (1636), to return to their communities, and, through their leadership, to reify social, political, and religious structures and governance in the church and society.

If young girls were educated at all, they were taught alongside very young boys in "dame schools." Dame schools were structured similarly to what we now call a home daycare setting. Young boys of wealth or stature in the community later attended grammar school; however, it was unlikely that young girls would receive any additional formal schooling beyond their time at the dame school.

Outside of the Bay Colony and beyond the Puritan schooling efforts, children of families of marked affluence were educated typically by tutors secured at the family's expense. Education for the masses was not yet a primary concern for the British colonizers in the "Bible Commonwealth," Virginia, and other settlements. Whether in basic schools with tutors, or in Latin grammar schools, students were taught by teachers with little, if any, formal preparation to be teachers.

Education, or the rudimentary beginnings thereof, in colonial Massachusetts Bay Colony and New England was marked by social and political fragility. A careful balance between enabling literacy and limiting dissent and rebellion was constantly sought. Ironically, this very increase in literacy among the peoples of the early colonies (especially among women, slaves, and new immigrants) that the early schools promoted would unravel the system of education as a form of social regulation—schooling became "a hidden passage in the social control structure" (Kincheloe et al., 2000, p. 119).

A New Nation (1750–1830)

Beginning in the mid-18th century and continuing for almost the next hundred years, schooling and education became increasingly open ventures. Various types and configurations of schooling emerged: grammar schools, academies, petty schools, and common schools. Universities and colleges were also founded between the Revolutionary and Civil Wars. The numbers of children attending school increased as did the diversity of the student population. Although it remained primarily for upper-class, White boys and men, it was becoming common for young girls to gain at least some level of education even if that education occurred in the home or in dame schools. Missionary schools persisted in their goal of assimilating Native Americans and immigrants into the way of life of the New Land. Slaves, however, were educated only inconspicuously, often by women and White children in and around the home.

Teachers teaching in any one of these types of schools could have found their way there in any number of ways. Many young men, graduates of the university and college, took time to teach before ascending to more professional careers in law, ministry, or medicine. During this time, the student population grew, instigating a teacher shortage. Consequently, women who had been educated, or at least taught to read, were called upon to meet this increased need for teachers. Still, it was assumed that any formal apprenticeship or preparation to teach was unnecessary and the most important prerequisite to teach was "far more focused on religious orthodoxy than scholarly or pedagogical skills" (Fraser, 2007, p. 22). Simply, if one wanted to teach, was willing to be paid very little, and would work in less than desirable conditions, one could be a teacher.

Although there were few requirements for teachers, in the early to mid-19th century, there began a movement to encourage academies to address the teacher shortage in a more organized way. Fraser (2007) marks the important beginning in teacher education as when in the 1830s New York's Board of Regents became the first to develop a systematic teacher education program funded by the state that would teach students the "science of common school teaching" (p. 16). Reformers such as Catherine Beecher and Horace Mann viewed teacher preparation as a way to ensure basic standards in every classroom. It would remain true, however, for many, many more years that most teachers had no formal training to do the work of educating the young citizens of the growing nation.

The Early Feminization of Teaching (Circa 1800)

As the school-aged population increased, so too did the demand for schools and teachers. Although most schools continued to educate mostly the elite or upper classes, schools were popping up all over the new nation. Some classes met in churches, others in one-room schoolhouses. Mission schools, charity schools, and the like were accessible to a limited number of non-White children and citizens. The availability and quality of schooling were intimately linked to the availability and quality of teachers and schooling resources—in those communities where resources were available, schools were built, teachers were hired, and students attended. In communities where population, funding, and resources were scarce, educational opportunities lacked. While the public's demand for and perception of the importance of education and schooling grew, the new nation struggled logistically and ideologically to conceptualize public education for all.

As the need for teachers increased, female seminaries began to offer specialized education for women to become teachers in addition to their original aims of preparing democratic mothers and wives. At the call of women leaders such as Catherine Beecher and Emma Hart-Willard, teaching was put forth as an ideal profession for women, especially those with "strong morality . . . and social graces." Mount Holyoke and Troy Female seminaries, and later the Cherokee Female Seminary, were arguably the first professional schools for teachers (Fraser, 2007, pp. 28–29). The curricula in these first teacher education programs did not include a focus on pedagogy or skills of teaching; rather the curriculum was a liberal one that modeled good teaching. It was the first real opportunity for women to obtain a "college-level education" even though the rigor of study was similar to a present-day advanced middle school or high school program of study.

In addition to female seminaries, teacher institutes began to spring up in poor, rural areas. With limited access to such elite schools and a persistent need for teachers in the outstretches of the expanding nation, these institutes offered month-long training sessions that specifically targeted teaching women how to teach in poor schools, to build moral habits of mind, and to instill religious values and traditions in children.

These two ventures in teacher education, female seminaries and teacher institutes, led to the feminization of the teaching force. By 1870, more than half of the nation's teachers were women—in stark contrast to what was previously a male-dominated field for nearly 200 years. Teachers were largely middle class, European and Protestant, though a few exceptions did exist in the free communities in the north where a small number of African American teachers taught. Catholics and poorer women also made up a relatively small number of teachers.

Fraser (2007) explains candidly that during these formative years of teacher education and the humble beginnings of public schooling, a troubling compromise was made: Women's participation in society was limited, but they were allowed complete control of the domestic sphere. It was during this time that teaching came to be seen as "women's work" and as a profession with less prestige than medicine, law, and the like. In many ways, the problematic negotiation of who would be teachers and why set the stage for decades of debates about gender, institutional structure, curriculum, and professionalism in teaching.

From its humble beginnings, public schooling in the United States was riddled with complications and did not progress in a seamless, organized way, but it was in fact a significant part of what some would later call "the Great American Experiment"—the great quest, the unique journey of a nation seeking to be an independent, successful, powerful, and democratic place where its people were literate and educated. The mid-18th century witnessed a surge in public education and attempts to move toward cohesion

---

Missed Historical Moment 1: Women and Teaching

Rather than paint the profession of teaching as one of high calling and prestige, society and stakeholders minimized the import of education and teaching from the very inception of public schooling. If one became a teacher, it was either because he was on his way to a better career or because she was biologically, morally, and emotionally well suited for teaching—not intellectually gifted or vocationally talented.

In 1840, just 30% of teachers were women. By 1920, women made up nearly 85% of the population of all school teachers; even today, women comprise just more than 70% of our classroom teacher population. The explicit sociocultural turn toward "republican motherhood" enabled an increase in female literacy as well as the reasoning that teaching was a logical extension of a woman's "motherly duties" (Kincheloe et al., 2000, p. 142).

As Joel Spring (1997) notes, "What was considered the natural subordination of women to men provided a social basis for creating a hierarchical educational system in which role expectations were the same as those in more general social situations. Thus, the function of women in the common school was to be . . . teachers, guided and managed by men holding positions of authority" (pp. 123–124). Women were paid lower salaries than were their male counterparts, often lived in less than desirable conditions, and were encouraged to remain single to uphold their moral standing. Although teaching offered women a professional venture of their own, it came at great cost: Women were "schoolmarms" never "schoolmasters."

Remnants of this hierarchical system and its inevitable inequities linger today as evidenced by the disproportionate representation of women in teaching and men in administration, the resistance of society to increasing teacher salaries, and the undervaluing of teaching as a professional career.

and organization. From this point forward, public education and schooling confronted conflicting ideals, philosophies, and stakeholders on many fronts. Critical questions remained to be answered: For whom was schooling intended? What should constitute the curriculum and why? Who should be teachers? In the next hundred years, policymakers, administrators, clergy, parents, missionaries, and other stakeholders in education attempted to engage these questions and set out to (re)form education for the democracy.

Normal Schools for Good Citizens (1830–1920)

In the next iteration of public education, the normal school promoted education as a means by which to "mold good citizens through concerted state action" (Fraser, 2007, p. 46). Normal schools marked a sharp turn toward the centralization of schooling and education in the young nation and remained a stronghold in education (and teacher education) for nearly a century. New mechanisms of state control were implemented, boards of education formed, and mandates for curriculum and instruction were imposed on education in an effort to provide stability and structure to a very loosely conceptualized and unorganized public school system.

Mann and his supporters viewed the normal school as having a critical role in solidifying national unity with a common language, English, and common religion, Protestantism. Although critics of Mann and his new school system denounced his agenda as inherently undemocratic and costly, the normal school model proliferated with much influence until the Civil War, especially with regard to training teachers. The normal school marked the beginning of one of the most dynamic periods in education, schooling, and teacher preparation. Over the next hundred years, teacher education grew, expanded, struggled, and surged in ways that might never have been previously conceived.

The same uniformity that was sought through normal schools was promoted as the best way to prepare teachers. It was thought that teachers would be best trained for their work through a common preparation experience. In 1838, funding was allotted to develop uniform programs of teacher education in Massachusetts. The curriculum in these programs differed from usual academic study. The teacher education curriculum was designed to prepare students in *all* the subjects being taught in the common school and allowed for practice teaching in a model school. Teacher education was to last approximately 1 year and would focus on the acquisition of high levels of content knowledge, development of skills in pedagogy and classroom management, and observation and practice of good teaching in a fashion similar to present-day student teaching (Fraser, 2007).

As normal schools sprung up across the country, attendance increased; however, the number of "trained" teachers remained low. Normal school students were transient, in and out of school, and many of the students who did complete the curriculum either never taught or only taught for a short while because they viewed their normal school education as a "step up" from rural life. Normal schools had a great impact on the future of teacher education in both structure and composition.

Teacher Institutes: The Next Best Thing (1830–1920)

The normal school model grew and replicated, but access to normal school education was limited—and limiting. Not only was a normal school education costly but also time consuming to complete, requiring a solid year to finish a course of study to teach. Attendance, affordability, and the access to a complete normal school program of teacher education were challenges for many citizens, especially for working-class, rural, and/or poor individuals.

Teacher institutes began to move into the teacher education arena about the same time that normal schools were gaining popularity and support. These two types of schools shared similar curricula and supported developing content knowledge, skill in teaching, and a sense of community. The differences were stark but simple: Teacher institutes aimed to prepare teachers in a short amount of time and provide more access to more prospective teachers whereas normal schools provided limited access. Four- to 6-week teacher institute sessions were held a few times throughout the year, and it was thought that attendance at these seminars for duration of 3 years was the equivalent of a normal school education, given the mobility and inconsistency of attendance at the normal schools. Perhaps most important, the number and popularity of teacher institutes grew because of the outpacing need for teachers compared to the numbers of teachers being educated in normal schools, academies, and colleges. In the surge from 1840 to 1920, teacher institutes became "the most prevalent teacher preparatory agency in America and touched the lives of more teachers than any other educational institution" (Mattingly, 1975, p. 71). Additionally, in a time when it was not legal to allow teachers to teach "unlicensed," teacher institutes helped to fill the gaps of normal schools and to improve failing schools. A majority of the certified teachers in the late 19th century and early 20th century held certificates gained by examination and attendance at teacher institutes (Fraser, 2007).

Just prior to the Great Depression, teachers typically attended institutes once a year, even after certification. Institutes served as pre-service training as well as in-service continuing education for practicing teachers. Grassroots organizations and teacher's groups emerged across the country, building a strong sense of community among both private and public school teachers. Increased attempts to regulate and control teacher education were met with increased propagation of alternative opportunities all aimed at supplying the nation's growing number of new classrooms with qualified teachers.

A sharp and salient shift from a scarcity of teachers before the Great Depression to a surplus during and after led the nation's teacher preparation entities—normal schools, institutes, colleges, academies—quickly and significantly to increase teacher qualification standards. Because there were more teachers than necessary, districts and schools could be more selective in their hiring. The teacher institutes, the very structures that supplied a majority of the teachers in the growing nation, became the casualty of economic crisis and educational reform.

Expanding Education at Public Expense: The American High School (Circa 1830)

In the early 19th century, something of a bridge between primary/grammar schools and colleges and academies was built: the high school, or city normal school. Viewed as an opportunity to offer an education to a wider audience and to do so entirely at public expense, the new high schools offered education for advanced stations in industry and community. Moreover, high schools quickly became the preferred location for preparing the nation's teachers (Fraser, 2007) and served to reify the feminization of teaching by offering separate, often shorter normal courses and curricula almost exclusively for girls.

The high school movement began in the cities and by the early 20th century had also expanded to most rural areas. As the new, preferred means of preparing teachers, this was an important contribution to rural schooling where previously teachers had been less educated and of lower social class. Simply put, high schools offered more teachers with more education and served as the foundation of reformers' efforts to produce teachers from and for normal schools. Courses were graded and hierarchical based on age and achievement.

Although boys and girls were admitted at almost equal rates, the majority of graduating students were girls. For young women seeking a professional place in society, high schools and city normal schools offered an opportunity for a real career in teaching. Because of their intense focus on preparing teachers, high schools tended to be almost exclusively single-gendered. Eventually, high schools evolved to offer a 4-year program with an additional year of professional study that was then followed by a short period of what is now called student teaching. During this final phase, which usually lasted a few months, students were to observe, practice, and learn the business of the school and classroom management. Fraser (2007) pointedly notes, "The normal course [in the high school] came more and more to be a girls' ghetto, sometimes a very large ghetto within the budding comprehensive high school" (p. 86).

Also during this time, the first high school for African American teachers emerged and aimed to improve educational opportunity for African American children in rural, often one-teacher-one-room schoolhouses. Resources, financial and logistical, were scarce and very few African American teachers were trained. Later, country training schools became a substantial part of the 20th-century rural high school teacher education movements and provided opportunities for African American teachers and students.

The Roaring Rise: From Normal School to College (1870–1920)

The normal school, typically entered upon completion of high school, became the promise of teacher education—though ironically it never prepared the majority of America's teachers. With the surplus of teachers during and after the Great Depression, teacher education responded by raising its standards regarding the number of years of study, courses, curriculum, and certification requirements. The normal schools had a large constituency and the curriculum included a focus on content, pedagogy, and commitment—head, hand, and heart (Fraser, 2007).

The first normal school was founded in 1839. Just 30 years later, there were 35 schools, and by 1927 there were nearly 200 normal schools in 46 of 48 states. Normal schools in the South were segregated. Born out of the common school movement, the normal school grew from requiring just some level of elementary or common school education to selecting students who had something more similar to a high school diploma and some evidence of good moral character. The normal schools offered a curriculum that was most like the last 2 years of present-day high schools and the first of typical college curricula. By 1920, nearly a century after the first normal school opened, most offered a 4-year course of study and had moved to the college designation.

Whereas most agreed that a normal school education was ideal for teacher preparation, relatively few students actually completed a full course of study. Consequently, states began to award certifications based on levels of completion. For those who completed only some preparation, certification was offered for a limited amount of time. For others who completed their teacher education programs, certifications were valid for a lifetime. During this time, while certification standards were becoming less flexible and more stringent, the American Normal School Association (later the National Education Association) was founded and began investigating programs and curricula with the aim of making recommendations for certification. This group claimed as their responsibility the governance of curriculum and expectations in the normal school as well as qualifications to teach.

Normal schools were essentially teachers colleges, and although White normal schools seemed to thrive, those that served African Americans continued to be starved and stagnated by lack of resources and funding. Mandates for curriculum, teaching, and certification imposed stringent guidelines on normal schools, and in 1920, the Carnegie Report called for all teacher education to be moved to the college level. Still, normal schools had an undeniable impact on teacher education—although not producing high numbers of teachers, perhaps the affordability and accessibility of the normal school as compared to the university or academy were its greatest contributions to education.

With the metamorphosis from normal school to college came more rigid standards and limited admissions policies. These new colleges required that all students entering have satisfactory completion of secondary schooling. New standards and higher entrance requirements supported the continued growth of the high school, the demand for more teachers in the high school, and thereby increased the numbers of candidates for the baccalaureate degree. Cyclical in nature, one development or progression supported another—the pipeline of American education was becoming more clearly articulated in the early years of the 20th century, from the elementary/grammar school all the way through to the college and university. Still, there remained a large and growing number of youths and citizens who remained outside of the *normal* system, unconsidered and unaccounted for by most.

Teaching a Separate and (Un)Equal America: Preparing African American Teachers, City Teachers, and Teachers for New Immigrants (1870–1940)

It is an understatement to note that in the early years of the new nation, education and schooling opportunities were limited across the young, growing nation, especially for African Americans, Native Americans, Catholics and Jews, and new immigrants. From the mid-19th century to the middle of the 20th century, a few institutions began to open their doors to a more diverse core of potential young teachers and thereby extended educational opportunity in revolutionary ways.

Most striking, education for African Americans—especially those in the South—was limited and harshly restricted. Many African Americans, both enslaved and freed, learned in secret, taught by the few who were at the time literate and learned. Following the Civil War, an intense movement began among African Americans and their allies for equal access to quality education. Still, schooling and educational opportunities remained narrowly conceptualized and inaccessible for young Black children. It is significant to note here that in schools where African American children were learning to read and write, they were taught by African American teachers. The magnitude of the importance of the presence (albeit limited) of Black teachers in these early schools would not be fully understood until many years later.

As noted in the previous section, a handful of high schools developed to serve African Americans who wanted to be teachers and prepared them to work in the most challenging of conditions—schools where there were limited supplies, poor resources, dilapidated school buildings, and very high student–teacher ratios. Although "free" and available, educational opportunities for African Americans continued to be harshly limited by Whites harboring resentment and racial hostility in both the North and the South following the Civil War.

In the late 19th century, formal preparation for African American teachers began; however, the progress of this preparation was slow. In 1917, the majority of African American teachers held only temporary or emergency certificates. It was not until the 1930s that normal institutes, missionary colleges, and training schools would significantly contribute to the numbers of Black teachers, specifically in the South. Among the first normal schools to prepare African American teachers was the Hampton–Tuskegee Normal School that offered studies in both academic subjects and pedagogy and prepared teachers for the elementary certificate.

African American teachers understood that their calling was "much more than teaching skills—they were to uplift a race" (Fraser, 2007, p. 96). However, the Hampton–Tuskegee model and ideology was one of marginalization and assimilation to second-class citizenship conceptualized by White stakeholders. Funding for schools that trained African American teachers was predicated on the assumption that schooling and education for African Americans were to prepare freedmen and women (and their children) to assume their place in an inherently unequal system dominated by wealthy White European men and women. Not only was the ideological foundation of these schools inherently disenfranchising, these schools also expected their "students" to work in the fields, kitchens, and shops of the institutions themselves. This philosophy did not go unchallenged.

During this time as well, missionary colleges formed and led by both White and Black groups relied on a classic, liberal curriculum and did not focus solely on the training of teachers or the economic and social disenfranchisement of its students. Supported by the American Missionary Association (AMA), the goal was to have "schools of high grade" in all major centers in the South where African American children were taught by African American teachers. The AMA did not limit its impact to high schools alone; it also funded colleges and universities that sought to uplift and provide opportunities for Blacks. The first of its kind, Fisk University in Nashville, Tennessee, was founded in 1867 "on the shared dream of an educational institution that would be open to all, regardless of race, and that would measure itself by the highest standards, not of Negro education, but of American education at its best" (Fisk University, n.d.). The excitement and progress were short lived. Growth and proliferation of colleges and universities that served African Americans, Native Americans, and immigrants were paralyzed by a shortage of money, college-ready students, and other logistical issues.

By 1935, country training schools had emerged as a force within the teacher education movement for African Americans. Offering a 4-year program, these schools mirrored high schools and served as both multipurpose high schools and teacher training institutes. Teacher training curricula included observation and practice teaching, and principles of teaching and school management. Teachers in many of these schools also taught beyond the scope of "industrial education," focusing more on classical subjects. Using their literal distance and freedom from mandates and oversight (not to mention, ideological racism), these schools taught beyond the scope of prescribed courses in an act of covert resistance (Fraser, 2007).

Although opportunities were emerging and the AMA was operating in a "deeply racist White nation," resources remained severely unequal for the education and schooling of African Americans. Even so, W. E. B. DuBois (1939) noted that schools had begun an educational revolution among African Americans in the South by providing schools with Black teachers and virtually eliminating illiteracy among Black people. Likewise, Fraser (2007) acknowledges, "If one looks at teacher education as a field that always involved questions of moral values and commitment as well as content knowledge and professional pedagogical skills, then in the end, these schools did something in the arenas of values that few other educational endeavors could match" (p. 113).

The Struggle to Be Inclusive and Responsive

In 1868, amid the intense accreditation pressures and shortage of teachers, the New York Board of Regents voted to establish the Daily Normal School (later renamed the Normal College of the City of New York) for females and gave it power to grant teaching certificates without further examination. It also ruled that no teacher could teach without a certificate, thereby ensuring survival of a school as a certification granting body. There were strict admissions tests to ensure there was no hint of political or social favoritism. The school felt a great tension from its inception to serve as many young women

---

Missed Historical Moment 2: Racism in Education

In his book *Racist America* (2000), Feagin explains, "From the colonial era to the present, educational institutions have been critical to the transmission of the racist ideology. . . . Elites have long maintained power in part by controlling the processes of learning and knowledge dissemination through public, religious, and other private schooling" (p. 76).

Embedded in society, American education is racialized. We cannot ignore race as a factor that has and continues to influence educational opportunity (Kozol, 2005) and that therefore influences teacher expectations and student achievement (Marshall, 2002; McKenzie, 2001; Winfield, 1986). Situated among a racial hierarchy with White and Black as opposites (Ladson-Billings, 2000), the racialization of society can be seen "not only in the social, economic, and cultural resources passed along generations . . . but also in [White] dominance of the economic, legal, educational, and political arrangements" (Feagin, 2000, p. 206).

As explained in this section, education and teacher preparation were inherently unequal ventures. It was in this problematic inception that the roots of inequity and systemic racism took hold and continue to permeate many aspects of public education and schooling today. Many schools, urban and rural, continue to suffer from a lack of resources and adequate funding. Funding structures remain unequal and more often than not privilege some while marginalizing others (Kozol, 2005). Dilapidated school buildings, out-of-date texts, and underqualified teachers serve the most vulnerable youth. The inherently separate and unequal two-tiered educational system born 400 years ago remains the foundation of a public education system intended for all—but failing many.

as possible or to serve only those intellectual, if not financial, elite. Although most of the students at the Normal College of the City of New York were indeed middle-class, White, Protestant women, some Catholics, Jews, and African Americans attended. At this time, it was rare for any college, school, or university outside of Historically Black Colleges and Universities (HBCUs) to admit African Americans. It was an attempt to diversify the well-educated teaching force; however, social class distinctions proved more salient, and it remained that normal school graduates did the teaching while university graduates did the supervising and determined the curriculum.

Administrative Progressives, or reformers, began to emerge with a strikingly different agenda for city training schools than those who were doing the work of teacher education in normal schools around the 1920s. Taking as their view that decisions and standards for teaching and teacher education should flow from the top down, they imposed standardized regulations that left schools the ability to certify courses of study but gave to professional examining agencies the ability to grant teaching licenses. Again, like the cyclical nature mentioned earlier, by controlling the examinations, agencies were able to influence, if not dictate, the courses of study in schools. In short, the normal school 4-year program was no match for the increased standardization, narrowed curriculum, and abbreviated course of study in city training schools. Normal schools were losing their grip on teacher education, and city training schools were surging to meet the growing demands of schools and teaching—as were the emerging colleges and universities (Fraser, 2007).

Colleges and Universities: More (Un)Certainty and Standards (Circa 1920)

Across the nation, schoolchildren were still being educated mostly by teachers with little more education than the children had and usually no formal training. Most teachers during the late 19th century and early 20th century were common school graduates hired based on need and availability of funds—if one wanted to teach and the money was available, a teacher was hired. Teachers took examinations in "common branches of learning" and sometimes pedagogy, and some attended teacher institutes and/or returned for advanced education later. Even with the recommendations of national education groups, initial movements to train teachers at the college level went underutilized with regard to preparing classroom teachers because there was relatively little demand for college-educated teachers. In short, the need for teachers, any teachers, was more pressing than the benefits of having college-educated teachers. It wasn't until the mid-1900s that colleges and universities began to prepare a significant number of classroom teachers.

Universities in Iowa and Michigan were among the first to appoint full-time faculty in education, and the states later would designate universities as separate entities qualified to authorize the granting of teaching certificates without the approval of local authorities. This catapulted the prestige and importance of the university to new levels in the realm of teacher education. Perhaps more than any other university, Columbia University did more to establish a clear and necessary place for a university-based school of education. With Columbia University resisting the beginning of a teacher education program, the New York College of the Training of Teachers was founded in 1887 and chartered in 1889 to grant bachelor's, master's, and doctoral degrees. By 1892, Teacher's College, as it was renamed, enjoyed the affiliation with Columbia and its autonomy as a degree-granting institution and became the center of progressive educational thought, theory, and research in the United States. American education was becoming increasingly hierarchical in the era of college and university proliferation, and other universities saw their role as one to prepare the top tier of the hierarchy.

Universities began to offer summer extension programs and professional development for teachers and to nudge out the more typical school-district-led programs and teacher institutes. A rapid expansion in college attendance occurred as access to high school increased and as universities insisted that high school teachers be prepared at the university level. This time of synergy and growth had a significant impact on teacher education that affected almost all levels of education. Normal schools began to require a high school education for admission, high schools transformed teaching into a highly differentiated endeavor, and high schools wanted college- and university-trained teachers. Paradoxically, while the standards and educational requirements to become and be a teacher were rising, especially at the high school level, there remained evidence of contradictions with regard to access, quality, and expectations. Disproportionately, high school teachers were male and graduates of the university, and elementary school teachers were female and more typically normal school graduates. Moreover, as the accreditation movement began in the final years of the 19th century, universities staked claim to a monopoly in teacher education, thereby marginalizing normal schools and their graduates simultaneously. Finally, amid growing national racism and segregation, the universities and colleges that aimed to serve African Americans and prepare teachers of Black children were constrained by the widely supported Hampton–Tuskegee model—a model that served to disenfranchise African Americans rather than educate them. While seeking to secure a place in teacher education, the university also asserted itself as the natural place for the beginning and flourishing of educational research—although these two aims often contradicted each other. Those who wanted prestige and recognition directed their attention and resources to research; others trained teachers (Fraser, 2007). University engagement in teacher education has been difficult from the start.

In the 1930s, the "distinctions between normal school, high school, college, and university were still quite vague, in Black and White schools. Nevertheless, the teacher education programs were, as in most universities, offered at the pre-college level" (Fraser, 2007, p. 179). What was not vague, however, was the level of prestige associated with normal schools and colleges, with more attributed to the latter. By making a big leap from offering what was typically a ninth-grade level of education to providing 1- or 2-year college-level courses of study, normal schools moved to college designation more and more. These new "teacher's colleges" emerged in Massachusetts, Pennsylvania, and even in southern states. However short lived, these budding teacher's colleges were a strong force in strengthening and solidifying standards and curriculum in teacher education.

Just as quickly as teacher's colleges were birthed, they were transformed into multipurpose institutions, inviting a wider constituency of students and offering broader courses of study but simultaneously marginalizing teacher education. No longer was the preparation of teachers a priority at the college and university level—it was relegated to schools, colleges, and departments of education. Moreover, as the recruitment and preparation of teachers moved from private and local entities to state-controlled bodies, teacher education curricula narrowed and certification was more strictly regulated, so that by 1960 school districts and hiring bodies were forced to require a college degree to teach. Although many a state required a college degree from a university to teach, the very same state was governed by state education department standards. Here a conflict began—conflict between the university standards and those of state departments of education. As Fraser (2007) notes, it was almost without exception that teacher education suffered as a result of this restructuring and (re)form movement.

In 1930, the National Survey of Education of Teachers was published. Findings suggested that the number of certified and educated teachers was growing but still insufficient, especially at the high school level. The most underprepared teachers were teaching in rural areas that served the poorest of students. Importantly, for the first time in history, this survey offered

Missed Historical Moment 3:
The Abandonment of Teacher Education

In 2007, Darling-Hammond wrote: "Despite a growing consensus that teachers matter, the role of teacher education in teachers' effectiveness is a matter of debate. Education schools have been criticized as ineffective in preparing teachers for their work, unresponsive to new demands, remote from practice" (p. 19).

Although written some 80 years after the initial birth of colleges and universities as teacher preparation sites, there is evidence in Darling-Hammond's statement that the chasm between school, schools and colleges of education, and universities is vast and no doubt had its beginnings very early in the history of schooling and teacher education. The isolation and marginalization of teacher education and the narrowing of the curriculum and standards compounded the ideological debates about and the structure and implementation of teacher education programs around the country. The separation of teacher education from normal schools and the encapsulation of programs within departments of education apart from the general mission and focus of the multipurpose university left teacher education lingering somewhere between important and ignored. Colleges and departments of education at the university, and the professional faculty therein, attempted to use research to garner support for the importance of a strong foundation for teachers in not only knowledge but also pedagogy. Conversely, traditional academic departments and university structures as a whole minimized the importance of pedagogy and teaching courses while placing their emphasis on academic subjects—making the claim that all that was necessary to be a good teacher is knowledge in a core subject.

Teaching became an undervalued, low-status vocation in the United States very early on—and teacher education an "even lower-status enterprise" (Darling-Hammond, Bransford, & Lepage, 2007, p. 277) as the proliferation of colleges and universities ensued. University faculty members working to prepare teachers were paid less and did the often "time-consuming work with prospective teachers and schools" while other faculty focused on research and writing, a trend that continues to this day. Moreover, they were often not granted tenure, the premium currency and seal of approval at the university. Further complicating the problematic existence of teacher education at the university level were issues that included but that were not limited to inadequate time allotted for mastery in the many areas necessary to be a good teacher (i.e., subject matter, child development, learning theory), fragmentation of coursework, uninspiring teaching by faculty members, superficial curricula, and traditional (read: narrow and exclusive) views of schooling; these issues remain. They are but a few of the critically ineffective conditions undermining teacher education programs in higher education (Darling-Hammond et al., 2007).

There was, for a moment, the opportunity to elevate the status of teaching and teacher education as well as expand and enhance the curriculum as programs moved to colleges and universities. Unfortunately, for teachers and students, this opportunity went unrealized and teacher education remains undermined by bureaucratic inadequacies and structural inefficiencies in higher education.

commentary on the status of African American education and teacher education in the country. Survey results indicated that 80% of the nation's African American population was living in the south and the District of Columbia and that African American children were attending legally segregated schools. While tremendous gains were made in the education and literacy rates of African Americans from before the Civil War to 1930, curricula in teacher training schools, pay for teachers, and standards for education and certification were still disparate when compared to those for White teachers and students. There were few—slightly more than a handful—normal schools and colleges preparing African American teachers for African American students, and the education of teachers in these schools was predicated upon the Hampton–Tuskegee ideology discussed previously in which assimilation took precedence over an education intended to promote learning and intellectual growth. The first of many calls, the survey suggested that if separate was ever to be equal, far-reaching changes were needed. It was up to the country to respond.

Sputnik, Civil Rights, and the Contentious Act of Teaching (Circa 1950)

The launch of *Sputnik* in 1957 catapulted education and teacher education (and the scathing critiques of both) into the national and international spotlight. By 1960, teacher education was a university monopoly, and the divide between teacher educators and faculty in other, more traditional disciplines was deep and growing. Significant reform efforts supported by large funds of private monies sought to unite these two competing entities to work under the assumption that it was not only the responsibility of the colleges of education to educate teachers but of the entire university. They should be providing a well-rounded liberal education, extended subject knowledge, professional knowledge, and classroom management skills. Fifth-year programs proliferated, and states began to rely on certification-based programs while dictating what courses future teachers needed to complete. Professional educators took the reins of teacher education curricula and programs while the academic community sat idly by—complacent and uninterested.

Teacher education had become the unruly step-child of the comprehensive, scholarly university. It was a less than important educational endeavor, and professional education courses, and the faculty who taught them, were viewed as worthless and unnecessary. The proverbial storm was brewing and the debates over teacher education were pouring down like torrential rains.

Many a critic offered his commentary. In 1953, Bestor presented his scathing perspective in *Educational Wastelands: The Retreat From Learning in Our Public Schools* and claimed that the academic study of education had become detached from the academic disciplines and was thereby ineffective. He challenged the alliances between school administrators, superintendents, and principals who he believed sought to silence educational researchers as effective critics of schools. Karl Bigelow (1954) quickly retorted that Bestor had oversimplified his critique and grossly underestimated the complexity of teacher education and the quality and quantity of skills that exceptional teachers needed. Others chimed in throughout the decade. In 1963, James Koerner produced another frightfully harsh critique of teacher education, this one based on interviews with teacher education students. In *The Miseducation of Teachers*, Koerner (1963) cites several issues with teacher education including a clear lack of evidence supporting one sound method or program of teacher education, the need for more routes to teacher education supported by the lack of evidence for one best program, and the ineptitude of education as a stand-alone "discipline." He also critiqued the relationships between education programs and schools as a "top-heavy bureaucracy" and identified the "inferior intellectual quality of the Education faculty [as] *the* fundamental limitation in the field" (pp. 12–21, emphasis in original). While the debates raged, teachers were (under)trained, students were (ill) taught, and schools remained largely unchanged.

Sputnik launched a conversation, Civil Rights were on the move, and contentions about how and what the art and practice of effective teaching should be percolated through much of the country; however, as the teacher shortage raged on, as women continually met resistance in careers other than teaching, and as teacher education became a lucrative endeavor for colleges, the status quo prevailed. In 1965, after reviewing the curricula at nearly 100 schools of education Walter K. Beggs wrote, "There is no indication at present that any major changes will be made in this general format" (p. 42). Teacher education in the 1970s looked much like it did in previous years, and all indications signaled that it would remain a haphazardly conceived, overly regulated, and problematically unresponsive venture for some time to come.

"We Don't Need No Education": Teaching and the New Millennium (1960 to Present)

Leading up to and following the launch of *Sputnik*, a strong movement developed outside of colleges and universities that sought to bring about

Missed Historical Moment 4: Conflicts of Interest

Critique of and disagreement about (and within) teacher education were certainly not new phenomena in the mid-20th century, but the conflict seemed to escalate at this time. As Sarason et al. (1986) note, "The criticisms took on cascading proportions" following the launch of *Sputnik* when Americans were feeling desperately inept, having been intellectually and technologically outpaced by the Russians (p. i). Moreover, while the country was wrestling with its own systemic prejudice and inequality, few could reach consensus about who was to be educated and how best to do so (Stevens, 1999). Although critique and constructive debate are healthy, offering opportunities for change and productive growth, infighting and political wrangling overshadowed this moment for a (re)conceptualization of teacher education and schooling—we had become "a nation at risk."

Professional educators have long been viewed by academics, politicians, and industry alike as "mushy, wooly-minded, misguided and misguiding intellectuals who [have] made shambles of our schools" (Sarason et al., 1986, p. i). Conversely, educators view politicians, academics in traditional disciplines, and business as arrogantly unconcerned with education and misinformed when it comes to informing teaching, learning, and curriculum. Conscientious and thoughtful study and articulation among all stakeholders of education and teacher preparation were lacking, and the goals of education were absent—replaced instead by insults, stalemates, and a lack of consideration for the students that public education intended to serve. The federal monies flooding education that aimed to improve the experiences of schoolchildren (especially those in urban, newly integrated schools) and teachers and to uplift a society struggling to find its identity and strength were misused. Ultimately, this crescendo of debate and critique resolved itself to a fruitless end, and little about teaching and schooling changed for better or for worse.

Fatalistic perceptions and political wars served to stifle the transformation of teacher education and schooling. These disabled any productive conversation about teacher education in this historical period and continue to do so even today—psychologically, politically, logistically, and pragmatically. To this end, Joel Spring (1998b) notes: "If current trends continue, then public schools will primarily serve the interests of business and politicians; the curriculum will be narrowed and ideas restricted in the classroom by pressures from interest groups; and education will be in continual financial crises" (pp. 200–201). We must turn our focus and energies to the transformation of education and schooling—not (re)forming political agendas or blaming teachers and schools for the ineptitudes of society.

change to education and teacher preparation under the assumption that if real and meaningful change could not be realized within the structures of academic institutions, perhaps it could be instigated in other spaces. Programs developed to bypass the "traditional" undergraduate course to teaching and meet the "increasingly urgent needs of the nation's cities and the schools and children of those cities" (Fraser, 2007, p. 216). The Teacher Corps and Peace Corps Programs for Urban Teaching both aimed to reach students and schools with an intellectual fervor and commitment to social justice by employing those who would not complete traditional programs of study at the university. Although these programs thrived for a few years, they dwindled as the need for teachers was met with a surge in the number of teachers remaining in the classroom. This left teacher education to colleges and universities—if young people were to consider teaching at all.

In 1984, the Center for Educational Renewal was begun under the administration of John Goodlad, Kenneth Sirotnik, and Roger Soder. In the years leading up to the development of the center, Goodlad (1970) wrote, "Nothing short of a simultaneous reconstruction of pre-service teacher education, in-service teacher education and schooling itself will suffice if the [educational] change process is to be adequate" (as cited in Fraser, 2007, p. 220). Although the center and team produced major works in 1990, the outlook and promise for real change was grim. It appeared that the real question was the one that remained following the intense debates and educational wars of the previous decades: To what extent would the community support the "mass democratic education for the nation's children, beyond slinging barbs at the schools and/or education faculties"? (Levin, 1990, p. 46) and How, if at all, will schools and education professionals (re)form themselves to meet the needs of a dynamic and most deserving population of public schools, teachers, and children? It seemed that teacher preparation was caught between the proverbial rock and a hard place. Judith Lanier spoke to this in the Holmes Report in 1990: "There is an inverse relationship between professorial prestige and the intensity of involvement with the formal education of teachers" (as cited in Fraser, 2007, p. 222). It seemed that our history had delivered us at a complicated moment. On the one hand, society wanted and clamored for the best education for its best—its children; however, on the other hand, the role of teacher carried with it little regard and the role of teacher of teachers even less.

During the 1980s, education became a major political issue and organized activity by special interest groups increased dramatically (Spring, 1998b). In 1986, the landscape of teacher education was redefined, in theory at least. Two reports in that year, *A Nation Prepared* by the Carnegie Forum on Education and the Economy and *Tomorrow's Teachers* from the Holmes Group of Education Deans, set out to restructure teacher education and set an agenda "to make the education of teachers intellectually more solid." Although few could argue with such an auspicious goal, each report outlined

basic tenets that were debated, argued, supported, and refuted in the literature for years to follow. The diagnoses of the problems were not unlike those
offered in the critiques in years prior; however, unlike years past, many of
the proposed reforms were implemented at a very rapid pace. The reports
included recommendations for the following:

- Create a National Board for Professional Teaching Standards
- Restructure schools to provide a professional environment for
  teaching
- Restructure the teaching force
- Require a bachelor's degree in the arts and sciences
- Develop a new professional curriculum in graduate schools of
  education
- Mobilize the nation's resources to prepare minority youth for careers
  in teaching
- Relate incentives for teachers to school-wide performance
- Make teacher's salaries and opportunities competitive

Schools of education almost immediately began to alter certification
laws, require a major in a liberal arts discipline, strengthen clinical experiences, and raise academic standards. Most teacher education programs
include components that support teachers' knowledge of the "subject matter
they are to teach, the psychological and physical natures of those they plan
to teach, the political and social structures of the institutions in which they
will be teaching, the methods by which people learn, and the best methods
for teaching a particular subject" (Spring, 1998a, p. 45). Although teacher
education programs were undergoing reform, the larger sociocultural issues
(i.e., restructuring the teaching force and increasing incentives to teach)
persisted.

One final reform effort proposed by the Holmes Group aimed to shift
much of the core of teacher preparation to professional development
schools—places where research, teaching, planning, and internships would
be fostered and supported (Goodlad, 1990; Lucas, 1997). The goal was to
build a more solid, intellectual, and practical connection between the university and the public schools. With this suggestion, the Holmes Group proposed that the public school, not the university, become the center of action
in teacher education. It *seemed*, perhaps for the first time, that teacher education would be notably enhanced and the partnerships between universities

and public schools would be forged to promote promising educational futures for all students.

Efforts also began to address the critical need for and glaring absence of a quality educational experience for minority children. Moreover, the Carnegie Report recognized the importance of preparing minority teachers for America's public schools. Ironically and tragically, the strong African American teaching force present before the U.S. Supreme Court's 1954 *Brown v. Board of Education* was virtually eliminated with mandates to integrate White schools and close Black ones (Fraser, 2007). Although initiatives to recruit and retain minority teachers were begun, little success was realized and the achievement gap between students of racial/cultural/ethnic/linguistic minority groups and their White counterparts continued to grow. Any real connection and substantial improvement between learning and teaching for children of color in America would remain a dream deferred.

There *appeared* to have been notable accomplishments in the decades leading up to the new millennium. Moreover, with the reauthorization of the Higher Education Act and Title V, "Shaping the Profession That Shapes America's Future," intense calls for "highly qualified" teachers in the No Child Left Behind (NCLB) Act, and a number of textbooks and reports published on the state of education, teacher education and how best to ensure teacher quality (see, for example, Hess, Rotherham, & Walsh, 2004), it seemed that teacher education might finally garner the focus it deserved—for better and for worse.

(Re)envisioning Teacher Education: Promising Possibilities

The first step we can take toward changing reality—waking up from the nightmare that is the present state of public miseducation—is acknowledging that we are indeed living a nightmare. The nightmare that is the present—in which educators have little control over the curriculum, the very organizational and intellectual center of schooling.

Pinar, 2004, p. 5

We find ourselves at the end of the first decade of the 21st century. College and university programs continue to prepare the next generations of teachers, and so too do the multiple and alternative routes to teacher certification. Debates continue to rage over the "best" way to become certified, what constitutes an "effective" teacher, how "rigorous" programs should be, and who should be admitted. Conflicting ideals and competing agendas have a strong hold on education, teacher preparation, and the future of our public schools. Educational researchers and parents alike claim that teacher disposition is important, whereas politicians and media pundits claim that a social justice agenda in education is little more than a distraction from the core academic subjects and strict accountability.

Further complicating matters, standards for the credentialing of teachers have been consistently and incongruously reduced while standards and measures of student achievement seem always to be on the rise. Our schools and classrooms are crowded with the oppressive and reductionist focus on high-stakes tests and accountability measures. Creativity and critical thinking among teachers and students are discouraged in exchange for a greater focus on basic skill acquisition, rote memorization of facts, and scripted curricula. We have young people who want to teach but who leave the profession in large numbers within 5 years of entering the classroom citing deplorable, unbearable working conditions and little, if any, administrative support. We have become a nation of strikingly persistent and shamefully counterproductive educational paradoxes. While we, as an intellectual field and a society, continue our political banter and wallow around in self-righteous indignation about the state of our schools, our children (and their futures) are reduced to little more than collateral damage. Even at the time of this writing, it remains questionable whether we as a society and a profession will learn the lessons of our past and realize the promising possibilities of a new, brighter, and more equitable future.

Few are satisfied with the status of education (and teacher education), and rightfully so. Walk into any school building today and you can find students sitting in the hallway, excluded from instruction because their teacher does not know how to deal with their behavior and meet their basic needs. Study a school's achievement data and note the disproportionate numbers of minority students and poor students failing and not making adequate yearly progress while an equally disproportionate number of the same school's White and wealthier children are identified as gifted and talented and enrolled in Advanced Placement (AP) courses. Visit a school cafeteria and find that many of the children are receiving a free or reduced lunch that hardly meets the nutritional needs of a growing body and learning brain. Sit in the teachers' lounge and listen—you're certain to hear tales of "bad kids" and a growing lack of morale and apathy about teaching and engaging the future of our society. Look a bit more closely into the qualifications of teachers in today's classrooms and note that our most vulnerable students are being taught by the most unskilled and inexperienced teachers. Examine the pay scale of most districts compared to cost of living indices and you will quickly realize the challenge of providing for a family on a teacher's salary. Venture into a college of education classroom and note seats full of young, White, middle-class women, many of whom have chosen to pursue a career in education as a "second choice." They are unengaged in critical discussions about how to instigate real and meaningful change in our public education system that address racism, classism, sexism, and homophobia. If we are to really envision something different for ourselves, we must deal candidly and assertively with the realities in our schools, the inadequacies of teacher education, and the persistent failings of our past and present.

There are calls for a dramatic and sweeping restructuring of teacher education, recruitment, and professional development as well as the reforming of professional standards for certification, accreditation, and assessment. The careful reader knows that this is nothing new. With each wave of reform efforts comes a new wave of criticism and recommendations. National groups (including the National Commission on Teaching and America's Future [NCTAF] and the National Education Association [NEA], among many others) have organized to "create new policies and practices for dramatically improving the quality of teaching" (as cited in Fraser, 2007, p. 235), and stakeholders (politicians and parents, business and clergy) at all levels are calling for change. In what ways will these organizations and current stakeholders shape the future of teacher education? Perhaps the more appropriate questions are: What lessons will we learn from the past so that we may look forward to a brighter future? What will it take to *transform* teaching and teacher education?

In each of the four missed historical moments discussed in this chapter lie opportunities for study, growth, and de/re/construction of practice and ideologies that can support the transformation of our philosophies and goals for education and teacher education. The following recommendations offer a place to begin as we (re)focus our reflections so that they inform our intentions.

We must celebrate and elevate the art and act of teaching as a profession—in society, schools, and universities—and respect and nurture (in word and deed) those who choose to spend their life in service to our youth as teachers. Whether in school buildings where teachers' opinions are respected and heard and teachers are nurtured as creative, knowledgeable, and compassionate professionals or in university settings where the status of teaching and those who prepare teachers is upheld as critical to the survival of our democracy, we must, as a nation, rethink our commitment to education and teaching, and therefore teachers. The old adage "Those who can, do; those who can't, teach" must be left behind as a great misconception. We orphaned our teachers and in so doing abandoned the education of our children. As a profession and society, we must move beyond "rhetorical commitment" and recognize the need to sincerely value our teachers and be willing to do the hard work of educational reform on all levels (Goodlad, 1990). We can no longer sit idly by and allow teacher education to continue as it has in its haphazardly conceptualized past. We know our students better, we are more knowledgeable about how best young people learn, and we know our shortcomings. Money alone will not solve the problems, but it is necessary to achieving equity, quality, and prestige. Perhaps even more important than funding is the realization that education is not a peripheral enterprise in a democracy; it is the foundation.

Our universities are but a place to start, offering the freedom and space to envision theoretically and practically a new direction in teacher education in such a way that teachers, schools, and students may be touched and transformed in powerful ways. Institutional change must include not only changes in ideology but innovative ideas and conceptions about how that ideology may be realized in practice and praxis. Attention must be focused on the institutional structures at work in the university and on seeking better, more productive ways to develop and sustain collaborations across colleges and faculties. Careful attention must be paid to the relationships between universities and colleges and public schools. These partnerships are essential to preparing our future teachers for their future students. Finally, and perhaps most important, universities must turn a critical eye on themselves with the understanding that change is not delegated but embraced to create a context in which teacher education can flourish. "The benefits of investing in strong preparation for all teachers will repay the costs [of doing so] many times over" (Darling-Hammond et al., 2007, p. 342).

We must acknowledge our own complicity in building and reinforcing the structural inequities of our educational system and work tirelessly to ensure that future generations of immigrant children, youth of racial/ethnic/ cultural/linguistic minority groups, and poor children do not have to endure the racism, classism, and marginalization of those who came before them. It is no longer acceptable or excusable (no matter what the reason) that the

United States maintains a two-tiered, apartheid system of education that serves some students while alienating and discarding others. We must address the practices that serve to marginalize, isolate, and hinder the success of many of our children. Crumbling school buildings, inadequate resources, out-of-date texts, underprepared teachers, limited access to technology, mediocre curricula, racist teachers and school policy, class-based assumptions about what is to be valued, censorship by special interest groups, and an overreliance on standardized methods of assessment are but a few of the issues screaming out for attention in our schools today. Numerous scholars (see, for example, Delpit, 1995; Kozol, 2005; Ladson-Billings, 1994; Lewis, 2003; Spring, 1998a, 1998b) have noted that these problems and practices are the most harmful to our most vulnerable students. If we are to realize the goal of educating well *all* children, then we must attend to *all* of our failures, structural, social, psychological, political, personal, and intellectual. In a dynamic, engaged society that recognizes its possibilities and works determinedly to realize and nurture the potential of all people, classrooms are places where teachers understand, appreciate, and embrace difference both between and among themselves and their students. Curriculum in effective classrooms is responsive to *all* students *all* year long—not only on celebratory holidays or during a month marked by superficial historical remembrance. In this realization, the content and context of *what* and *how* children learn are as important as our selection and preparation of their teacher.

Finally, we must (re)claim a unified voice as informed and committed educators and immediately cease to allow bureaucratic policies, mindless procedures, self-serving political agendas, and special interest group pandering to continue to dictate what happens in and about our schools. Our schools, the teachers working therein, and the students and families we serve deserve more than a passive consumption of mandates, scripted curricula, and the reductionist, dehumanization of teaching and learning. As Joel Spring (1998b) critically explains: "There are certain elements in the current political structure of American education that inhibit the free flow of ideas and information through the schools and allow certain individuals to gain privileges over others. They include: (1) the problem of majoritarian control; (2) the power of special-interest groups; (3) the political use of schools; and (4) the economics of education" (p. 195). Moreover, "right-wing reform has rendered the classroom a privatized space or domestic sphere in which children and their teachers are, simply, to do what they are told" under "control, disguised by apparently commonsensical claims of 'accountability'" (Pinar, 2004, p. xiii).

What is largely missing (purposefully silenced, I would contend) is the voice of teachers. It is our job, our responsibility, our urgent call to arms if you will, as teachers and teacher educators, to (re)move ourselves from the suffocating clutch of industry, politicians, private foundations, and other seemingly benevolent groups that have overwhelmingly and decisively weakened our ability to assert ourselves as knowledgeable, skilled, and critical scholars and intellectuals in our own field. We must obligate ourselves absolutely, as teachers, to the academic, intellectual, pragmatic and personal understanding of ourselves, our students, education, and society "despite our public and private subjugation, despite the anti-intellectualism around us and within us . . . [and] recommit ourselves to the study of our history, to work toward our future" (p. 255). It is not enough for us to ask our students to "understand themselves and the world they inhabit" and to prepare them to be contributing, active, and purposeful participants in their democracy. It is our responsibility as their teachers to model this in our every word, action, and deed. We must no longer be silent on the issues important to our students and their families, to our children and our grandchildren. We must no longer allow the scapegoating of our colleagues and our profession. We can no longer close the door and hide in our classrooms and allow others to determine what is best for our children. It is time we focus our energies on (re)enVISIONing teaching and teacher education. "When we listen to the past we become attuned to the future. Then we can understand the present, which we *can* reconstruct" (Pinar, 2004, p. 258).

Notes

1. It is important to note that in a study of the history of teacher education, many dates overlap; reforms and new programs were begun sometimes in a chronological order and at other times simultaneously in different parts of the country depending upon demand for teachers, financial resources, student needs, and political agendas. Moreover, names of institutions (e.g., common schools, normal schools, colleges) often were used interchangeably and to describe various organizations of schooling and education. This brief overview of the history of education outlines major movements, milestones, and moments but is not intended to be an exhaustive history of the field. For the most thorough history of teacher education documented to date, see Fraser (2007).

References

Beggs, W. K. (1965). *The education of teachers*. New York: Center for Applied Research in Education.

Bernard, B. (1972). *Education in the forming of American society.* New York: W. W. Norton.

Bigelow, K. W. (1954). How should America's teacher's be educated? *Teachers College Record, 56*(1), 20–24.

Button, H. W., & Provenzo, E. F., Jr. (1989). *History of education and culture in America.* Upper Saddle River, NJ: Prentice Hall.

Cremin, L. A. (1961). *The transformation of the school: Progressivism in American education, 1876–1957.* New York: Knopf.

Cubberly, E. P. (1919). *Public education in the United States.* New York: Houghton Mifflin.

Darling-Hammond, L. (2006). *Powerful teacher education.* San Francisco: Jossey-Bass.

Darling-Hammond, L., Bransford, J., & Lepage, P. (2007). *Preparing teachers for a changing world: What teachers should learn and be able to do.* San Francisco: Jossey-Bass.

Delpit, L. (1995). *Other people's children: Cultural conflict in the classroom.* New York: New York Press.

Dubois, W. E. B. (1939). *Black folk, then and now.* New York: Henry Holt.

Feagin, J. (2000). *Racist America: Roots, current realities, and future reparations.* New York: Routledge.

Fisk University. (n.d.). *Fisk's storied past.* Retrieved February 27, 2010, from http://www.fisk.edu/AboutFisk/HistoryOfFisk.aspx

Fraser, J. W. (2007). *Preparing America's teachers: A history.* New York: Teachers College Press.

Goodlad, J. I. (1970). The reconstruction of teacher education. *Teacher's College Record, 72*(1), 61–72.

Goodlad, J. I. (1984). *A place called school.* New York: McGraw-Hill.

Goodlad, J. I. (1990). *Teachers for our nation's schools.* San Francisco: Jossey-Bass.

Hess, F. M., Rotherham, A. J., & Walsh, K. (Eds.). (2004). *A qualified teacher in every classroom? Appraising old answers and new ideas.* Cambridge, MA: Harvard Education Press.

Hofstadter, R. (1963). *Anti-intellectualism in America.* New York: Knopf.

Kincheloe, J. L., Slattery, P., & Steinberg, S. R. (2000). *Contextualizing teaching: Introduction to education and educational foundations.* New York: Longman.

Koerner, J. (1963). *The miseducation of teachers.* Boston: Houghton-Mifflin.

Kozol, J. (2005). *The shame of the nation: The restoration of apartheid schooling in America.* New York: Crown.

Ladson-Billings, G. (1994). *The dreamkeepers: Successful teachers of African American children.* San Francisco: Jossey-Bass.

Ladson-Billings, G. (2000). Fighting for our lives: Preparing teachers to teach African American students. *Journal of Teacher Education, 51*(3), 206–214.

Levin, R. A. (1990). Recurring themes and variations. In J. I. Goodlad, R. Soder, & K. A. Sirotnik (Eds.), *Places where teachers are taught* (pp. 40–83). San Francisco: Jossey-Bass.

Lewis, A. (2003). *Race in the schoolyard: Negotiating the color line in classrooms and communities.* New Brunswick, NJ: Rutgers University Press.

Lezotte, L. (1994). The nexus of instructional leadership and effective schools. *School Administrator, 51*(6), 20–23.

Lucas, C. J. (1997). *Teacher education in America: Reform agendas for the twenty-first century.* New York: St. Martin's Press.

Marshall, P. L. (2002). *Cultural diversity in our schools.* Belmont, CA: Wadsworth.

Mattingly, P. H. (1975). *The classless profession: American schoolmen in the nineteenth century.* New York: New York University Press.

McKenzie, K. B. (2001). *White teachers' perceptions about their students of color and themselves as White educators.* Unpublished doctoral dissertation, University of Texas at Austin.

National Center for Educational Statistics (NCES). (n.d.). *Common Core of Data.* Retrieved April 2, 2009, from http://nces.ed.gov/ccd

Pinar, W. (2004). *What is curriculum theory?* Mahwah, New Jersey: Laurence Erlbaum Associates.

Santayana, G. (1905). *Life of reason.* New York: Charles Scribner's Sons.

Sarason, S. B. (1962). *The preparation of teachers: An unstudied problem in education.* New York: Wiley.

Sarason, S. B., Davidson, K. S., & Blatt, B. (1986). *The preparation of teachers: An unstudied problem in education* (Rev. ed.). Cambridge, MA: Bookline Books.

Spring, J. (1997). *The American school: 1642–1996* (4th ed.). New York: McGraw-Hill.

Spring, J. (1998a). *American education* (8th ed.). Boston: McGraw-Hill.

Spring, J. (1998b). *Conflict of interests: The politics of American education* (3rd ed.). Boston: McGraw-Hill.

Stevens, R. J. (1999). *Teaching in America's schools.* Upper Saddle River, NJ: Prentice Hall.

Winfield, L. (1986). Teacher beliefs toward academically at risk students in inner urban schools. *Urban Review, 18*(4), 253–267.

Woodson, C. G. (1919). *The education of the Negro.* Washington, DC: Associated Publishers.

2

LIBERAL PROGRESSIVISM AT THE CROSSROADS

Toward a Critical Philosophy of Teacher Education

Nathalia E. Jaramillo

If educational theory goes beyond its proper limits, if it pretends to supplant experience, to promulgate ready-made formulae that are then applied mechanically, it degenerates into dead matter. If, on the other hand, experience disregards pedagogical thinking, it in turn degenerates into blind routine or else is at the mercy of ill-informed or unsystematic thinking.

Emile Durkheim, *Moral Education*

Since the beginning of formal education in the United States, philosophy has played an important role in shaping institutional practices and teacher–student relationships and generating the ideals and promises of schooling for a democratic society. It is impossible to discuss the central tenets of each philosophical tradition of education within the context of this chapter, but it is possible to interrogate key educational movements in the United States and how educators have relied on philosophy to address teacher practice, student learning, and increasing diversity in schools. Philosophers of education have attempted to contribute to our understanding of the relationship between schooling and society and the critical role that education plays in transmitting and reproducing the American ideals of citizenship, ethics, and values reflected in the legal doctrines and constitutional frameworks. Equally, educators serve a formidable function in the duplication of the American archetype, themselves distracted by the spinning wheels, levers, and ideological smoke that portray our democracy.

In the epigraph, Durkheim (2002) illuminates the discord that undergirds the teaching encounter—a "doing" versus "thinking" conundrum. A great proportion of teacher education programs today emphasizes skill sets over philosophy and standards training over pedagogy. When educators are introduced to the abstract, philosophical questioning that can lead to a more nuanced understanding of the basis of school settings, it is commonplace to hear the quip, "What does this have to do with my everyday practice?" To some degree, this knee-jerk reaction that many educators have to theory and philosophy is to be expected. But educators who develop an understanding of philosophy's contribution to our notions of teaching and learning and who reflect on its relevance to the 21st century are better equipped to serve an increasingly diverse student population who will confront changing economic conditions, cultural shifts in the social-political scene, and demands to excel on standardized measures of academic achievement. It is important for both new and more experienced educators to look to the past and present to better understand where philosophy in teacher education has been and perhaps where it needs to go. The key is for educators to begin to see themselves as active participants in shaping how teaching and learning are conceived, to build upon their knowledge about being a part of society, and to generate new theories and practices (praxis) that can help transform the legacy of exclusion that has affected so many generations of youth living in poverty and who experience various forms of racial-ethnic-gender discrimination. In other words, educators need to see themselves as philosophers of praxis, working under conditions that will advance human nature (McLaren & Jaramillo, 2007).

There has always been a noticeable concern for how to pair teaching and learning with the needs of society. Philosophers, politicians, business leaders, researchers, religious leaders, and so forth advance particular ideas, laws, and practices in education intended to *improve* societal outcomes. Every proposal stems from a particular worldview, a place from where people speak and act in the world. For the purposes of this chapter, I focus on the general tendencies of progressive educational philosophy as one of the fundamental building blocks of teacher education. I do this because it is often considered one of the most significant achievements of the liberal education movement and because, I argue, it has fallen short of where philosophy in teacher education needs to be. I then analyze the shifts that have taken place in education reform since the late 1980s and I propose a series of questions that educators must begin to ask about the purposes of schooling and its relationship to society. This chapter ends with a series of propositions intended to encourage debate and critical reflection for incoming generations of educators.

Progressive Education

The progressive educational tradition is most closely aligned with the work of the educator John Dewey. Dewey developed a philosophy of education based on his growing preoccupation with the dissonance between youths' experience in the classroom and the actual conditions and interactions of student experience in society. Dewey's ideas became known as *social pragmatism*, a term that referenced his concern with the relationship between the mind and body, communication, and how students' experiences could provide a basis for intelligent problem solving. Experience, for Dewey, was *social interaction* (Garrison, 1994) and a continuation of how people related to their natural environment and being in the social world. In this sense, Dewey's pursuit of *true ideas* in the *natural unit of society* (Hardie, 1962) was a move that attempted to help educators make sense of how knowledge came about. For Dewey, the mind was the embodiment of social practices (Schneider & Garrison, 2008) so that the structures of reality were always constructed by the "interactions of events" (Garrison, 1994, p. 7). Put simply, Dewey advocated for an active form of inquiry that would result in knowledge about what was taking place in the world. In the words of Jim Garrison, *"As Dewey saw it, we are participants in an unfinished universe rather than spectators of a finished universe"* (1994, p. 8, italics in original).

Preceding Dewey was an extended philosophical tradition that questioned the relationship between mind–body and knowing–doing. Philosophers have debated the connection between perception (ideas) and objects (matter) and whether human beings could ever truly know the world around them. Is knowledge solely a question of the mind? Is it a question about how people interact with the material world around them? Or is it both? Dewey became concerned with how educators, over time, had separated the mind from the body and how they pursued teaching practices that focused primarily on raison d'être without questioning its relevance to students' experiences and the interactions that constituted social life. For such reasons, Dewey adamantly opposed ranking knowledge from the "higher" cognitive world of ideas to the more mundane world of doing (or vice versa). For Dewey, the interaction between thought and action led to a "securer, freer and more widely shared embodiment of values in experience by means of that active control of objects which knowledge alone makes possible" (1929, p. 30).

In John Baldacchino's (2008) assessment, Dewey's educational thought "teaches us how to philosophize. By his example, we are taught how to move around and understand a multiplicity of experiences that are different and indeed diverse in nature and import" (p. 151). Philosophy, in other words, can be the basis for establishing an educational praxis linked with the pursuit of pluralism (i.e., diversity of views). Key to Dewey's conception of knowledge was a process of reflection that entailed the power of reasoning. Baldacchino asserts (following Biesta, 1994) that Dewey's philosophy was most concerned with the exchange of ideas and conjoint student activity as a form of democratizing *communication*. The argument proposes that by reflecting on the development of ideas that takes place in everyday activities we approach clarity of thought. With clarity of ideas:

> understanding cannot be subservient to anything but the truth that we recognize (sic) by dint of our growth and by which we lay claim upon an open-ended form of reflective thinking through the development of our own dispositions. Truth, therefore, does not emerge from a grammar of clarity. Rather, any grammar of clarity emerges from the dispositional truth by which humans exercise their power of reasoning. (Baldacchino, 2008, p. 151)

Here, reason as a discovery of truth is grounded in a reflection of one's surroundings and experiences. In Dewey's words, "reason affords the basis of certainty . . . we ascend from belief to knowledge only by isolating the latter from practical doing and making" (1929, p. 26).

The pragmatist view of education is at the heart of the liberal/progressive movement in U.S. education. Linking the formation of knowledge with the direct experience of students in the context of their environment established (in theory) more participatory and inclusive models of educational practice that sought to overturn the authoritarian focus of schooling. Rather than catering to the educator as the all-knowing deliverer of ideas and beliefs, students and their environments became the focus of educational practice, building upon the notion of democracy as a mode of associated living. Here, the communication of experience established the consensus of difference. Moving away from the Cartesian[1] preoccupation with the mind and consciousness, the liberal progressive tradition attempted to emphasize communication as "participation in conjoint activity" (Biesta, 1994). Educators were asked to abandon their tendencies toward rote memorization and curricular control and advance in their stead grounded methodologies and practices that were shaped largely by the level of the "unknown." Unknowing in this sense is driven by an intellectual imperative toward knowing so that the realm of student experience and context refracted the always partial understanding that an educator had about her subject matter and students with whom she worked. In these educational spaces, the locus of control has much less to do with affirming an educator's rank or grasp of material, and more with the inherent possibilities of generating knowledge that has direct relevance to students' experiences and interactions. Teacher educators, in turn, were conceived as social scientists, with the capacity and ability to organize educational practice based on their assessment of students' needs and experiences. Students—their lives and experiences—became the center of inquiry, in the hopes of generating meaningful knowledge that could be applied to real-world events. The importance of developing agency on behalf of the educator and student alike became the bedrock of radical liberalism, and social intelligence came to be conceived as the conduit for social change vis-à-vis rational conduct (Brosio, 1990).

Dominant Drift of Teacher Education

To understand the tendencies of teacher education and the system of beliefs and ethics that inspire reform, it is necessary to think about the changes that schools have undergone in the 20th century. Since the early 1980s, we have witnessed a spate of dramatic shifts and turns in U.S. education policy. Motivated by an urge to decrease government spending on public services and to roll back the so-called welfare state, politicians have introduced free market reforms to replace public, judicial, and democratic attempts to reversing the historical legacy of increased economic, racial, and social segregation in public schools. While education critics such as Jonathon Kozol (2005) have decried the creation of what he calls "apartheid schooling" the wealthy, powerful, and predominantly Anglo-Saxon student populations of the country continue to reap the benefits of U.S. schooling. They receive greater material (in the form of tangible sources—more qualified teachers, books, materials, labs, etc.) and social benefits (opportunities to pursue better employment, living wages, and political representation) than their racially and economically stratified counterparts do. This sometimes glaring disparity between student populations is often discussed in terms of structural or deep racism, and, less frequently, class-based alienation, or a form of racial *and* class stratification. However, what remains largely ignored in these discussions has to do with the basic foundation upon which many of these social disparities hinge. In other words, the link between the fundamental social relations of capitalist society and education reform is relatively unexamined and uncontested.

The dominant drift of educational reform refers to a set of processes that take place along the continuum of dominant ideas, norms, and values of society and the concrete, real, and historical conditions that have shaped educational philosophies and practices. For the remainder of this chapter, the dominant drift is discussed in terms of the *Imaginary* and *Real* conditions that shape teacher education in capitalist society. Here, the Imaginary refers to ideology—the categories and ideas that we draw on to recognize ourselves in society—and the Real corresponds to the structural determinants and social relations of capitalist society in which the Imaginary operates. We can say that as historical and social human subjects our understanding of the social world in capitalist society is shaped by the very ideals and representations that gain meaning in the circulation of texts (media, language, and otherwise) that are largely separated from how people actually come to know themselves and the world around them. These very ideas, or ideology, operate on an unequal field, where economic and social disparities exist and where public institutions, such as schools, transmit and produce knowledge differentially. Historically, efforts have been made in educational philosophy and practice to attend to the structural hierarchies and inequities among social groups and student populations. In the liberal-progressive tradition discussed earlier, attempts were made to remedy social inequalities by democratic means by changing both the organizational structure of teaching and learning and the different ways that teachers and students alike pursue knowledge formation. For example, rows of desks were discouraged, authoritarianism was considered counterproductive, and experimentation, creativity, and problem solving were brought into the curriculum. I maintain, however, that what is needed is a critical philosophy of teacher education that questions the presuppositions of liberal-progressive education reform and that epistemologically breaks from traditional paradigms of knowing, or imagining the world, revealing the smoke and curtains, so to speak, of how educational philosophies and practices operate in capitalist society.

To an unhealthy degree, a hierarchical educational system and structure that separate the have-nots from the haves (or the have-mores, according to some political circles) are considered an unpleasant but unavoidable commonplace in capitalist society. Where reform and reformers attempt to make their mark is not in contesting the very system that advances inequity and disparity a priori, but rather in regulating the educational market to allow more of the have-nots to incorporate into the haves and have-mores. In effect, what we are witnessing is the marrying of individualism and capitalism similar (yet philosophically opposite) to the alchemist tradition of creating a magnum opus or great work of renowned achievement. Politicians, lobbyists, CEOs, political advisors, and the like come together in the golden chambers of Congress, writing, devising, and experimenting with a series of proposals designed to enhance social policy in the so-called free market society of capitalism. *Competition, individual choice, accountability,* and *standards of achievement* are the keywords associated with this movement, and teachers are expected to deliver quality services to their clients (i.e., students). The point is that successive waves of education reform have been remarkably successful in altering the state of education across the country and in aligning the development of its citizenry with the implicit goals of capitalist society. Production and consumption in capitalist society and the beliefs, values, and ethics implicit in the formation of knowledge and practice in U.S. school settings are profoundly intertwined, pressing teacher education reform into the ideological coordinates and organizational structures of dominant reform initiatives. The liaison between neoliberal social and education policy and a population that equates having more with an idealized sense of being more is difficult to break, given the lack of critique or questioning about the social-economic system that underwrites U.S. citizenship.

In the field of education, welcoming gestures toward capitalist schooling are relatively noticeable. Free market principles under the rubric of school choice in educational legislation have been established (conflating choice with notions of democracy building; see McLaren & Jaramillo, 2007). In common speech it sounds something like this: If you're not getting what you need, then pay for it elsewhere. We have also witnessed legislation advancing educational reform in the spirit of national security, competitiveness in the global market, military recruitment, monolingualism as an index of national identity, Judeo-Christian values in the curriculum (see McLaren & Jaramillo, 2007), and/or strictly positivist conceptions of scientific research that serve to regulate schooling and advance private and/or nationalist interests.

Some argue that this is the natural and inevitable path that education must take precisely because the United States as the world's superpower depends on the advancement of capital, cultural homogeneity, and militarism in the face of terrorism as indexed by the horrific attacks of September 11, 2001. Others posit that the liberal and progressive tendencies of education reform from the 1950s through 1960s did nothing to increase student achievement or teachers' qualifications to provide service to an increasingly diverse student demographic. Missing from either of these arguments is the critical questioning necessary for a democratic and pluralistic society to flourish. Teacher educators, students, and communities need to be given the opportunity to ask questions that speak to their histories and to their participation in education. Some of the questions may include: Whose needs or interests are being met in education reform today? What is the social and political context informing education reform? What are the ideals of a so-called capitalist democracy and how do those ideals translate to educational practice? Is democracy compatible with converting education into a business-centered venture, where public services are taken over by private entities? What is the prevailing philosophy that shapes teacher education and how does it differ from philosophical tendencies of the past?

While blind belief in the inevitability of capitalism and its ability to regulate itself has been challenged by the current global crisis of capital, it remains the case that historically there has never been a clear line of separation between the needs of an evolving U.S. capitalist economy, a maturing system of governance, and educational measures aimed toward *patria.* There was a time, however, when working people could partially depend on the welfare state for supplying essential health and educational benefits. That is all but gone in the 21st century and education as one of the primary social benefits historically afforded to peoples as a local state responsibility is being increasingly usurped by the intensification of the corporate complex assuming ownership of public services. As Henry Giroux and Ken Saltman (2008) note, steady efforts to

> disinvest in public schools as critical sites of teaching and learning and govern them according to corporate interests is obvious in the emphasis on standardized testing, the use of top-down curricular mandates, the influx of advertising in schools, the use of profit motives to "encourage" student performance, the attack on teacher unions and modes of pedagogy that stress rote learning and memorization. (p. 1)

The logic of neoliberalism and the ethic of individualism have systematically etched away at the collective sensibility associated with caring for a citizenry through public means. At the same time, nationhood has translated into better production and consumption of capitalist goods. In education, this translates to teacher educators, students, researchers, and communities alike being placed in a position to accept and comply with the reform measures undertaken by government (vis-à-vis neoliberal social policy) rather than participate from the bottom up in building a nation predicated on resurrecting the ideals of pluralism, sovereignty, and the development of personhood and agency.

The natural unit of society (as sociable and interacting peoples) as the field from which to establish educational practices has been trumped by wider political-economic and institutional relations that, at first glance, seem far removed from everyday life. A philosophic shift in how the teaching encounter is conceived and in how educators, students, and communities are asked to think about the relationship between the economy, politics, and culture and the formation of youth in U.S. schools has taken place.

Democratic Education in the Imaginary and Real America

The dominant drift described earlier has been accompanied by a sustained and increasingly complex system of beliefs and ideals that circulate in the capitalist commonplace, or what we might call the capitalist Imaginary. At question here is the necessity for educators to develop an awareness of the dominant discourses and tropes that shape teacher education reform and to understand the historical relationship that exists between education and capitalist society. Too often a detheorization of the teaching encounter has taken place, stripping educators of the opportunity to develop a critical awareness or consciousness of education as a central and important practice and setting for the formation of our subjectivities and our political agency. Instead of introducing educators to history and theory and encouraging the development of a philosophical praxis, many of our teacher education programs, both in the United States and abroad, focus on the managerial, instrumental, or technical (i.e., delivery system) aspects of the profession (see Huerta-Charles, 2004).

Teacher education is both a business and a high-stakes field that requires practical and deliberative action. Educators pay for their credentials, and hiring agencies require numerous tests for placement purposes. Teacher educators want to keep it simple, "tell us what we need to know so that we can work" is one of the many daily mantras heard in teacher education programs. But teacher educators require and can benefit from a language and a schema that can assist them in charting out the educational enterprise. It cannot be only self-interest that motivates teacher educators, but a moral and ethical imperative to provide service to a citizenry in addition to the knowledge and technical skills that make education possible. When it comes to a philosophy of education we are faced with two choices: We can either overcomplicate matters to the extent of unintelligibility, or follow Albert Einstein's dictum: "make things as simple as possible, but not simpler."

In the late 1980s, the communications theorist and social critic Anthony Wilden wrote a groundbreaking text, *The Imaginary Canadian*, where he adopted key terms (similar to, but not identical with) from the psychoanalytic philosopher Jacques Lacan—the Imaginary and the Real—to designate the individual and structural determinants that shape hierarchical relations within capitalist society. Wilden attempted to personalize the abstract dimensions of consciousness and develop a typology to explain how people from dominant and subordinate positions in capitalist society related to one another in real economic and social terms. Writing specifically about the Canadian context, Wilden (1980) describes the Imaginary thusly:

> The Imaginary presently dominates our understanding of social and economic relationships. This means that we do not primarily perceive and understand our relationships to the many different kinds of people in Canadian society on the basis of real images and real concepts. Rather we depend on Imaginary images and Imaginary concepts. These are in effect socially defined and accepted fantasies which are commonly assumed to be real. (p. 65)

For Wilden, an analysis of Imaginary relations consisted of two basic components: one, the distinction between Imaginary relationships and Real ones, and second, the "contradictions and inconsistencies within the Imaginary viewpoint itself" (p. 65). The general architecture of capitalist society, for Wilden, rested on human experience and interactions predicated on the Imaginary. Imaginary images and concepts represented the socially defined and accepted "fantasies" that, for Wilden, were commonly assumed to be real by the majority of the public. The central determining characteristic of the Imaginary is the image. Here we can substitute for *image* the concepts that give society their meaning, whether it is *democracy*, *equal opportunity*, or any other term that we hold steadfast in our everyday practice. Wilden's analysis attempts to contrast prevailing beliefs—their formation and circulation—against the concrete, real social and economic terms in which people operate on an everyday basis. Wilden further notes:

The dominance of the Imaginary over our actual social and economic relations in our kind of society is a collectively experienced and collectively supported system of mirages. This collective experience leads to apparently individual and apparently psychological behavior. In fact, this behavior has its primary source in social and economic relations. The reason that it may appear "inherent" in the "individual" is simply that this behavior is characteristic of the social and economic system which brings us up to behave as we actually do. (p. 66)

By adapting Wilden's contributions on the Imaginary and the Real to the U.S. context, we can consider society as a series of constraints that we often discuss in binary terms: man versus woman, Black versus White, poor versus rich, and so forth. The tensions that emerge between people (depending on how they are socially categorized) are often considered along individual terms, based on the *patterns* of individual behavior. But what is often missed in understanding how social constraints emerge, and as Wilden elaborates, is the acknowledgment of how our socioeconomic system co-establishes the conditions in which people interact. For instance, racial, sexual, ethnic, and cultural hierarchies are constitutive elements of the general economic system of capitalist society. And as Wilden insightfully notes, they assume individual and *imaginary* qualities that often "explain away" concrete sources of oppression within hierarchical social structures. This brings to mind George Orwell's remark: "To see what is in front of one's nose needs constant struggle." The point to be made in situating Wilden's insights within the social and political dimensions of teacher education, socially and politically, is to reveal how schools—as social media—are the expression of real social and economic conflicts. They constitute, in other words, not binary oppositions in some metaphysical domain, but real dependent hierarchies.

A central feature of the U.S. Imaginary has historically been shaped by the notion that capitalism is compatible with democratic social formations. From the onset, schooling in the United States has served an important purpose in an evolving capitalist economy, supporting the values of individualism and merit most closely aligned with fitting a populace to the demands of capitalist democracy. Consequently, formal legal frameworks and social institutions such as education—the face of government—emphasized the notion of equal opportunity as the central characteristic of a capitalist democracy. Constitutional amendments, Supreme Court rulings banning the racial segregation of public schools, and federal education policy aimed

at alleviating poverty and cultural/linguistic discrimination in schools' curricula and operating structures made important gains in remedying the historical legacy of sexism and racism in the country, but they did so still
operating within the Imaginary ideal of U.S. society.

The problem with the Imaginary of equal opportunity in capitalism is
that it consequently obscures the structural limitations and boundaries that
condition human activity in social institutions, such as schools. Rather than
drawing attention to the social organization and social relations between and
among different actors in education, the Imaginary of capitalist democracy
reproduces the belief that academic failure is largely the result of individual
characteristics. Whether the blame is placed on educators and administrators
as ineffective, lazy, unqualified, and so forth or on the families themselves as
poor, uninformed, culturally dissonant, or otherwise, the predominant belief
systems in education attribute blame to either or both groups for paltry
academic outcomes. This forms part of what Wilden calls the projection,
identification, and objectification of the "other" for legitimizing the pervasive Imaginary social view.

As Wilden writes, an Imaginary projection of the other "is the process
by which we are induced, by the combination of apparent personal experience and social norms, to select a particular other or a group of others as the
supposed source of the alienation we feel, and to blame these others for our
alienated feelings" (1980, p. 67). In the context of education, we can consider
the feelings of alienation that an educator might feel when she does not
speak the language or share cultural attributes with her students. Her perceived problem is not that she lacks the repertoire or knowledge to move
outside her immediate feelings of discomfort and into a productive pedagogical space where she can identify with her students, but that her students are
the sole cause for her inability to connect with them. The Imaginary processes of identification and objectification differ from projection in that they
reflect processes by which we "identify the image of our 'self' with the image
of the other; or else we identify our 'self-image' in opposition to the other.
In both cases, we are defining the image of the other (as distinct from the
reality of the other) as essential to the image of our self" (p. 67).

Here, the other satisfies the image of that we prefer not to become, or
identify with; the other becomes an object separate from ourselves. By sepa-
rating our image from others, we can differentiate—confirm or discon-
firm—how we choose to see ourselves. "I" can judge my actions, values,
ethics based on what "I" find missing/extreme in the other. This is qualita-
tively different from identifying difference among us; it implies a moral,

ethical, and cultural response to objectifying the other based on the value we place on him/her/them to construct our self-image. And when the history of social difference and hierarchies that have contributed to a collective image of both the self and other upset our subconscious, we can more readily blame the other for our sense of alienation. In other words, there is not self-image without the other; they are always mutually constitutive. We are always already self/other.

In 2008, the French film *Entre les murs* (*The Class*) made international headlines after receiving awards, nominations, and accolades at the 2008 Cannes Film Festival and the U.S. Academy Awards. The film is "based on an autobiographical novel by author and former teacher François Bégaudeau, about working at a tough multi-ethnic school in the Parisian banlieux" (Bradshaw, 2009). Bégaudeau is a teacher of French language and literature who is both passionate about his subject matter and students' learning, but who also experiences great discomfort and difficulty when his students seemingly lash out at him or at one another. The film has been summarized as follows:

> The trickiest member of the class is Souleymane (Franck Keita), a boy from Mali with family problems and a temper. Souleymane cheekily tells François that he has heard the teacher "likes men"—and insolently says that this is not his own accusation, just something he has heard. Happily, François finds a way to get through to Souleymane: he turns out to take great photos of his family on his mobile phone and François gets him to use these pictures in an autobiographical class project: it is a euphoric breakthrough. But things turn very sour when two girls are allowed to sit in on a staff discussion on standards and behaviour and gleefully report some disobliging remarks back to Souleymane, who is deeply angry and hurt after his class-project triumph, with no vocabulary to express his sense of betrayal. François himself is coldly furious at the girls' indiscretion and accuses them in class of behaving like "pétasses"—"skanks"—crucially losing his cool and compromising his authority. That crude insult ignites a violent row, which becomes toxic when François neglects to mention the "skanks'" provocation in his official report. When challenged, François airily insists he was not saying that they were "skanks," merely that they were behaving as such—the same species of dishonest sophistry that Souleymane used with his "gay" jibe. (Bradshaw, 2009)

Bégaudeau's case is not exemplary or out of the ordinary; he exposes one of the essences of being human, of being a contradictory and flawed professional. We could think of Bégaudeau, to some extent, as the only "true" Frenchman in the classroom—he dominated the language, the literature, and the customs. His students, primarily immigrant and working class, had different realities, concerns, and experiences. Perhaps Bégaudeau could see himself as the true Frenchman in relation to the un-Frenchness of his students. And yet in the end, he too resorted to slurs and epithets that he had associated with the undisciplined other. It is in this way that we are always self/other.

These are complicated arguments to make, and my intent here is not to suggest that educators must undergo intensive psychoanalytic training to help make sense of how they do or do not relate to students who differ from themselves. But Wilden's points on the Imaginary do offer important insights that help make sense of the tensions, contradictions, and relationships that transpire in educational settings.

Too often educational practice is severed from the symbolic, subjective, and concrete realms that condition human interactions. My purpose is to illuminate the two governing worldviews that have historically characterized U.S. society. There is the world of the Imaginary, where dominant ideas and beliefs about the role of education in a capitalist society is to operate as a mechanism for distributing equal opportunity to its citizens, and the concrete worldview shaped by the actual historical and social contexts that people inhabit. The Imaginary world has a prescient quality. The concrete worldview includes an analysis and understanding of the hierarchies that take place in real time and on real terms. The concrete worldview expresses real social and economic conflicts and demonstrates an awareness of the dominant-subordinate hierarchies within capitalist society.

Many of the gains made in expanding equal opportunity in education to marginalized student groups have resulted from the concrete struggle of peoples who, on the one hand, understood how social hierarchies operated within U.S. society and who, on the other, believed in the imaginary ideals of a capitalist democracy. Following the civil rights movement and the Great Depression of the 1930s, social stratification along race, ethnic, gender, and class lines assumed greater significance as the courts and education systems began to remedy the historically *unequal* structural dynamics that limited educational opportunities to the other—non-White, female, poor, or any combination thereof. In light of the unequal distribution of educational opportunities and outcomes for the colonized and dominated peoples of U.S. society—indigenous peoples, women, low-wage laborers, the formerly enslaved, and immigrants—educators and philosophers began to question the underlying ideals communicated through differential educational systems and their effect on nascent democratic formations. Put in Wilden's terms, the Imaginary was contrasted with the concrete, and people struggled to surpass the contradictions between what was and what could be.

Liberal Progressive Attempts to Remedy Education

In education, the liberal-progressive tradition emerged as an attempt to restructure teaching and learning in pursuit of reconciling the ideals of democracy with historically unequal educational practices. Operating against the seemingly detached and authoritarian practices of what has been called the essentialist or perennial tradition in education—a teacher-centered approach that privileges principles over the pursuit of truths, canonical texts over literatures based on diverse experiences, the teaching of basic skills to fulfill a function in society over the development of human agency to change society—social pragmatism began to gain momentum and its impact on education was both profound and endearing. It was not so much that the wider economic and political arrangements associated with the social stratification inherent in capitalist society came under question; rather, a focus on the capacity for intelligent problem solving across peoples irrespective of race, class, or gender differences was given greater significance for alleviating social ills.

Over time, the ideas of social pragmatists such as Dewey have garnered greater attention and have been adapted into various teacher education efforts to make the classroom more experiential, less teacher centered, and more sensitive to the realities and experiences of students. In short, greater focus has been given to the creation of *cooperative communities* where students come together to problem solve, experiment, and develop both moral and academic reasoning. Communication plays a central role in such settings, and students are expected to tap into the affective dimensions of their actions and conflicts with others/nature. Social equality is also given primacy as all participants in the educational process are considered able and free to pursue inquiry. Within these settings teachers are encouraged to facilitate, to create, and to see themselves as participants within the class community.

These Dewey-inspired efforts are not issues of concern if and when we think of education as separate from the social structures that condition human experiences. But when we recognize that the everyday and seemingly individual characteristics of experience generate commonalities as well as differences, and that life outside the classroom is as much a part of the individual experience as what takes place inside, then we recognize that communication alone cannot bring about new knowledge(s) or new practice(s) in and of itself. Communication is a necessary component of democratic formations and of generating more inclusive, ethical, and pedagogical means of helping students connect with their environment, the mind with the body, and so forth. But communication as reasoning is not a value-free practice. Lacking a critical interrogation into how people perceive reality, why they perceive it the way that they do, and the historical context of such reasoning, communicative interactions tend to reproduce the very Imaginary worldview from which dominant ideas originate. Obscuring the real contexts of relations between people as "relations of communication" has the tendency to support the representation of the Imaginary as "relations between subjects and objects" (Wilden, 1980, p. 75). A closed communication system between a person and her immediate social setting or between people within a structured educational setting, with its rules and social customs of conduct, leads to an either/or relationship in the Imaginary. Or as Wilden puts it, "In the Imaginary, there is only one subject in the world—you (or me!) and in this either/or relationship in the Imaginary, everyone else is simply an object floating around in your 'field of view' (or mine)" (p. 75).

Dewey's philosophy can be useful in expanding our discussion of the Imaginary. Dewey recognized the constraints placed on educators and educational practice at a time in U.S. history when capitalist, private control over public services was relatively minor as compared to today. He strongly supported the formation of teacher and professorial unions as a way to safeguard against the "business mind-set" that threatened an educator's freedom and legal protection for teaching and engaging in serious research, some of which might be deemed in conflict with prevailing ideological sentiments or conventional social reasoning. And his determined belief in the facts about "human activity" signaled a move away from the Imaginary realm of unquestioned ideas and images about society and into the Real, concrete and material formations that shape experience. The issue at hand has more to do with the various mainstream and traditional interpretations of Dewey's philosophy that on one hand recognizes the unequal opportunities within society but that supports, on the other hand, the belief that adjustments to the system vis-à-vis establishing lines of communication and dialogue can bring forth a more democratic society.

Toward a Critical Philosophy of Teacher Education

Teacher educators and teacher education programs across the country will always be asked to direct their attention to the state of the nation's schools.

With every new presidential administration, or new Congressional term, there is—undoubtedly—a plea, a reform initiative, or a new idea about how to fix U.S. schools. Teacher educators find themselves at the crossroads. In one direction, they can think back to a historical legacy of progressive educational reform and philosophies that have attempted to restore the ideals of democracy in schooling. In another direction they are being asked to toughen up, work harder, and ensure that youth acquire the skills and habits that demonstrate "proficiency." Teachers may be told that theory and philosophy are irrelevant; that what matters is the mastery of subject matter to deliver to students. Such oppositions in teacher education are unnecessary. Who can argue that knowing a subject is not important for teaching? And who can rightfully state that the ideas and values that we carry about the social world do not shape our *knowing* of a subject? A critical philosophy of teacher education does not assume an either/or position.

In light of these developments, it is imperative for teacher educators to gain knowledge of and insight into a wide array of educational philosophies and to ground their teaching practice historically and socially in the communities they serve. In closing, I discuss—albeit briefly—some central tenets of a critical philosophy of teacher education.

At the forefront of a critical philosophy of teacher education is the realization that history is a necessary component to understanding how present conditions have enabled or disabled individuals to become independent, sovereign subjects, able to exercise their agency in the realm of social life. A critical philosophy of teacher education requires the historicity of teaching and learning in U.S. schools and a grounding of teacher education in an understanding of the dominant philosophies and practices that have shaped Western thought (often in opposition to non-Western and indigenous systems of knowledge) in general and the teaching encounter more specifically. This brings into focus a reinterrogation of the notion of ethics, values, and epistemic formations in teacher education.

On the question of epistemology and epistemic justice, a critical philosophy of teacher education examines dominant ways of knowing and being (the ruling epistemes) set forth in Western philosophy, dating back to the formative Greek thought of Socrates, Plato, and Aristotle (the foundation of what is referred to as Idealist and Pragmatist philosophy) and proceeding forward with the various manifestations and iterations that educational philosophy undertook in the context of Colonial America and the post–Civil Rights era. At the basis of such questioning is the imperative to undo the mythic status of the Imaginary and to situate philosophical thought in the real and concrete dimensions that govern knowledge formations. Interrogating the basis of philosophical thought leads to the following questions: What is the relationship between the mind (thinking) and body (doing) in dominant Western philosophy? What is the relationship between mind, body, and the logic of colonial domination in America? How has knowledge been affected by the inherent hierarchies of an evolving capitalist society? How is knowledge both race-/ethnic-specific and gendered? Here, it may be useful for teacher educators to visit the work of scholars and philosophers working outside the dominant center of Western philosophy who provide insights into Western knowledge formations. Consider, for example, the ideas set forward by Ramon Grosfoguel, a sociologist who works within the decolonial Imaginary:

> Rene Descartes, the founder of modern Western philosophy, inaugurates a new moment in the history of Western thought. He replaces God as the foundation of knowledge in the Theo-politics of knowledge of the European Middle Ages with (Western) Man as the foundation of knowledge in European Modern times. All the attributes of God are now extrapolated to (Western) Man. Universal Truth beyond time and space, privilege access to the laws of the Universe, and the capacity to produce scientific knowledge and theory is now placed in the mind of Western Man. The Cartesian "cogito ergo sum" ("I think, therefore I am") is the foundation of modern Western sciences. By producing a dualism between mind and body and between mind and nature, Descartes was able to claim non-situated, universal, God-eyed view knowledge. This is what the Colombian philosopher Santiago Castro-Gomez called the "point zero" perspective of Eurocentric philosophies (Castro-Gomez, 2003). The "point zero" is the point of view that hides and conceals itself as being beyond a particular point of view, that is, the point of view that represents itself as being without a point of view. It is this "god-eye view" that always hides its local and particular perspective under an abstract universalism. Western philosophy privileges "ego politics of knowledge" over the "geopolitics of knowledge" and the "body-politics of knowledge." Historically, this has allowed Western man (the gendered term is intentionally used here) to represent his knowledge as the only one capable of achieving a universal consciousness, and to dismiss non-Western knowledge as particularistic and, thus, unable to achieve universality.

The point to be taken from the preceding excerpt from Grosfoguel is that philosophy, like education, is not a value-neutral or bias-free discipline. The very origins of Western philosophical thought were grounded in the ethic of colonization, the forced removal of peoples across the globe, and their subsequent incorporation into a burgeoning capitalist formation. The "point zero" perspective of all knowledge being born in the universal conceptions of being and doing in Western philosophical thought are recaptured in the Imaginary ideals and visions of U.S. society. Understanding philosophy's development over time, in real space and under concrete conditions, sheds light on the contradictions and tensions inherent in Western thought and their subsequent implementation in educational practice. From the onset, the nation's schools have been characterized by a small yet increasingly diverse student population, all of whom enter the system shaped by their particular histories and genealogies.

Questioning the governing premises that shape teachers' personal and practical classroom knowledges and formal teaching practices creates the spaces for a critical positioning between dominant modes of thought and the "other" knowledges that students bring into the class setting—or those knowledges that are never brought in under "normal" circumstances. Here, an evolving critical philosophy of teacher education begins at the point of critique and pursues a dialectical form of creating knowledges and modes of understanding that finds its grounding in the abstract ideals of so-called democracy but that pairs such thinking/doing with the actual and everyday conditions of communities. In this case, democracy is not considered a priori as an established condition that is obtained in society but rather is questioned and actively pursued in conjunction with communities themselves. In this case, communication takes on a critical dimension and not only signals the democratic exchange of human experience but also provides the context for evaluating and determining the spaces that can enable democratic knowledge formations to emerge. Paulo Freire discussed this in terms of problem-posing education, where teaching/learning was moved forward by a sustained criticality and questioning of the environment and the concrete places/conditions that people inhabited. In a similar vein, what I propose here requires the additional dimension of historicity and attention to the particular genealogies that shape the teaching encounter.

Summary

Philosophizing is an underdeveloped skill in teacher education, even though it has the decisive duty to help us understand the relationship between society and schools. Connecting a critical doing with a critical thinking in teacher education allows educators to begin to exercise their capacities and abilities for fully engaging the teaching encounter. In the absence of one over the other (thinking over doing, or vice versa), teacher education follows the well-traveled path formed by dominant ideas, values, and belief systems that remain unchallenged and that—to a remarkable extent—are unfounded. Those living in the United States can click their heels and utter the word *democracy* thrice over, but they still won't find themselves in Oz. Perhaps French sociologist Emile Durkheim (2002) brought our attention to the misguided practice of teacher education best when he wrote:

> If educational theory goes beyond its proper limits, if it pretends to supplant experience, to promulgate ready-made formulae that are then applied mechanically, it degenerates into dead matter. If, on the other hand, experience disregards pedagogical thinking, it in turn degenerates into blind routine or else is at the mercy of ill-informed or unsystematic thinking. (p. 2)

Needed is a critical language and the sustained development of ideas, conjugated with a praxis of knowledge construction (or questioning) that can enable teachers to pull back the curtains and see for themselves the spinning wheels, levers, and the ideological smoke that diminish a great idea like democracy.

Progressive education, once a hopeful model for participatory educational practice, has been usurped by society's overarching ideologies—causing the dominant shift of teacher education. Teacher education struggles with the tension between capitalist society and democratic education; the Imaginary of a complex system of beliefs that herald individuality, materialism, and patriotism competes with the Real or lived experiences of disenfranchised learners. The liberal-progressive attempts to reconcile the Imaginary and the Real proposes epistemological decentering as a vehicle for true democratic change, a fundamental mechanism for educators and students to understand how people perceive America's social realities. The promise of a critical philosophy for teacher education is not doing or thinking, but doing and thinking.

Notes

1. *Cartesian* refers to the philosophy of René Descartes, a French philosopher who is considered the father of modern Western philosophy.

References

Baldacchino, J. (2008). The power to develop dispositions: Revisiting John Dewey's democratic claims for education. *Journal of Philosophy of Education, 42*(1), 149–163.

Biesta, G. (1994). Pragmatism as a pedagogy of communicative action. *Studies in Philosophy and Education, 13,* 273–290.

Bradshaw, P. (2009). *The class.* Retrieved February 27, 2009, from www.guardian.co.uk/film/2009/feb/27/the-class-entre-les-murs

Brosio, R. A. (1990). Teaching and learning for democratic empowerment: A critical evaluation. *Educational Theory, 40*(1), 69–81.

Castro-Gomez, Santiago. (2003). *La hybris del Punto Cero: Biopolíticas imperiales y colonialidad del poder en la Nueva Granada (1750–1810).* Unpublished manuscript. Bogotá, Colombia: Instituto Pensar, Universidad Javeriana.

Dewey, J. (1929). *The quest for certainty: A study of the relation of knowledge and action.* Chicago: Southern Illinois University Press.

Durkheim, E. (2002). *Moral education.* New York: Dover Publications.

Garrison, J. (1994). Realism, Deweyan pragmatism, and educational research. *Educational Researcher, 23*(1), 5–14.

Giroux, H., & Saltman, K. (2008). *Obama's betrayal of public education? Arne Duncan and the corporate model of schooling.* Retrieved December 21, 2008, from www.truthout.org/121708R

Grosfoguel, R. (in press). Decolonizing political economy and post-colonial studies: Transmodernity, border thinking, and global community. In R. Grosfoguel, J. D. Saldivar, & N. Maldonado (Eds.), *Unsettling postcoloniality: Coloniality, transmodernity and border thinking.* Durham, NC: Duke University Press.

Hardie, C. (1962). *Truth and fallacy in educational theory.* New York: Teachers College Press.

Huerta-Charles, L. (2004). A forgotten issue in the education of teachers in Mexico. In J. O'Donnell, Marc Pruyn, & Rodolfo Chavez Chavez (Eds.), *Social justice in these times* (pp. 117–145). Greenwich, CT: Information Age Publishing.

Kozol, J. (2005). *The shame of the nation: The restoration of apartheid schooling in America.* New York: Crown Publishers.

McLaren, P., & Jaramillo, N. (2007). *Pedagogy and praxis in the age of empire: Towards a new humanism.* Rotterdam: Sense Publishers.

Schneider, S. B., & Garrison, J. (2008). Deweyan reflections on knowledge-producing schools. *Teachers College Record, 110*(10), 2204–2223.

Wilden, T. (1980). *The imaginary Canadian.* Vancouver, British Columbia: Pulp Press.

PART TWO

IMPLEMENTING VALUE-ADDED TEACHER TRAINING AND DEVELOPMENT

3

DISPOSITIONS MATTER

Advancing Habits of the Mind for Social Justice

Valerie Hill-Jackson and Chance W. Lewis

Watch your thoughts; they become words.
Watch your words; they become actions.
Watch your actions; they become habits.
Watch your habits; they become character.
Watch your character; it becomes your destiny.

Frank Outlaw, *Watch Your Thoughts*

Teachers must possess the professional triumvirate of knowledge, skills, and dispositions to be effective. Researchers have built the backbone of teacher education describing knowledge (Heibert, Gallimore, & Stigler, 2002; Leinhardt, 1990) and skills (Freiberg & Driscoll, 2000) needed to engender quality teachers. Yet the third construct, dispositions, has failed to garner the same type of gravitas in the field. Despite its marginalization in teacher education (Schussler, Bercaw, & Stooksberry, 2008), the critical study of dispositions for social justice may help to characterize its academic worth (Murray, 2007; Villegas, 2007) and serve as the linchpin for recognizing and selecting quality educators for the twenty-first century.

Diverse students, who have historically underperformed in America's schools compared to their White counterparts (Lee, 2002), need teachers with dispositions for social justice. The research has been discounted but clear—teachers with a disposition for social justice positively affect the achievement of diverse learners (Moll, 1992; Nieto, 2000; Ogbu, 1999; Tharp & Gallimore, 1998; Viadero, 1996). "The overriding goal of the social justice agenda in teacher education is to prepare teachers who can teach

61

all students well" (Villegas, 2007, p. 372). If teacher quality encompasses dispositions, then the development of teacher dispositions with an emphasis on educating the underserved is as important as the exploration of knowledge and skills and is the responsibility of colleges of education committed to democratic practice.

In the poem cited at the beginning of this chapter, popular culture figure Frank Outlaw charts how thoughts progress to become our words and habits, shaping our destiny of self. In other words, our attitude or ideologies are the precursors to our habits and behavior. *Attitudes* and *dispositions* are terms that are often used interchangeably; although related, these terms have different meanings. Allport (1935) demarcates attitudes as mental and neutral states of readiness, organized through experience, exerting a directive or dynamic influence upon the individual's response that directly influences behavior. Katz (2007) defines dispositions as habits of the mind. Murrell and Foster (2003) concur and describe dispositions as attitudes and beliefs that are manifested in behavior and professional activity. The link between attitudes/beliefs and dispositions has created mounting interest to reveal:

> Research on the relationship between educators' beliefs and practices indicates that the former assist educators in determining what is and what is not important in their practice. Beliefs act as a filter through which a host of instructional judgments and decisions are made. This supports Comb's (1972) contention that people's beliefs follow and flow from their perceptions of a situation. Thus beliefs help identify how one is disposed to behave, one's disposition. (cited in Huber-Warring & Warring, 2006, p. 39)

Giroux (1988) agrees that teachers' beliefs, or their ideologies, are a cogent force to understanding teacher practice and should be explored as we continue the arduous task of preparing the best leaders for America's classrooms. Kincheloe and McLaren (2002) declare that a *critique of ideology* must be one of the main objectives to make sense out of how ideologies are produced and reproduced. The pair proclaim:

> As long as our vision is obstructed by the various purveyors of ideology, our effort to live in democratic communities is thwarted. Power wielders with race, class, and gender privileges have access to the resources to promote ideologies and representations in a way individuals without such privilege cannot. (Kincheloe & McLaren, 2002, p. 104)

This provocative statement proposes that societal beliefs are transmitted by the power brokers of ideas and helps us to comprehend the current, pervasive, and dominant ideologies found in every aspect of American society. Bourdieu (1973) describes this succession of ideologies as a process known as social reproduction in which the societal norms are created, maintained, and replicated by those who constitute the dominant class. Delpit (1988) explains that the rules of culture and power are a reflection of the rules of the culture of those who have power. That is, those who craft and conduct the art of teaching often reproduce their culture in the field, which trickles down to the classroom. Because education is a mirror of society, it would follow then, the philosophy and ideological stance of education reflect that of the prevailing beliefs of those at its helm. For this reason, it becomes necessary to inspect the ideology of America's teaching force, a primarily White teaching cadre.

Landsman and Lewis (2006) explain the paradox that exists in teacher education: The power brokers. White pre-service teachers (WPTs), are the same critical mass who will be teaching in America's diverse schools and the same group that resists diversity. At the time of the printing of this book, 40% of learners in our classrooms are children of color (Gay, 2002) while 85% of the teachers continue to be White, middle class, and Christian (Applied Research Center, 2000). Villegas (2007) confirms:

> The line of research shows that prospective teachers generally enter teacher education believing cultural diversity is a problem to overcome and that students of color are deficient in some fundamental way. . . . teacher beliefs about students significantly shape the expectations they hold for student learning. . . . As Madom and colleagues (1997) put it, "teachers do indeed develop erroneous expectations for their students, and these expectations predict motivation and achievement." (p. 374)

The central argument of this chapter proposes that a *critique of ideology* is essential to the training and selection of quality teachers and

> given the need for teachers with the belief systems and the predispositions to effectively relate to diverse children . . . there can no longer be any question that selecting those with appropriate dispositions determines the usefulness of any subsequent teacher education program offered them. (Haberman, 2005, p. 11)

It is time to consider the many ways in which the teaching profession might determine whether teachers' ideologies are injurious or innocent to our learners. Teachers' thoughts lead to their classroom disposition, or pedagogical destiny, which becomes surreptitiously inserted into the classroom environment as part of the hidden or latent curriculum (Apple, 2004).

This chapter begins with a discussion on the definitions and rationale of dispositions for social justice in teacher education. We share research on WPTs and classify two competing ideologies that lead to teachers' pedagogical destinies. Second, we share the significance and methodology of a prior study on WPTs' dispositions in which their narrative was captured for critical review; we sifted their words as a means to decipher their attitudes and ideologies. Third, the results from this prior study shed light on future teachers' ideologies by highlighting five salient dispositions. Fourth, a short discussion on who should teach in diverse classrooms is warranted. Fifth and finally, this chapter closes with some recommendations for the critique of ideology in the preparation of future teachers.

Dispositions Matter: Social Justice and the Status Quo

Dispositions for Social Justice

The definition of *dispositions*, or habits of the mind, is often opaque and has many orientations (Schussler, 2006). *Habits of the Mind: Thinking in the Classroom* (Thompson, 1995) introduces the origin of the phrase "habits of the mind":

> Alexis de Tocqueville commented on the "habits of the heart" of the American people. Late in the 19th century, into the 20th, William James, then John Dewey, counseled teachers that life is a "mass of habits" and that education "consists in the formation of wide-awake, careful, thorough habits of teaching." (p. x)

The long history of the exploration of teacher habits has evolved over the years to a newly formulated charge in teacher education that encourages the field to prepare teachers in an effort to connect with, communicate with, and educate diverse learners effectively (Darling-Hammond & Bransford, 2005). In 2002, the National Council for Accreditation of Teacher Education (NCATE) defined *dispositions* as follows:

> the values, commitments and professional ethics that influence behaviors toward students, families, colleagues and communities and affect student learning, motivation and development as well as the educator's own professional growth. Dispositions are guided by beliefs and attitudes related

to values such as caring, fairness, honesty, responsibility and social justice. (p. 53)

Similarly, the definition of social justice is also vague and receives little attention in teacher education. Sleeter (1996) defines social justice as "having the perspective that allows one to take social action against social structural inequality and an understanding of oppression and inequality which allows greater insight into methods of eradicating them" (p. 239). The concept of social justice is richly explored in educational research and has come to represent a process and a goal (Bell, 1997); a fluid construct (North, 2006); liberatory consciousness (Love, 2000); affirmation of difference and self, but a challenge to the status quo (Ladson-Billings, 1995); a continuous act of suspending habitual acts of domination (McLaren, 1998); and a set of principles for equity pedagogy (Cochran-Smith, 2004). Villegas (2007) clarifies the complexity of social justice and defines it as "a broad approach to education that aims to have all students reach high levels of learning and to prepare them all for active and full participation in a democracy" (p. 372).

Dispositions and social justice are inextricably attached and require mindful inquiry that forces us to reflect on the many ways that our disposition, that is, thoughts put to action, can oppress or empower learners. Although it is the intention of this chapter to focus on social justice, we define social justice as a frame of mind, or ideology, and assert that multicultural education is one of the many mechanisms for achieving social justice in teacher preparation (Sleeter & Grant, 2007). The first author does, in fact, use multicultural education courses as the conduit for teaching social justice ideas.

Over the years, NCATE presumably has provided accountability for multicultural education related to social justice in accredited teacher preparation programs. However, the effectiveness of these multicultural classes has been questioned (Garmon, 2004; Lesko & Bloom, 1998; Wideen, Mayer-Smith, & Moon, 1998) because most colleges of education are disobeying this directive by offering only one course that is at best dismissive and pacifist, and at worst negligent in meeting the needs of diverse learners. Colleges of education have scrambled to assemble their own versions of disposition checklists. For example, at our university the current NCATE disposition directory, shared with all teaching faculty, refers to such habits of the mind as oral and written communication, attire, tardiness, work habits, initiative, critical thinking, and respect for others—in all, a total of 13 dispositions that omit culture, diversity, and justice. A preliminary and informal review of several notable colleges of education around the country reveals that a serious acknowledgment of culture and social justice is missing from the professional criteria in the assessment of teacher disposition.[1]

As numerous educational researchers have documented, existing public schools are profoundly unequal, stratified by race and class. All across the nation educators face many challenges attending to the needs of diverse groups. Especially troublesome are the economic, social, and political contexts that make difficult our attempts to address differences and oppression in schools and society. Yet, in the face of these challenges, teacher education has failed to make significant changes in the preparation of future teachers. McDonald (2005) proposes that the study of social justice among pre-service teachers is important because it can help them develop conceptual and practical tools related to the needs of marginalized students. We argue that dispositions for social justice can be operationalized to assist pre-service teachers in (a) understanding the sociopolitical context of schools and communities, (b) advocating for disenfranchised students, and (c) promoting and evaluating culturally relevant pedagogy among our primarily White teaching force.

A Note on White Pre-Service Teachers: The Wielders of Ideological Power

The overwhelming presence of whiteness in the teaching population (Sleeter, 2001), along with the growing student diversity, should propel the field to produce teachers who have dispositions for social justice. An ideological lens on teachers informs us that they are not neutral beings (Viadero, 1996); the resistant behavior and decisions made in the classroom reflect the opposing ideology of the teachers and the profession. Every teacher disposition, regardless of proclaimed objectivity, has an acute effect on the learners in the classroom. Because WPTs make up 85% of the teaching force, their ideology is pervasive and influential. For sure, WPTs are the ideological power wielders in America's classrooms, given the weight of teachers' views and expectations of diverse learners. Teacher expectations are directly related to achievement; low expectations of students lead to low student achievement (Madom, Jussim, & Eccles, 1997; Rosenthal & Jacobson, 1968).

Researchers have described the particular attitudes, beliefs, and behaviors that accompany the many expressions of theorizing the whiteness identity within the White racial group. *Whiteness* has many definitions including privilege (McIntosh, 1988), sameness (Marshall, 2002), racial exclusion and control (Carter, 1997; Roediger, 1991; White, 1994), of property (Harris,

1993), and invisibility (Frankenberg, 1993). But social theorists (Feagin, Vera, & Batur, 2001) and the new critical scholarship (Giroux, 1988) recognize whiteness as an ideology of the status quo.

The expanding research on whiteness is also raising the pedagogical issue of what it means to rearticulate whiteness in oppositional terms to enable WPTs to become culturally competent pedagogues (Levine-Rasky, 2001) and able to interact with and teach students from cultures different from their own (Causey, Thomas, & Armento, 2000; McFalls & Cobb-Roberts, 2001). In the field, we have determined that attitudes such as care, dialogue, fallibility, moral character, and so forth are necessary to enhance cross-cultural competency, but we have not been able to address covert or unconscious discrimination that may accompany underlying attitudes and perspectives that often undermine equity pedagogy and student achievement. Moule (2009) details current racist behaviors, specifically those acts that are unintentional. Despite the prevailing thinking that "good people do not discriminate," Moule finds that those who declare to have no biases do show much partiality through their actions. She affirms, "It is important to note that the well-intentioned are still racist" (p. 325). Marx (2004) advocated intercession on the effects of deficit thinking for White individuals in teacher education. These ideas are echoed in a genre of research efforts to elucidate whiteness in America and teacher education (Bell, 2002; Kincheloe, Steinberg, Rodriguez, & Chennault, 1998; Sleeter, 2001).

Although WPTs preparing to enter the field are acquiring the necessary knowledge and skills pertinent to multicultural education (Kemp, 1993; Sparapani, 1995), they lack culturally responsive practices, attitudes, and perspectives (Gallavan, 1998; Schultz, Neyhart, & Reck, 1996). This evaluation is particularly burdensome for WPTs in multicultural education courses who erect a "wall of resistance"—an invisible barrier of dispositions that reject multicultural education or the social justice mandate. Few have challenged the observable fact that most teachers in America who are primarily White, female, and middle class do not come to teacher preparation programs with a social justice ideology (Haberman, 2005; Marx, 2006); they require multicultural learning experiences to get them there (Hill-Jackson, 2007). We propose that teachers' ideologies occupy one of two domains: an advocacy–social justice ideology or a resistant–status quo perspective.

Two Ideological Camps That Influence Teacher Dispositions

Two ideological camps have arisen from our preliminary research with WPTs: advocates and resisters of social justice (Hill-Jackson, Sewell, &

Waters, 2007). Teachers who are advocates of social justice symbolize a social justice ideology and seek equity pedagogy as their goal. Equity pedagogy exists when teachers modify their teaching in ways that make possible academic achievement of students from diverse racial, cultural, gender, and social class groups (Banks, 2004). Advocates of social justice believe in social change so that current social systems are reimagined to benefit all types of Americans across all types of differences. Teachers who portray a social justice ideology seek to disrupt conventional thinking by holding high expectations for all learners and use various teaching techniques to inform and empower their learners. Advocates are WPTs who positively respond cognitively (mentally) and affectively (emotionally) to information presented in multicultural courses. Levine-Rasky (2001) describes advocates as individuals who usually identify with social justice, support critical pedagogy and multicultural education, and have the desire to understand the effects of history and social domination.

Conversely, the resistant or status quo ideology is the maintenance of the existing societal conditions or state of affairs and is embraced by many in the dominant culture. Those who have a status quo ideology fear the support of social change that may lead to the redistribution of resources (Jost & Hunyady, 2005). Love (2000) rationalizes, "This happens because humans are products of their socialization and follow habits of mind and thought that have been instilled in them. The institutions in which we live reward and reinforce behaviors that perpetuate existing systems and resist efforts toward change" (p. 472). King (1991) eloquently elucidates this dangerous dogma among WPTs in her multicultural courses:

> Most of my students . . . are anxious about being able to "deal" with all the diversity in the classroom. Not surprisingly, given recent neoconservative ideological interpretations of the problem of diversity, many of my students also believe that affirming cultural diversity is tantamount to racial separatism, that diversity threatens national unity, or that social inequality originates with sociocultural deficits and not with unequal outcomes that are inherent in our socially stratified society. With respect to this society's changing demographics and the inevitable "browning" of America, many of my students see a diminution of their own identity, status, and security. Moreover, regardless of their conscious intentions, certain culturally sanctioned beliefs my students hold about inequity and why it persists . . . take White norms as givens. (p. 133)

The resisters who assume a status quo ideology do not use effective multicultural educational practices in their classrooms (Gallavan, 1998) and do not use multicultural skills beyond the mandatory diversity course. Garmon (2004) reports: "Students who bring strong biases and negative stereotypes about diverse groups will be less likely to develop the types of professional beliefs and behaviors most consistent with multicultural sensitivity and responsiveness" (p. 202).

Ladson-Billings (2006) surmises:

> In some cases, preservice teachers participate in a teacher education program that requires them to have at least one field experience in a diverse classroom and/or community setting. When such field experiences are poorly done, this requirement becomes just another hoop through which students jump to earn a credential. Students in these circumstances regularly speak of "getting over" their diversity requirements. (p. 38)

These findings suggest that WPTs are resisting social justice issues in preparation courses, not likely to incorporate equity pedagogy beyond their one-course mandate, and simply take the required diversity course as part of the ritual for completing their teacher preparation program. Gillete (1996) concurs and depicts resisters as teacher candidates who have an overall unreceptive attitude toward multicultural education.

To further explain dispositions of advocacy and resistance, formed by ideologies of social justice or status quo, we find it necessary to share the results of a prior research endeavor performed by the first author. This earlier study enhances the growing body of literature that explores equity pedagogy and White teacher resistance but also seeks to interrupt these opposing, yet connected dialogues.

Watch Your Words: They Become Your Actions

This section[2] of the chapter reports the results of research with WPTs. Using teacher voice as the theoretical framework, the study presents insights into the issues and difficulties that can be encountered by Anglo-European students in a teacher preparation program. Findings from this study suggest that future teachers in training arrive at their teacher preparation programs with established ideologies that may or may not conflict with the social justice mandate in teacher education. Critical theories seeking social justice do not offer a concrete means of envisioning equity pedagogy as more than teacher idealism. However, equity pedagogy, when applied to the critique of teachers' disposition and ideology, support a way of addressing teacher bias and discrimination.

WPTs' thoughts and ideologies are easily hidden, but attitudes become unveiled through their silences (Ladson-Billings, 1996) and words (Hill-Jackson et al., 2007). Kincheloe and McLaren (2002) advise that "unraveling ideological codings" is essential to understanding how people make sense of their realities. Haworth (1999) claims that Bakhtin's ideas can be used to decipher meaning for dialogic talk where sociocultural principles for learning are the goal. The interrogation of future teachers' words, to uncover their attitudes and ideologies, offers a means to reveal the contradictions that exist between teacher talk and their pedagogical destiny. Lesko and Bloom (1998) explain that discourse analysis can be a powerful way to understand how participants in multicultural classrooms use language to communicate meanings. In this portion of the chapter, then, we describe the subjects and approach for completing the study.

Participants and Methodology

The racial and gender composition in the first author's multicultural courses superseded national averages: Nearly 95–99% of classes were typically White and female. Throughout the yearlong study, the WPTs were consistently split between those who embraced and those who resisted social justice or multicultural ideas and concepts. The study's original goal was to examine the impact of critical issues in multicultural education with a sample of 200 WPTs.

The summative research experiences unearthed many conclusions. However, the obvious acceptance or denial of multicultural precepts by most WPTs interrupted the original study and forced the researchers to ask reflectively: What are the multicultural dispositions that should be developed in WPTs? And, how can the knowledge of multicultural dispositions serve as a strategy for the creation of equitable pedagogues?

During a full semester, several members of the research team, including two peer WPTs who had taken the course in a prior semester, observed participants during class discussions. Using their voices, views, and values, participants responded to multicultural concepts. At times, the first author, as the teacher educator and part of the research team, shared her views and values so that WPTs would be encouraged to reveal their opinions on the critical issues discussed in class. Other members of the research team joined her in keeping field notebooks during observations and research journals that chronicled their experiences over 4 months of investigations.

The researchers also wanted to hear from the dominant voices in class. These were WPTs who were passionate about their position, for or against, on multicultural issues. Self-selected WPTs were interviewed at length about issues of difference, including gay and lesbian issues, social class, religion, and ethnicity. These in-depth interviews were performed with three groups of eight WPTs and encompassed nearly 12 hours of data. The focus group researchers included White female graduate and undergraduate students so that student participants would be more inclined to respond openly and honestly. These interviews were audiotaped and transcribed. The WPTs on the research team, former students in the multicultural course, helped to analyze the respondents' voices and provided a form of member checking as it relates to the credibility of their assertions.

In addition to these in-depth interviews, the authors collected journals from self-selected participants. WPTs were given compact discs, with directions for use, to anonymously record their reactions to topics discussed in class and observations made in their private lives. These discs were confidentially left in and retrieved from a drop-off box outside the classroom. Moreover, anonymous pre- and post-surveys were administered to the entire sample so that WPTs could respond privately to the issues presented in class.

After the data were collected and coded, several salient themes surfaced. The data made clear, through discourse analysis of transcribed spoken data (Brown & Yule, 1983), that certain WPTs were potential advocates for multicultural education, while many remained resistant to the knowledge, skills, and attitudes needed for multicultural education. Members of the research team became interested in the advocacy and resistant discourses that emerged from the study and scrutinized equity pedagogy and resistance studies to formulate a dispositions model.

Five Dispositions of Advocates and Resisters in the Multicultural Classroom

Drawing on the research on whiteness, teacher education, and dispositions and using mixed methods that incorporated discourse analysis identified previously, five dispositions of advocates and resisters were identified in multicultural education courses.[3] WPTs' attitudes toward multicultural education were based on five interconnected and interdependent dispositions gathered from the authors' review of the literature: cognitive complexity, worldview, intercultural sensitivity, ethics, and self-efficacy (see Table 1).

Cognitive Complexity

Cognitive complexity relates to overall sophistication inherent in thinking and problem-solving skills (Marshall, 2002). WPTs with high cognitive

TABLE 1
Five Dispositions of Advocates and Resisters
in the Multicultural Classroom Model

Advocates	Resisters
Disposition 1: Cognitive Complexity	
Cognitive complexity relates to the overall sophistication inherent in our thinking and problem-solving skills (Marshall, 2002).	
High Cognitive Complexity	**Low Cognitive Complexity**
"Low expectations lead to low classroom engagement, which leads to high dropout rate [for Hispanics]; this is how the self-fulfilling prophecy gets fulfilled."	"I can't get any college scholarships; all of the money out there is for minorities. There's nothing out there for White people."
Disposition 2: Worldviews	
A worldview is a person's ability to organize information about the world around him or her; it serves as the basis for one's perspective, which is informed by culture (Helms, 1994). Worldviews influence our perceptions, and pre-service teachers hold worldviews that may influence how they perceive themselves and others (Marshall, 2002).	
Multifocal Perspective	**Unifocal Perspective**
"We need to be conscious of the lived experiences (of others)."	"I did not make the laws that discriminated against other races, and now I don't feel like I owe them an apology."
Disposition 3: Intercultural Sensitivity	
Teachers who display empathy toward the students in their classroom are shown to have students who achieve higher and are more motivated (McAllister & Irvine, 2002).	
Empathy	**Apathy**
"It's a sad thing, to think that an entire culture [Native American] is disappearing. Educators have to tell the truth about their culture in our classrooms."	"They [university officials and teacher educators] keep shoving this diversity thing down our throats."
Disposition 4: Ethics	
Multicultural education for teachers is a moral and ethical imperative (Goodlad, 1990).	
Ethical	**Immoral**
"It helps them [learners] see everyone as a contributor."	"I had it [life, childhood, etc.] hard too and nobody ever gave me anything. Why do we have to learn about this [multicultural education] stuff?"
Disposition 5: Self-Efficacy	
Yerrick and Hoving (2003) discovered that two types of pre-service teachers can emerge based on their own sense of self-efficacy: (a) those who demonstrate an ability to reflect on and revise their practices and engage in the production of new teacher knowledge; and (b) those who seemingly deflect efforts to shift their thinking and instead reproduce their own educational experience with a new student population.	
High Self-Efficacy	**Low Self-Efficacy**
Pre-service teachers had a willingness to create adaptations to their curricula to better meet the needs of the many different cultural groups in their classroom (field note, November 2005).	"I mean you have to be careful—that is their culture—and you don't want to step on anyone's toes."

complexity can use theories from various courses and apply them across the curriculum. On one occasion, the authors sat spellbound as a WPT systematically connected the current high rate of dropouts among Hispanic youth with the self-fulfilling prophecy theory. This teacher-to-be skillfully explained how teachers' low expectations of learners may lead to decreased engagement, followed by a decreased interest in education, and then to a high dropout rate among learners. Therefore, Hispanic youth remain in low-status jobs; then, poverty and undereducation remain within the culture as generational burdens. A high cognitive complexity enables WPTs to bridge the gap successfully from lived experiences to history, concepts, and knowledge.

Conversely, WPTs with low cognitive complexity perceive knowledge and concepts in unsophisticated ways. Hunt (1971) explains that teachers with low cognitive complexity perceive events in one-dimensional ways. Resisters lack understanding of how multicultural education directly relates to them as a collective, and they often fail to see how they have unconsciously benefited from the privilege of being White in America (McIntosh, 1988). One pre-service teacher angrily asserted, "I can't get any college scholarships; all of the money out there is for minorities. There's nothing out there for White people."

WPTs' concern with scholarships resonates with White America at large (Schmidt, 2004). WPTs fail to see how White people consistently surpass persons of color in educational outcomes, which encompass high school graduation rates (National Center for Educational Statistics, 2004) and future economic outlooks (Webster & Bishaw, 2006). WPTs look at fairness from an individual, as opposed to a collective, perspective and struggle with the bigger picture of social domination and institutionalized racism that prevent generations from achieving group success (Feagin, Vera, & Batur, 2001). In this case, the one-dimensional analysis of equity and historical oppression prevents a greater understanding of contemporary racial and ethnic issues steeped in inequality. WPTs do not grasp that injustice is an institutional and collective idea with sweeping, contemporary ramifications.

Worldviews

A worldview is a person's ability to organize information about the world around him or her; it serves as the basis for a person's perspective, which is informed by culture (Helms, 1994). Brown (2005) argues that WPTs, exposed to new information in a multicultural course, accept or reject data according to their entrenched worldviews.

Most advocates have a special ability to see and accept life experiences from multiple points of view (a *multifocal* perspective). During a presentation on Native American learners, one WPT responded, "We need to be conscious of the lived experiences (of others)." This comment allowed students to understand the importance of realizing how different cultures' experiences affect who individuals were and are, past and present.

Alternatively, resisters in class have dramatically different views on issues discussed and are unable to accept new information; this is called cognitive dissonance (Festinger, 1957). Many resistant WPTs are unaware of their own cultures or the multiple realities of other racial groups' experiences. Very early in the semester, many WPTs explained, "I have no culture, I am White."

Howard (1999) illuminates that White people are not accustomed to relating to themselves as racial beings. For many White people, race and diversity belong to "others." They feel that their heritage or culture does not exist; they are "normal" or American without anything making them unique. They resist, partially, because they believe that their identity is not affirmed. In class, many WPTs sat stone-faced, disinterested, and yet supportive of one another if one denounced a multicultural theory or principle. Brown (2005) informs:

> Avoidance strategies are used to protect the student's worldview and maintain acceptance within their current out-of-class reference groups. These strategies are evidenced when students neglect to prepare for class, disengage from class discussions and activities, and evade cross-cultural interactions. (p. 326)

Resistant WPTs see the world in one way—from a *unifocal* perspective—and refute, ignore, or deny information that does not align with their worldviews. One strategy for teacher educators may be to recognize and discuss cultures that exist in these White students so that the students can begin the process of learning and validating others. A discussion on White historical and contemporary figures is a great way to highlight White culture and activism.

Intercultural Sensitivity

Characteristics such as care, dialogue, fallibility, and empathy are necessary to enhance cultural understanding in classrooms (Haberman, 1996; Moule, 1998). Teachers who display empathy toward students in their classroom are shown to have students who achieve higher, are more motivated, and are keenly attracted to issues of injustice (McAllister & Irvine, 2002).

Advocates of multicultural education have the ability to "wear the shoes" of other cultures and imagine life as the cultural "other." One student lamented, "It's a sad thing, to think that an entire culture (Native American) is disappearing. Educators have to tell the truth about their culture in our classrooms." This WPT's ability to empathize with others allowed for a greater understanding of the struggles of another culture. New awareness could be implemented in her future classroom content in hopes of inspiring effective instruction and enriched curricula.

Resisters are indifferent and do not exhibit care for other groups and their plight in America. They generally have a naïve view about discrimination and feel that individuals can pull themselves "up by their bootstraps" to succeed. After a semester of discussing a 400-year legacy of discrimination against African Americans, one resister insisted, "I did not make the laws that discriminated against other races, and now I don't feel like I owe them an apology."

WPTs immediately take the discussion personally, feeling attacked and guilty for past injustices against people of color. The job of a WPT is to move beyond personal guilt, acknowledge history of oppressed groups, and connect the past to contemporary academic phenomena, and then to work on bridging academic achievement gaps.

Ethics

Gordon and Sork (2001) explain that people who enter the field of education generally have a high degree of internalized moral values—implying that multicultural education would be a philosophy that appeals to prospective teachers. Sirin, Brabeck, Satiani, and Rogers-Serin (2003) find that "ethical sensitivity toward issues of racial and gender intolerance is related to coursework in ethics and multicultural issues and attitudes toward multiculturalism, women's equality, and racial diversity" (p. 231).

Advocates of multicultural education expressed, "Multicultural education is not just for others, it is for all people." Or, "It helps them (learners) see everyone as a contributor." Advocates recognize the philosophical stance of multicultural education and quickly understand the implications for all learners in the classroom.

In contrast, resisters are ethically deficient—failing to understand the moral imperative of multicultural education. Though multicultural courses deal with topics historically and scientifically, WPTs interpret institutional inequality as blame and subjective political opinion. Resisters responded with, "They [university officials and teacher educators] keep shoving this diversity thing down our throats." And, "I sometimes feel like you're [teacher educator] blaming us. I always feel angry when I leave this class." Also, "I had it [life, childhood, etc.] hard too and nobody ever gave me anything. Why do we have to learn about this [multicultural education] stuff?" Resistant WPTs do not grasp the moral and ethical obligations for learning about others (Gay, 2002; Goodlad, 1990; Marshall, 2002) and lack the moral conviction to incorporate multicultural education into future classrooms.

Self-Efficacy

Self-efficacy is the belief that one's personal efforts as an educator can positively affect learners. Yerrick and Hoving (2003) discover that two types of pre-service students can emerge from coursework based on their own sense of self-efficacy. There are students who: (1) demonstrate an ability to reflect on and revise their practices and engage in the production of new teacher knowledge; and others who (2) deflect efforts to shift their thinking.

For instance, as a part of WPTs' final course requirement, groups created a lesson to connect subject matter content, state standards, and teaching strategies to help peers adapt their instruction to meet the needs of different cultural groups in their future classrooms. Advocates were able to create lessons seamlessly and felt that they had gained some skills, knowledge, and strategies to meet the needs of their diverse learners. Bandura (1997) advises that people will act if they believe their efforts will be effective.

Resisters are quite the opposite and have a low sense of self-efficacy. These WPTs do not see the importance of multicultural education and fail to see how it could benefit their classrooms. They hold stereotypical views about their learners: Asians are high achievers; boys are smarter than girls; and African American children are loud troublemakers. Gillette (1996) reports that resisters attribute the success of underrepresented populations to luck, suggesting success for these students lies beyond the educator's control.

Resisters see no correlation between multicultural education and effective pedagogy. Their disposition on the importance of multicultural education ranged from *passive resistance* (apathy) to *active resistance* (anger, denial, or confusion). Resistant WPTs are resigned to the belief that the world operates a certain way and that they can have no real impact on changing the world through awareness of or participation in cultural diversity issues.

Lasch-Quinn (2001) expresses that White people maintain a "race etiquette"—careful not to unveil language or hidden perspectives about underrepresented groups. Murrell and Foster (2003) explain that the teacher candidate learns how to avoid committing discriminating behavior, "or at least, learns how not to be observed doing these things" (p. 47). Resisters were afraid of offending people they did not know, or spent time with, in their monocultural lives. In a focus group, one WPT stated, "I mean you have to be careful—that is their culture—and you don't want to step on anyone's toes."

When resisters discussed educating students in an urban environment, they focused on beliefs that students are not self-disciplined and lack respect for teachers, emphasizing their desire to teach in their monocultural comfort zone (Lesko & Bloom, 1998). Rushton (2003) suggests that pre-service teachers have preconceived ideas about urban environments but come to grow and change their beliefs after new experiences. Resisters did not welcome new knowledge presented in the course that would improve their pedagogy.

During one class session, a WPT bravely admitted, "I don't think that I can teach there [in an urban school district]. I just don't think I can do it." Consequently, WPTs with low self-efficacy are less likely to employ multicultural practices and equity pedagogy in their future classrooms (Garmon, 2004). When an educator has this disposition, the goals of multicultural education—student achievement for all—is not actualized.

Attentiveness to these dispositions is not the answer to changing injurious to innocent ideologies but does remind us that those dispositions for social justice can be a profitable opportunity to select the best educators for America's diverse classrooms.

Only Those With Dispositions for Social Justice Should Teach

We may have placed the proverbial cart before the horse in the discussion about dispositions: Why are we assuming that we can affect teacher behavior before having a discussion about their thinking? Haberman (2005) imparts the overarching thesis of this chapter that maintains that a *critique of ideology* is essential to the training and selection of quality teachers. Cochran-Smith (2004) reminds us of the demographic imperative for America's primarily White female teaching force to seek emancipatory teaching approaches for the increasingly diverse student body. However, it is difficult to assess whether prospective teachers who enter teaching programs have the dispositions to teach all children equitably. There is potential in every student, and a teacher's attitude and actions can leave lasting impressions. Effective teachers have dispositions for social justice. Awareness of the five dispositions of advocates and resisters can serve as a ruler by which to measure one's pedagogical perspective, a reflective strategy to defer resistant behaviors, an instigator to dialogue on equity pedagogy, and a means to break down the wall of resistance in multicultural education. The study found five dispositions for social justice in the multicultural classroom that include an elevated cognitive complexity, expansive worldviews, a soaring degree of intercultural sensitivity, ethical receptiveness, and a high sense of self-efficacy.

The literature continually points to the same conclusions about teachers as they are: maintaining and projecting racist and discriminatory attitudes and behaviors (Marx, 2004); refusing to teach topics or issues associated with multicultural education and resisting the responsibility of ensuring equity for all (Gallavan, 2007); entering and exiting teacher programs with unchecked cultural biases and stereotypes (Brown, 2005); denying biased structures and policies; and failing to recognize the sociopolitical context of teaching. Understanding the perspective of oppressed groups is an important concept for educators because it influences students' lives and the way they learn. Because most pre-service teachers' childhoods, places of worship, and school environments reflect little cultural diversity, many are not familiar with the cultural backgrounds of their future students (Moll & Gonzales, 2004).

A pervasive, perverse, and faulty presumption exists in teacher education—that all teachers are just "good people" (Moule, 2009), consequently their ideologies are beyond reproach. Gay (2000) shares that an overwhelming number of practicing teachers possess negative attitudes toward diversity while Hill-Jackson (2007) identifies the same outcome with pre-service teachers. The origin of this resistant behavior is a status quo ideology. This ideology becomes problematic because it creates a demographic and pedagogical chasm; teachers' unexamined ideologies create an environment that does not affirm difference, empower learners, and improve academic performance (Gay, 2000).

The NCATE mandate that requires dispositions for social justice is being side-stepped by teacher preparation programs throughout the country as a result of ideological resistance in the field, society, and at the university level. Entrance requirements do not adequately address attitudes and behaviors that signify competency and readiness. Haberman (2005) points out that teacher preparation programs require little more than a certain GPA and an essay on "why I want to be a teacher." Similarly, Villegas (2007) shares the difficulty in selecting teacher candidates:

> For one thing, judgments faculty make about applicants to the program
> are solely on a review of materials found in the application packets and

information gleaned from an interview with them, not observable actions in classroom settings, as the assessment of the disposition in question calls for. (p. 376)

Because of this difficulty in assessing dispositions among candidates, Murrell and Foster (2003) contend, "It would be pointless to set professional standards like . . . 'teachers must have positive attitudes about diversity' because there simply is no way to verify them in teaching performance" (p. 47). Haberman (2005) counters this position and asserts that there is a way to assess teachers' attitudes and shares three questions that get to the core of the ideology of star educators (i.e., advocates for social justice) who serve children and youth in poverty:

1. What is the role of schools serving diverse children?
2. What is the teacher's expectation regarding having problem students?
3. And how do stars explain what causes students to be successful? (p. 98)

Haberman (2005) elucidates that star teachers understand that they are teaching more than subject matter and are engaged in the business of saving lives, expect students to come with problems and react in a mature manner, and recognize that success is often a measure of effort and not innate ability. The ideology of star teachers or advocates of social justice is connected to the inherent belief that all students have unique experiences and their diversity is an opportunity and not an obstacle. Additionally, stars and advocates of social justice believe in the untapped promise of all learners if the learners are given encouragement and opportunity to thrive.

Skrla, Scheurich, Garcia, and Nolly (2004) propose a unique leadership tool that can be used to uncover, understand, and change inequities that are internal to schools and districts in three areas: teacher quality, educational programs, and student achievement. This tool serves as an equity audit and can be instrumental in determining whether democracy operates in theory or practice. Along a similar line of logic, *ideology audits* should also be performed as a primary prevention tool at colleges of education before novice teachers enter America's classrooms. An ideology audit is a set of broad assessment practices used by teacher educators and colleges of education that help to determine the beliefs and attitudes that pre-service teachers bring to teacher preparation programs. The primary purpose of this chapter is not to outline the work in this area that has begun on the fringes of teacher education. Instead, we provide a name for this critical process of determining prospective teachers' attitudes and begin a conversation on the importance of untangling the ideological positions of future teachers because we have shown that teacher ideology affects behavior. We have established that there are two chief ideologies that typify pre-service teachers' belief systems: an advocacy–social justice ideology or a resistant–status quo perspective.

The goal must be, therefore, to impress upon future teachers the benefit of teaching for democracy. As stated earlier, it is time to consider the many ways in which the teaching profession might determine whether teachers' ideologies are injurious or innocent to our learners. Teachers' thoughts lead to their classroom disposition, or pedagogical destiny, which becomes surreptitiously inserted into the classroom environment as part of the hidden or latent curriculum (Apple, 2004). Research from some of the most respected scholars in education continues to be overlooked—that teachers with a disposition for social justice positively affect the achievement of diverse learners. Ladson-Billings (1994) and Ogbu (1999) show that African American achievement is enhanced by teachers who practice culturally relevant pedagogy; Nieto (2000) and Moll (1992) conclude that teachers who employ a sociocultural perspective positively affect Hispanic learners' achievement; Viadero (1996) declares that educators who can communicate cross culturally with diverse groups are more effective; Takaki (1993) reminds us of the myriad ways that Asian learners are overlooked and how educators can better support them; Harbeck (1992) provides a tome of research that speaks to the value of providing positive role models and curricula that can protect and empower gay and lesbian students; Zigmund, Levine, and Laurie (1985) reveal that teachers hold low expectations of their students with learning disabilities and do very little to accommodate them in the classroom, hence student performance suffers; and Kozol (2005), Haberman (2005), Freire (1998), and Anyon (1997) explain that children from impoverished communities can thrive when educators practice liberatory or equity pedagogy. To be sure, the field of education has amassed enough research to substantiate that teachers' dispositions matter in relation to the achievement and performance of diverse learners.

The implications for assessment of ideologies are profound because this area is by nature subjective and is often dictated by personal philosophies. The assessment of ideology to determine disposition toward teaching diverse learners carries weight with various entities, but it also carries significant apprehension. To prevent possible bias in the assessment of ideology, it is necessary to consider the nature and definition of dispositions and the best way to measure selected dispositions objectively. Applebaum (2009), in "Is

Teaching for Social Justice a Liberal Bias?", responds to critics who suggest
students in higher education are being indoctrinated with the ideological
imposition of social justice. Critics allege that social justice is too broadly
defined and has no systematic way to assess teacher candidates. The ideological debate continues as teacher candidates continue to enter and leave teacher
preparation programs with their attitudes unexamined (Brown, 2005). Careful assessment of attitudes and behavior is necessary to protect the integrity
and veracity of teacher education programs.

Following are a few suggestions for assessing the ideology of prospective
future teachers to predict future teachers' dispositions. Without question,
these four proposals need more development because further discussion in
this area of ideology inquiry is needed.

Recommendations: Advancing Habits of the Mind for Social Justice

1. **Critical reflection.** Reflection is the most critical skill in teacher
   training and development (Schon, 1996; Zeichner & Liston, 1987)
   and can bring individuals to greater self-actualization. Further, the
   *Five Dispositions of Advocates and Resisters in the Multicultural Class-
   room Model*, shared in this chapter, can serve as a valuable reflective
   tool for WPTs to gauge their individual commitment to classroom
   instruction and equity pedagogy as White teachers who must come
   to terms with their own ideological position, and then choose to
   participate in social justice/multicultural issues. The model shared in
   this chapter forces teacher candidates to rethink basic truths, assumptions, claims, and motivations so that they might experience pedagogical transformation (Dewey, 1933).
2. **Teacher educators and classroom dynamics.** WPTs can easily con-
   ceal their ideologies. But the observant teacher educator should pay
   attention to the words of WPTs because their remarks can provide
   powerful insight into their pedagogical predilections. The Association of Teacher Educators (ATE) has approved a new set of standards
   that help affect student learning. ATE's Standard 2 insists that
   teacher educators apply cultural competence and promote social justice in teacher education.[4] Understanding oppressive ideology, in the
   context of the struggles of the diverse learners in the classroom, is the
   chief objective for critical education researchers of ideology. More

whole classroom instruction with critical dialogue can be used in teacher preparation classes in general and multicultural education courses in particular to spawn reflective talk and to help the teacher educator identify faulty ideologies. Innovative constructivist strategies such as films, multicultural literature, field trips, discussions, and service-learning have proved effective for promoting a social justice character among pre-service teachers. The teacher educator can be a powerful gatekeeper to the teaching profession and use the university classroom as a powerful site of ideological inquiry.

3. **Teacher preparation programs and credentialing.** Universities and colleges accredited by NCATE are facing the prospects of measuring dispositions related to teaching (Diez, 2006; Hillman, Rothermel, & Scarano, 2006). The NCATE mandate for social justice continues to be an overlooked and unaddressed feature in teacher credentialing. Ajzen (1991) finds "attitudes toward the behavior, subjective norms with respect to the behavior, and perceived control over the behavior are usually found to predict behavioral intentions with a high degree of accuracy" (p. 206). Several attitude surveys exist for determining pre-service teachers' dispositions, but most do not include criteria for evaluating dispositions for social justice.

Huber-Warring and Warring (2006) provide a user-friendly rubric for disposition analysis for social justice that assesses candidates in the areas of respect, critical inquiry, democratic participation, and ethical commitment. Credentialing and licensure programs must move beyond a teacher examination that is devoid of critical knowledge, skills, and dispositions to assess quality teachers. Novel disposition surveys that include social justice dispositions and move beyond generic professional dispositions must be part of the credentialing overhaul needed in teacher education; now is the time to hold teacher education accountable for social justice, and we have the means to do so.

Villegas (2007) and colleagues at Montclair State University (MSU) are using an innovative dispositions assessment technique that weaves an enriched teacher preparation curriculum, classroom observations, and other assessment techniques that are "principled and fair," and "evidence that dispositions related to social justice can be assessed in a fair and defensible way" (p. 378).

4. **Recruiting and selection.** There are many challenges in selecting committed teachers with a social justice ideology. However, organizations such as the Haberman Education Foundation (HEF), a

not-for-profit 501(c)3 foundation, is providing training to principals, school boards, site-based parent/teacher councils, teacher unions, and superintendents on how to interview teachers to identify those who will succeed with even the most challenging of students. The innovative Star Teacher Interview questionnaire is made up of 50 questions for which candidates are given three possible answers.[5] The instrument boasts a 95% accuracy rate in predicting which teachers will stay and succeed and which ones will fail or quit. High success rates result from the ability of the scenario-based interview to give a clear picture of the candidate's beliefs about teaching at-risk youth and predict how a candidate will behave on the job. Which ones will be able to handle the stress? The discipline? The unmotivated students? Those who learn differently? School districts would be wise to seek this or similar selection methods before hiring teachers who possess a deficit ideology.

Conclusion

Ideology informs dispositions; our thoughts (i.e., ideologies) and words are the predecessors of our habits. An appraisal of teacher ideology is an overlooked dimension in the field of teacher education. Additionally, the NCATE mandate to encourage dispositions for social justice continues to be flouted in the field of teacher education because a status quo line of thinking, held by the primarily White teaching force, wields a powerful ideological grasp over the field. Teacher dispositions for social justice, as established by NCATE, exist de jure, but de facto social justice remains elusive.

At the beginning of this chapter, Frank Outlaw poetically shares that our thoughts influence our words, words influence our actions, actions influence our habits, habits lead to our character, and our character influences our destiny. The ubiquitous ideology that dominates in this nation about diverse children is the same ideology that dominates our teaching force; it is an ideology that predisposes diverse children as deficient. One challenge for teacher preparation programs is to promote positive dispositions, or habits of the mind, about diverse children among pre-service teachers so that the future teachers might realize a promising pedagogical destiny.

In this chapter, a critique of ideology forms the theoretical framework and rationale for understanding future teachers' thoughts and behavior. Haberman (2005) advises,

> Given the need for teachers with the belief systems and the predispositions to effectively relate to diverse children . . . there can no longer be any question that selecting those with appropriate dispositions determines the usefulness of any subsequent teacher education program offered them. (p. 11)

The study of dispositions has failed to receive the type of serious scrutiny it deserves in teacher education and is neglected in the teacher selection process. As we develop this genre, let us avoid generic and cultureless orientations that do not force teachers to reflect sincerely upon the ideologies they bring to teacher preparation programs. Most of America's teachers are primarily White, female, and middle class, and this identity is political by its very nature, as many in this cadre refuse to accept social justice dispositions. A review of the literature notes that White pre-service teachers fall into one of two ideological camps: an advocacy–social justice ideology or a status quo–resistant perspective.

An earlier study performed with 200 White pre-service teachers, which included discourse analysis methods, is cited in this chapter. The purpose of the study was to sift through the words shared in multicultural courses to uncover cryptic thoughts or ideologies that may be injurious or innocent to diverse students in candidates' future classrooms. The study found that advocates embody an overall approach to teacher education that welcomes multicultural education, skills, and understanding that supports all learners' achievement. Advocates have problem-solving ability, see reality from many points of view, empathize with others whose culture is different from their own, are ethically aware of the democratic and moral necessity of multicultural education, and believe that they can employ strategies in the classroom that can change the academic lives of their learners. In contrast, resisters generally are unreceptive to ideas that support diverse learners. Resisters have difficulty understanding complex concepts, do not recognize their culture and see life through their own sense of reality, are apathetic about the plight of others, do not regard multicultural education as an ethical and moral imperative, and frequently blame the learners for their lack of achievement. Upon reflection, we have determined that the ideology canon is contentious, but we propose that only teachers with a social justice ideology should teach.

We briefly shared four recommendations for continuing the conversation on inspecting future teachers' ideologies. We are hopeful that ideology audits become further developed and can provide serviceable features in the art of reflection, in teacher preparation classrooms, and in credentialing and teacher selection. A teaching force that symbolizes habits of the mind for social justice can transform achievement and help realize bright futures for diverse students in America's classrooms. Dispositions matter.

Notes

1. The first author is undertaking a disposition study to assess the veracity of diversity and justice issues among the top teacher education programs around the country.

2. This section is based on Hill-Jackson, V., Sewell, K. L., & Waters, C. (2007). Having our say about multicultural education: Five dispositions of advocates and resisters in the multicultural classroom. *Kappa Delta Pi Record, 43*(4), 174–180.

3. *Multicultural education* and *social justice* are terms that are often used interchangeably. Like social justice, multicultural education has been described as a movement, idea, and a process. For the purposes of this chapter, multicultural education courses were used by the first author as the context for the original study cited herein and serve as the instrument for sharing social justice issues.

4. A full list of Standards for Teacher Educators is available for download from ATE's website, www.ate1.org.

5. Visit www.habermanfoundation.org to learn more about the Haberman Educational Foundation and the questionnaire.

References

Ajzen, I. (1991). A theory of planned behavior. *Organizational Behavior & Human Decisions Processes, 50*(1), 179–211.

Allport, G. (1935). Attitudes. In G. Murchison (Ed.), *A handbook of social psychology* (pp. 798–844). Worchester, MA: Clark University Press.

Anyon, J. (1997). *Ghetto schooling: A political economy of urban educational reform.* New York: Teachers College Press.

Anyon, J. (2005). *Radical possibilities: Public policy, urban education and a new social movement.* New York: Routledge.

Apple, M. S. (2004). *Ideology and curriculum* (3rd ed.). New York: Routledge.

Applebaum, B. (2009). Is teaching for social justice a liberal bias? *Teachers College Record, 111*(2), 376–408.

Applied Research Center. (2000). *46 years after* Brown v. Board of Education*: Still separate, still unequal.* ARC Research Brief. Oakland, CA: ARC.

Bandura, A. (1997). Self-efficacy. *Harvard Mental Health Letter, 13*(9), 4–7.

Banks, J. A. (1998). The lives and values of researchers: Implications for educating citizens in a multicultural society. *Educational Researcher, 27*(7), 4–17.

Banks, J. A. (2004). Multicultural education: Historical development, dimensions, and practice. In J. A. Banks & C. A. M. Banks (Eds.), *Handbook of research on multicultural education* (2nd ed., pp. 798–844). San Francisco: Jossey-Bass.

Bell, L. (1997). Theoretical foundations for social justice education. In M. Adams, L. Bell, & P. Griffin (Eds.), *Teaching for diversity and social justice: A sourcebook* (pp. 3–15). New York: Routledge.

Bell, L. A. (2002). Sincere fictions: The pedagogical challenges of preparing White teachers for multicultural classrooms. *Equity & Excellence in Education,* 35(3), 236–244.

Bogotch, I. E. (2000). *Educational leadership and social justice: Theory into practice.* (ERIC Document Reproduction service No. ED452585).

Bourdieu, P. (1973). Cultural reproduction and social reproduction. In R. Brown (Ed.), *Papers in the sociology of education: Knowledge, education, and cultural change* (pp. 71–112). London: Taylor & Francis.

Bourdieu, P., & Passeron, C. (1977). *Reproduction in education, society, and culture.* Beverly Hills, CA: Sage Publications.

Brown, E. L. (2005). What precipitates change in cultural diversity awareness during a multicultural course: The message or the method? *Journal of Teacher Education,* 55(4), 325–340.

Brown, G., & Yule, G. (1983). *Discourse analysis.* New York: Cambridge University Press.

Caldwell, B. J., & Spinks, J. M. (2007). *Raising the stakes: From improvement to transformation in the reform of schools.* New York: Routledge.

Carter, R. T. (1997). *Is White a race? Expressions of White racial identity.* In M. Fine, L. Weis, L. C. Powell, & L. M. Wong (Eds.), *Off White: Readings on race, power, and society* (pp. 198–209). New York: Routledge.

Causey, V. E., Thomas, C. D., & Armento, B. J. (2000). Cultural diversity is basically a foreign term to me: The challenges of diversity for pre-service teacher education. *Teaching and Teacher Education,* 16, 33–45.

Cochran-Smith, M. (2004). *Walking the road: Race, diversity, and social justice in teacher education.* New York: Teachers College Press.

Darling-Hammond, L., & Bransford, J. (2005). *Preparing teachers for a changing world: What teachers should learn and be able to do.* San Francisco: Jossey-Bass.

Delpit, L. (1988). The silenced dialogue: Power and pedagogy in educating other people's children. *Harvard Educational Review,* 58(1), 280–298.

Dewey, J. (1933). *How we think: A restatement of the relation of reflective thinking in the educative process.* Boston: D.C. Heath.

Diez, M. E. (2006). Assessing dispositions: Five principles to guide practice. In H. Sockett (Ed.), *Teacher dispositions: Building a teacher framework of moral standards* (pp. 49–68). Washington, DC: American Association of Colleges for Teacher Education.

Feagin, J. R., Vera, H., & Batur, P. (2001). *White racism: The basics* (2nd ed.). New York: Routledge.

Festinger, L. (1957). *A theory of cognitive dissonance.* Stanford, CA: Stanford University Press.

Frankenberg, R. (1993). *White women, race matters: The social construction of whiteness.* Minneapolis: University of Minnesota Press.

Freiberg, H. J., & Driscoll, H. (2000). *Universal teaching strategies* (3rd ed.). Boston: Allyn and Bacon.

Freire, P. (1998). *Teachers as cultural workers: Letters to those who dare to teach.* Boulder, CO: Westview Press.

Gallavan, N. P. (1998). Why aren't teachers using effective multicultural education practices? *Equity & Excellence in Education, 31*(2), 20–27.

Gallavan, N. (2007). Seven perceptions influencing teachers' self-efficacy and cultural competence. *Journal of Praxis in Multicultural Education, 2* (1), 6–22.

Garmon, M. (2004). Changing preservice teachers' attitudes/beliefs about diversity: What are the critical factors? *Journal of Teacher Education, 55*(3), 201–213.

Gay, G. (2000). Multicultural teacher education in the 21st century. *Teacher Educator, 36*(1), 1–16.

Gay, G. (2002). Preparing for culturally responsive teaching. *Journal of Teacher Education, 53*(2), 106–116.

Gillette, M. D. (1996). Resistance and rethinking: White student teachers in predominantly African-American schools. In F. A. Rios (Ed.), *Teacher thinking in cultural contexts* (pp. 104–128). Albany: SUNY Press.

Giroux, H. A. (1988). *Teachers as intellectuals: Toward a critical pedagogy of learning.* Westport, CT: Greenwood Publishing.

Goodlad, J. I. (1990). *Teachers for our nation's schools.* San Francisco: Jossey-Bass.

Gordon, W., & Sork, T. J. (2001). Ethical issues and codes of ethics: Views of adult education practitioners in Canada and the United States. *Adult Education Quarterly, 51*(3), 202–218.

Haberman, M. (1996). Selecting and preparing culturally competent teachers for urban schools. In J. Sikula, T. J. Buttery, & E. Guyton (Eds.), *Handbook of research on teacher education* (pp. 247–260). New York: Macmillan.

Haberman, M. (2005). *Star teachers: The ideology and best practice of effective teachers of diverse children and youth in poverty.* Houston, TX: Haberman Educational Foundation.

Harbeck, K. M. (Ed.). (1992). *Coming out of the classroom closet: Gay and lesbian students, teachers, and curricula.* New York: Harrington Park Press.

Harris, C. (1993). Whiteness as property. *Harvard Law Review, 106*(8), 1709–1791.

Haworth, A. (1999). Bakhtin in the classroom: What constitutes a dialogic text? Some lessons from social group interaction. *Language and Education, 13*(2), 99–117.

Heibert, J. H., Gallimore, R., & Stigler, J. W. (2002). A knowledge base for teacher education: What would it look like and how can we get one? *Educational Researcher, 31*(5), 3–15.

Helms, J. E. (1994). The conceptualization of racial identity and other "racial" constructs. In E. J. Trickett, R. J. Watts, & D. Birman (Eds.), *Human diversity: Perspectives on people in context* (pp. 285–311). San Francisco: Jossey-Bass.

Hill-Jackson, V. (2007). Wrestling whiteness: Three stages of shifting multicultural perspectives among White pre-service teachers. *Multicultural Perspectives, 9*(2), 29–35.

Hill-Jackson, V., Sewell, K. L., & Waters, C. (2007). Having our say about multicultural education: Five dispositions of advocates and resisters in the multicultural classroom. *Kappa Delta Pi, 43*(4), 174–180.

Hillman, S. J., Rothermel, D., & Scarano, G. H. (2006). The assessment of preservice teachers' dispositions. *Teacher Educator, 41*(4), 234–250.

Howard, G. R. (1999). *We can't teach what we don't know: White teachers, multiracial schools.* New York: Teachers College Press.

Huber-Warring, T., & Warring, D. F. (2006). Are you teaching for democracy? Developing dispositions, promoting democratic practice, and embracing social justice and diversity. *Action in Teacher Education, 28*(2), 38–52.

Hunt, D. (1971). *Matching models in education: The coordination of teaching methods with student characteristics.* Toronto: Ontario Institute for Studies in Education.

Jost, J. T., & Hunyady, O. (2005). Antecedents and consequences of system-justifying ideologies. *Current Directions in Psychological Science, 14*(5), 260–265.

Katz, M. S. (2007). Two views of teaching people to think. *Educational Theory, 26*(2), 158–164.

Kemp, L. (1993). *Encouraging pre-service teachers to understand student diversity: Pedagogical and methodological conditions.* (ERIC Document Reproduction Number ED 365 645).

Kincheloe, J. L., & McLaren, P. (2002). Rethinking critical theory and qualitative research. In Y. Zou & E. T. Trueba (Eds.), *Ethnography and schools: Qualitative approaches to the study of education* (pp. 87–138). Lanham, MD: Rowman & Littlefield.

Kincheloe, J. L., Steinberg, S. R., Rodriguez, N. M., & Chennault, R. E. (Eds.). (1998). *White reign: Deploying whiteness in America.* New York: St. Martin's Press.

King, J. (1991). Dysconscious racism: Ideology, identity, and the miseducation of teachers. *Journal of Negro Education, 60*(2), 133–146.

Koeppen, K. E., & Davison-Jenkins, J. (2006). Do you see what I see? Helping secondary preservice teachers recognize and monitor their teacher dispositions. *Action in Teacher Education, 28*(1), 13–26.

Kozol, J. (2005). *The shame of the nation: The restoration of apartheid schooling in America.* New York: Crown Publishers.

Ladson-Billings, G. (1994). *The dreamkeepers: Successful teachers of African American children.* San Francisco: Jossey-Bass.

Ladson-Billings, G. (1995). But that's just good teaching: The case for culturally relevant pedagogy. *Theory Into Practice, 34*(3), 159–165.

Ladson-Billings, G. (1996). *Silence as weapons: Challenges of a Black professor teaching White students.* San Francisco: Jossey Bass.

Ladson-Billings, G. (2006). "Yes, but how do we do it": Practicing culturally relevant pedagogy. In J. Landsman & C. Lewis (Eds.), *White teachers/diverse classrooms: A guide to building inclusive schools, promoting high expectations, and eliminating racism.* Sterling, VA: Stylus.

Landsman, J., & Lewis, C. W. (Eds.). (2006). *White teachers/diverse classrooms: A guide to building inclusive schools, promoting high expectations, and eliminating racism.* Sterling, VA: Stylus.

Lasch-Quinn, E. (2001). *Race experts: How racial etiquette, sensitivity training, and new age therapy hijacked the civil rights revolution.* New York: W. W. Norton.

Lee, J. (2002). Racial and ethnic achievement gap trends: Reversing the progress toward equity? *Educational Researcher, 31*(1), 3–12.

Leinhardt, G. (1990). Capturing craft knowledge in teaching. *Educational Researcher, 19*(2), 18–25.

Lesko, N., & Bloom, L. R. (1998). Close encounters: Truth, experience, and interpretation in multicultural teacher education. *Journal of Curriculum Studies, 30*(4), 375–395.

Levine-Rasky, C. (2001). Identifying the prospective multicultural educator: Three signposts, three portraits. *Urban Review, 33*(4), 291–319.

Love, B. J. (2000). Developing a liberatory consciousness. In W. J. Blumenfeld, X. Xuniga, M. L. Peters, R. Castenada, H. W. Hackman, & M. Adams (Eds.), *Readings for diversity: An anthology on racism, sexism, anti-Semitism, heterosexism, classism, and ableism* (pp. 470–474). New York: Routledge.

Madom, S., Jussim, L., & Eccles, J. (1997). In search of the powerful self-fulfilling prophecy. *Journal of Personality and Social Psychology, 72*(4), 791–809.

Marshall, P. L. (2002). *Cultural diversity in our schools.* Belmont, CA: Wadsworth.

Marx, S. (2004). Regarding whiteness: Exploring and intervening in the effects of White racism in teacher education. *Equity & Excellence in Education, 37*(1), 31–43.

Marx, S. (2006). *Revealing the invisible: Confronting passive racism in teacher education.* New York: Routledge.

McAllister, G., & Irvine, J. J. (2002). The role of empathy in teaching culturally diverse students: A qualitative study of teachers' beliefs. *Journal of Teacher Education, 53*(5), 433–443.

McDonald, M. A. (2005). The integration of social justice in teacher education. *Journal of Teacher Education, 56*(5), 418–435.

McFalls, E. L., & Cobb-Roberts, D. (2001). Reducing resistance to diversity through cognitive dissonance instruction: Implications for teacher education. *Journal of Teacher Education, 52*(2), 164–172.

McIntosh, P. (1988). *White privilege and male privilege: A personal account of coming to see correspondences through work in women's studies.* Unpublished manuscript, Wellesley College, Wellesley, MA.

McLaren, P. (1998). *Life in schools: An introduction to critical pedagogy in the foundations of education* (3rd ed.). New York: Longman.

Moll, L. (1992). Funds of knowledge for teaching: Using a qualitative approach to connect homes and classrooms. *Theory Into Practice, 31*(2), 132–141.

Moll, L., & Gonzales, N. (2004). Engaging life: A funds of knowledge approach to multicultural education. In J. A. Banks & C. A. M. Banks (Eds.), *Handbook of research on multicultural education* (2nd ed., pp. 699–715). San Francisco: Jossey-Bass.

Moule, J. (1998). *My journey with preservice teachers: Reflecting on teacher characteristics that bridge multicultural education theory and classroom practice.* Unpublished manuscript, Oregon State University, Corvallis, OR.

Moule, J. (2009). Understanding unconscious bias and unintentional racism. *Phi Delta Kappan, 90*(5), 320–326.

Murray, F. B. (2007). Dispositions: A superfluous construct in teacher education. *Journal of Teacher Education, 58*(5), 381–387.

Murrell, P. C., & Foster, M. (2003). Teacher beliefs, performance and proficiency in diversity-oriented teacher preparation. In J. Raths & A. McAninch (Eds.), *Teacher beliefs in classroom performance: The impact of teacher education* (pp. 43–64). Charlotte, NC: Information Age Publishers.

National Center for Educational Statistics. (2004). *The condition of education.* Washington, DC: NCES. Retrieved January 3, 2009, from http://nces.ed.gov/programs/coe

National Council for Accreditation of Teacher Education. (2002). *Professional standards for the accreditation of schools, colleges, and departments of education.* Washington, DC: Author.

Nieto, S. (2000). Placing equity front and center. Some thoughts on transforming teacher education for a new century. *Journal of Teacher Education, 51*(3), 180–187.

North, C. E. (2006). More than words? Delving into the substantive meaning(s) of social justice in education. *Review of Educational Research, 76*(4), 507–535.

Ogbu, J. (1999). Beyond language: Ebonics, proper English, and identity in a Black-American speech community. *American Educational Research Journal, 36,* 147–184.

Roediger, D. R. (1991). *The wages of whiteness: Race and the making of the American working class.* New York: Verso.

Rosenthal, R., & Jacobson, L. (1968). *Pygmalion in the classroom: Teacher expectations and student intellectual development.* New York: Holt, Rinehart & Winston.

Rushton, S. P. (2003). Two preservice teachers' growth in self-efficacy while teaching in an inner-city school. *Urban Review, 35*(3), 167–189.

Schmidt, P. (2004, March 19). Not just for minority students anymore: Fearing charges of discrimination, colleges open minority scholarships and programs to students of all races. *Chronicle of Higher Education.*

Schon, D. A. (1996). *Educating the reflective practitioner: Toward a new design for teaching and learning in the professions.* San Francisco: Jossey-Bass.

Schultz, E., Neyhart, K., & Reck, U. (1996). Swimming against the tide: A study of prospective teachers' attitudes regarding cultural diversity and urban teaching. *Western Journal of Black Studies, 20*(1), 1–7.

Schussler, D. L. (2006). Defining dispositions: Wading through murky waters. *Teacher Educator, 41*(94), 251–268.

Schussler, D. L., Bercaw, L. A., & Stooksberry, L. M. (2008). The fabric or teacher candidate dispositions: What case studies reveal about teacher thinking. *Action in Teacher Education, 29*(4), 39–52.

Shulman, L. S. (1986). Those who understand: Knowledge growth in teaching. *Educational Researcher, 15*(2), 4–14.

Sirin, S. R., Brabeck, M. M., Satiani, A., & Rogers-Serin, L. (2003). Validation of a measure of ethical sensitivity and examination of the effects of previous multicultural and ethics courses on ethical sensitivity. *Ethics & Behavior, 13*(3), 221–235.

Skrla, L., Scheurich, J. J., Garcia, J., & Nolly, G. (2004). Equity audits: A practical leadership tool for developing equitable and excellent schools. *Educational Administration Quarterly, 40*(1), 133–161.

Sleeter, C. E. (1996). Multicultural education as a social movement. *Theory Into Practice, 35*(4), 239–247.

Sleeter, C. E. (2001). Preparing teachers for culturally diverse schools: Research and the overwhelming presence of whiteness. *Journal of Teacher Education, 52*(2), 94–106.

Sleeter, C. E., & Grant, C. (2007). *Making choices for multicultural education: Five approaches to race, class, and gender.* New York: John Wiley.

Sparapani, E. F. (1995). *Preservice teacher education majors' understanding of issues related to diversity and exceptionality.* Paper presented at the Annual Meeting of the Association of Teacher Educators, February 19–22, Detroit, MI. ERIC ED 379 280.

Takaki, R. (1993). *A different mirror: A history of multicultural America.* Boston: Little, Brown.

Tharp, R., & Gallimore, R. (1998). *Rousing minds to life: Teaching, learning and schooling in social context.* New York: Cambridge University.

Thompson, L. J. (1995). *Habits of the mind: Critical thinking in the classroom.* Lanham, MD: University Press of America.

Viadero, D. (1996). Culture clash: When teachers and students come from different backgrounds, they may not speak the same language. *Education Week.* Retrieved September 24, 2005, from www.edweek.org/htbn/fastweb?getdoc+view4+ewi996+590+wAAA+%26%28native%american%

Villegas, A. M. (2007). Dispositions in teacher education. *Journal of Teacher Education, 58*(5), 370–380.

Webster, B. H., Jr., & Bishaw, A. (2006, August). *Income, earnings, and poverty data from the 2005 American community survey.* Washington, DC: U.S. Census Bureau. Available at: www.census.gov/prod/2006pubs/acs-02.pdf

White, T. W. (1994). *The invention of the White race volume one: Racial oppression and social control.* New York: Verso.

Wideen, M., Mayer-Smith, J., & Moon, B. (1998). A critical analysis of the research on learning to teach: Making the case for an ecological perspective on inquiry. *Review of Educational Research, 68*(2), 130–178.

Woods, P. A., Bagley, C., & Glatter, R. (1998). *School choice and competition: Markets in the public interest?* New York: Routledge.

Yerrick, R. K., & Hoving, T. J. (2003). One foot on the dock and one foot on the boat: Differences among preservice science teachers' interpretations of field-based science methods in culturally diverse contexts. *Science Education, 87*(3), 390–418.

Zeichner, K., & Liston, D. P. (1987). Teaching student teachers to reflect. *Harvard Educational Review, 57*(1), 23–48.

Zigmund, N., Levin, E., & Laurie, T. E. (1985). Managing the mainstream: An analysis of teacher attitudes and student performance in mainstream high school programs. *Journal of Learning Disabilities, 18*(9), 535–541.

4

TEACHER CANDIDATE SELECTION, RECRUITMENT, AND INDUCTION

A Critical Analysis With Implications for Transformation

F. Blake Tenore, Alfred C. Dunn,
Judson C. Laughter, and H. Richard Milner

I n this chapter, we examine teacher development through the lenses of three related components—teacher demographics, selection and recruitment into teacher education, and new teacher induction—and attempt to address the complexities inherent therein. The chapter begins with an analysis of the research literature guided and framed by the following questions: (a) Who are the pre-service teachers enrolled in teacher education programs and subsequently who teach in P–12 schools, and what do these teachers have in common? (b) How do teacher education programs select and recruit their teacher candidates? and (c) How do teacher education programs, districts, and states induct and provide support for their teachers once they have graduated and accepted teaching positions? We focus on these three related areas (demographics, selection and recruitment, and induction), critique the practices, and conclude with transformative recommendations.

Demographics in Teacher Education

Who teachers are in terms of their racial, ethnic, cultural, socioeconomic, and linguistic background is an important issue because research suggests that the teaching force needs to be more diverse to meet the needs of increasingly diverse P–12 students (Gay & Howard, 2000; Milner, 2006). The demographic divide rationale and imperative (Banks, 2003) are present in an important body of literature that makes a case for the preparation of teachers for the diversity they will face in P–12 educational contexts (cf. Gay & Howard, 2000; Zumwalt & Craig, 2005). Emphases on demographics in teacher education and subsequently P–12 operate on at least two levels: (a) teachers in teacher education programs (who are mainly White and female) need to be prepared to meet the needs of racially and ethnically diverse learners; and (b) teacher education programs need to be more persistent and innovative in selecting, recruiting, and inducting a more diverse teaching force.

Zumwalt and Craig (2005) report the most recently available statistics compiled by the American Association of Colleges for Teacher Education (AACTE, 1999) that map the demographic landscape of students enrolled in teacher education programs. They describe the shifting demographics of teacher education as follows:

> White students made up 80.5% of enrollment in [schools, colleges, and departments of education], a 2 percentage points decline since their initial study in 1989. African Americans increased their representation over the decade to 9%, a 40% increase, and Hispanics comprised 4.7%, or 80% higher than before. Asian and Pacific Americans and Native Americans comprised 1.7% and 0.7% respectively. (p. 115)

A comparison of teacher education demographic statistics with data available for practicing teachers at a similar point in time suggests that the teaching force is diversifying, however slightly. Analyzing statistics from the U.S. Department of Education, Gay and Howard (2000) explain that:

> 86% of all elementary and secondary teachers are European Americans. The number of African American teachers has declined from a high of 12% in 1970 to 7% in 1998. The number of Latino and Asian/Pacific Islander American teachers is increasing slightly, but the percentages are still very small (approximately 5% and 1% respectively). Native Americans comprise less than 1% of the national teaching force. (pp. 1–2)

However, whereas the pool of teacher candidates may be trending toward more racial and ethnic diversity in the teaching ranks, the dramatic demographic divide between teachers and pupils in P–12 schools continues to increase, as we discuss later.

Although the call for increased diversity in the teaching force is often couched in arguments that students are racially and ethnically diverse, Gay and Howard (2000) also maintain that "large numbers of European Americans and students of color really do not attend school with each other; nor are different groups of color in the same schools" (p. 2). Stated differently, when focusing on the student populations in P–12 contexts, discussions often focus on the "diversity" teachers will face. However, many teachers will find themselves in classrooms that are not very diverse at all in terms of race and ethnicity. For instance, students in urban schools are mainly African American and/or Latino/a American, and teachers in those schools must develop the knowledge, skills, attitudes, dispositions, and abilities to teach African American students and/or Latino/a students. Thus, although on a large scale students are increasingly becoming non-White, schools in the United States are increasingly not very diverse in terms of racial and ethnic makeup within each school.

Orfield (2001) writes, "The number of black and Latino students in the nation's public schools is up 5.8 million, while the number of white students has declined by 5.6 million" (p. 17). The trend in urban schools is even more profound:

> In 1998–1999 there were 26 cities with more than 60,000 students. These cities enrolled 4,715,000 of the nation's 48,392,000 public school students. While about a tenth (9.74%) of all students were enrolled in these districts, the districts served only a minute fraction of the nation's white students and a large share of the blacks and Latinos. (Orfield, 2001, p. 25)

Tables 1, 2, and 3 outline the demographics of teachers between 2003 and 2004 and of students between 2003 and 2007.

Research concerning the demographic divide includes gender, race, ethnicity, and socioeconomic background. For the purposes of this discussion, Tables 1 and 2 provide racial demographic data of teachers and of public school students. Cultural and racial congruence and incongruence are often used as frames to discuss the complexities embedded in preparing teachers to meet the needs of *all* students, including students of color. Because White teachers and students of color often possess different racialized and cultural experiences and repertoires of knowledge and knowing both inside and outside the classroom, racial and cultural incongruence may serve as a road block for academic and social success in the classroom (Irvine, 2003). However, as Gay (2000) asserts, "Similar ethnicity between students and teachers

TABLE 1

Teacher Demographics in Public Elementary and Secondary Schools,
2003–2004

Race	Elementary Public School	Secondary Public School
White (%)	81.6	84.2
Black (%)	8.8	7.5
Hispanic (%)	7.0	5.5
Asian (%)	1.3	1.3
Pacific Islander (%)	0.2	0.2
American Indian/Alaska Native (%)	0.4	0.6
More than one race (%)	0.7	0.7

Source: National Center for Education Statistics. (2007c). *Schools and staffing survey.* Retrieved November 24, 2008, from http://nces.ed.gov/surveys/sass/tables/state_2004_18.asp

TABLE 2

Student Demographics, 2003–2005

Race	2003	2004	2005
White (%)	60.5	59.9	59.4
Black (%)	14.9	14.9	14.8
Hispanic (%)	17.7	18.2	18.7
Asian (%)	3.6	3.7	3.7
Pacific Islander (%)	0.2	0.2	0.2
American Indian/Alaska Native (%)	0.9	0.9	0.9
More than one race (%)	2.2	2.3	2.3

Source: National Center for Education Statistics (2007a). *Digest of Education Statistics: 2007.* Retrieved November 24, 2008, from http://nces.ed.gov/programs/digest/d07/

TABLE 3
Student Demographics, 2006–2007

Race	2006[a]	2007[b]
White (%)	57.1	56.5
Black (%)	17.2	17.1
Hispanic (%)	19.8	20.5
Asian/Pacific Islander (%)	4.6	4.7
American Indian/Alaska Native (%)	1.2	1.2

[a] From National Center for Education Statistics. (2007b). *Public elementary and secondary school student enrollment, high school completions and staff from the common core of data: School year 2005–06.* Retrieved November 24, 2008, from http://nces.ed.gov/pubsearch/pubsinfo.asp?pubid = 2007352

[b] From National Center for Education Statistics. (2008). *Public elementary and secondary school student enrollment and staff from the common core of data: School year 2006–07.* Retrieved November 24, 2008, from http://nces.ed.gov/pubsearch/pubsinfo.asp?pubid = 2009305

may be potentially beneficial, but it is not a guarantee of pedagogical effectiveness" (p. 205).

In terms of gender, approximately 75% of teachers are female and even larger numbers of teachers in special education, early childhood education, and elementary education are female (Zumwalt & Craig, 2005). In terms of socioeconomic status, the field of teacher education seems to attract a range of candidates. Zumwalt and Craig (2005) explain that "the majority of teachers' parents still do not have high-school or college degrees, but the proportion with high-school- and college-educated parents has risen over the past 25 years" (p. 140). Research focusing on Black teachers suggests that teaching as a field was seen as a profession to gain entry into the middle class. With the increase in job prospects, prospective teachers are often selecting different careers (Milner & Howard, 2004; Zumwalt & Craig, 2005).

Teachers from any ethnic, cultural, or racial background can be successful with any group of students when the teachers possess (or have the drive and commitment to acquire) the knowledge, attitudes, dispositions, and beliefs necessary to teach all students well (Ladson-Billings, 1994). The question then becomes whether or to what extent teacher education programs are preparing teachers to teach a wide range of students and what roles selection, recruitment, and induction might play in teacher development. What are teacher education programs doing to attract and develop teachers for diverse learners? Are teacher education programs prepared to support these teachers? What happens to teachers once they have graduated? The next section of this chapter focuses on the selection and recruitment of candidates into the field of teacher education.

Selection and Recruitment in Teacher Education

In this section, we review the literature on selecting and recruiting potential teachers into a teacher education program. We make a specific distinction between *selection*, a process of establishing program-specific characteristics that potential teachers must meet, and *recruitment*, a process that involves the seeking out and encouraging of potential teachers with certain characteristics to enter a program. It appears that most programs opt for selection; however, as we discuss, teacher education programs may need to be more deliberate in developing processes and systems that place more emphases on teacher recruitment. This distinction, selection versus recruitment, prompts the question: In teacher education, are we relegated only to doing the best we can with those who enroll in a program?

The literature on teacher selection and recruitment in teacher education programs appears to be scarce. A search in the databases for peer-reviewed journal articles using the descriptors "teacher education selection criteria" and "teacher education recruitment" resulted in nearly 200 scholarly publications. However, searches using each descriptor resulted in merely 4 and 21 peer-reviewed, scholarly journal articles, which explicitly addressed recruitment or selection into preservice teacher preparation. The majority of the scholarship primarily focused on recruiting and selecting teachers into the P–12 schools and not into teacher education programs. In the mid-1980s and early 1990s, there was a brief surge in research looking at improving teacher quality through teacher selection criteria (Applegate, 1987) and the correlation between admission standards and scores on measures of achievement (Freeman, Martin, Brousseau, & West, 1989).

In our review of the literature, much of the research focusing on the effective use of criteria for admission into teacher education programs can be placed in one of two categories: (a) studies that address the underrepresentation of teachers and teacher candidates of color, and (b) studies that examine the correlation between variables such as candidates' grades and standardized test scores with student teaching performance.

The study of the underrepresentation of teachers of color is an area in which the teacher recruitment research continues to grow. Scholarship in this area tends to focus on the development and implementation of strategies for recruitment aimed at communities and organizations populated by people of color and/or lower socioeconomic status. Civic organizations, service agencies, and churches have been tapped as sites rich in potential for identifying people of color and those from lower socioeconomic statuses who may be strong teacher candidates (cf. Nunez & Fernandez, 2006; Villegas & Davis, 2007). Clewell and Villegas (1999) studied their process of recruiting teacher candidates from nontraditional sources such as the pool of paraprofessionals and uncertified/emergency-certified teachers. Further examples of the growth of literature focusing on the recruitment of teachers of color are research-based projects by Duncan-Andrade (2008) and Post and Woessner (1987). These scholars attempted to recruit high school students of color into teacher education.

Current efforts to diversify the teaching force are reactions to both the historically passive role teacher education has played in recruitment (Villegas & Davis, 2007) and the broadening racial, ethnic, and linguistic gaps among P–12 students and those enrolled in teacher education programs. The specific efforts of these researchers have led to the development of pathways into teacher education and strategies to support candidates personally, professionally, and monetarily that may be more attractive to and supportive of diverse candidates than the status quo. A permeating belief is that a more diverse pool of teacher candidates can shrink the demographic gaps among teachers and students and ultimately increase student achievement. Attention to diversity, however, is not a primary goal of the second line of inquiry that emerged from our review of the literature. Rather, the following studies focused on identifying characteristics of teacher candidates that may be correlated to teaching success.

Zeichner, Grant, Gay, Gillette, Valli, and Villegas (1998) write, "Students are admitted to teacher education programs largely on the basis of grade point average and scores on tests of academic skills" (p. 165). In fact, using Educational Testing Service (ETS) data, Mikitovics and Crehan (2002) report that more than 80% of states that assess teacher candidates' basic skills in math and reading require passing scores on the Pre-Professional Skills Test (PPST), which is also used for admissions screening by some colleges of education. However, research that examined correlations between teaching performance and some quantitative variable (e.g., Riggs, Riggs, & Sandlin, 1992) is inconsistent and inconclusive. For example, Mikitovics and Crehan

(2002) report that there was no predictive relationship between candidates' PPST scores and their student teaching performance ratings. On the other hand, Ehrenberg and Brewer (1994) find a positive correlation between the admissions selectivity of teachers' undergraduate institutions and their pupils' increased achievement, and Guyton and Farokhi (1987) report a positive correlation between teachers' college GPAs and their ratings on a performance-based assessment of their teaching (Allen, 2005).

In a 2003 synthesis of 92 studies on teacher preparation, Allen poses the question, "Is setting more-stringent teacher preparation program entrance requirements or conducting more-selective screening of program candidates, likely to ensure that prospective teachers will be more effective?" (p. 8). In response to this question, Allen found three studies (Ehrenberg & Brewer, 1994; Gitomer, Latham, & Ziomek, 1999; Guyton & Farokhi, 1987) that addressed the question, but none of them directly. Allen concludes that there is a demonstrated relationship between academic success and teaching success. However, similar to Mikitovics and Crehan (2002), he expresses concerns that these measures may disadvantage underrepresented student groups such as those who are not privileged in terms of race, ethnicity, and socioeconomic status. Allen (2003) is unable to make any policy recommendations as a result of the paucity of research.

The same paucity of research leaves us without clear answers regarding the connections that do or do not exist among quantitatively measured achievement variables and the likelihood of teaching effectiveness. Although some researchers call for raising the bar for entrance into a program, this is not without controversy, and we are reluctant to espouse such a stance given the available evidence.

Some studies fall outside the two categories of addressing the underrepresentation of teachers of color and examining the correlation between quantitative variables and student teaching performance. For example, Haberman (1993) claims that the success of urban teachers could be predicted based on the Urban Teacher Selection Interview. He developed the interview after observing effective urban classroom teachers to identify common attributes among the teachers he studied. Haberman (1995) uses the interviews to uncover similar attributes in prospective teachers as part of the admission criteria for a teacher education program. Such work calls for the recognition of strengths not measured by grades or test scores, strengths such as sociocultural knowledge about and experiences in a community (Villegas & Clewell, 1998). Lines of inquiry such as Haberman's are, to us, more promising than those exclusively focusing on a demographic divide or reinforcing the use of standardized measures. However, although research in this mold works to develop processes and procedures to select and admit candidates with certain experiences and dispositions, they are rare and leave unanswered the previous question: Are we relegated only to doing the best we can with those who enroll in a teacher education program?

In finding such little help in our review of the research, we decided to look for promising teacher selection and recruitment practices evident in current models of teacher education programs. Perhaps in analyzing these models, we can use the world of research to backtrack (Sleeter, 2001) and create models that can be useful for developing such promising programs more widely in teacher education.

Current Models of Selection and Recruitment

To address the issue of selection and recruitment into teacher education programs, we decided to investigate what some current teacher education programs are doing to select and recruit teacher candidates. We purposefully contacted three teacher educators to assist us in identifying promising programs because these teacher educators represent a range of geographic location (Delaware, Ohio, and Arizona), represent a range of experience as teacher educators (1, 4, and 7 years), and a range of specialization (social studies and history, English and literacy, and second language literacy). One teacher educator is an assistant professor interested in second language acquisition and completed her own teacher education in a foreign country. Another is a newly tenured faculty member who graduated from a traditional teacher education program in the United States. The third teacher educator is in his second year as an assistant professor and became a teacher through a nontraditional route before returning to graduate school. Each of the three educators we contacted was known to us previously and selected because he or she has had experiences that span across many university settings through work as doctoral candidates, teacher educators, and via collaboration with colleagues across the United States. We were confident in their familiarity with and knowledge about a variety of teacher preparation programs related to teacher recruitment and teacher selection.

We asked these three teacher educators to nominate and to describe three to five effective teacher education programs that varied in terms of their selection and recruitment criteria. Based upon the recommendations from our colleagues, the nominated programs became the focus of our own analyses of the criteria and procedures employed by each program. Although "community nominations" (Ladson-Billings, 1994, p. 147) are often used to understand individuals who exemplify a range of promising characteristics, we attempted to adapt the community nomination technique to one that allowed us to locate promising, yet imperfect, teacher education programs in terms of selection and recruitment. Teacher education programs nominated by our colleagues and included in this analysis are University of Georgia, University of Wisconsin-Madison, University of Nevada–Las Vegas, Indiana University, and Teachers College at Columbia University.

Teacher Selection

In reviewing the programs nominated by the teacher educators we queried, methods of selection and not recruitment were most common; in other words, the programs had criteria in place that were used to choose from among a pool of applicants rather than seeking and reaching out to desirable candidates. Two primary methods of selection used by teacher education programs emerged from the nominated programs and the research literature:

- Quantitative: Teacher education programs often select teacher candidates based on minimum levels of academic achievement as indicated by college entrance test scores (i.e., SAT or GRE), grade point average (GPA), and other academic or personal qualifications (Zeichner et al., 1998). Sometimes, market forces or accreditation policies intervene in defining these quantitative measures.
- Qualitative: Teacher education programs sometimes select teacher education candidates based on a specific end goal or by looking for specific qualities. For instance, evidence of preferred attitudes, dispositions, and previous experience may be used in determining a candidate's potential selectivity (Haberman, 1995).

From here, we describe these forms of selection with examples nominated by our teacher educators and the published materials of the programs.

Quantitative: University of Georgia

Some teacher education programs rely on the larger college or university to set quantitative minimums for admission. For example, undergraduate admissions to the University of Georgia are based largely on high school grades, high school curriculum difficulty, and standardized test scores (among other factors) aimed at selecting students "who have demonstrated high levels of maturity and personal integrity as well as commitment to serving their communities" (University of Georgia, 2008). There is no set formula used because the applicant pool changes from year to year and from student to student: "[A] student with a 3.0 GPA and an SAT of 1400 might not be admitted, if the student opts for no more than a standard college prep curriculum with few if any Honors, AP or IB courses" (University of Georgia, 2008). Once students have been admitted to the university, they may apply for admission into the college of education, typically in the sophomore or junior year. To do so, applicants prepare a dossier that includes their course transcripts and a record of their cumulative GPA. Admission decisions are made based on a selection committee's determination of the applicants' qualifications as evidenced by their dossiers (P. Graham, personal communication, October 3, 2008).

We found that selection criteria often are presented through a profile of the most recent entering class. For example, the University of Wisconsin–Madison (2008) publishes a *Profile of Admitted Freshmen* that provides the middle "50% range for each indicator." For example, 50% of the most current students had GPAs between 3.5 and 3.9, scored between 26 and 30 on the ACT, and published SAT scores between 1770 and 2010. This method of presentation allows prospective teachers to compare themselves with those most recently selected.

Quantitative: UNLV

In addition, although teacher education programs seek to develop teachers of strong ability, sometimes market forces intervene. For instance, some teacher education programs are compelled to prepare teachers to fill a district's or state's needs every year. The University of Nevada at Las Vegas has to place upward of 3,000 new teachers a year to meet the needs of rapidly expanding communities. Criteria in these programs are specific for graduation, not for entrance to the program, and often mirror the requirements for state licensure, comprising a combination of successful coursework and PRAXIS test scores.

The accreditation process can also influence the selection of teachers. Two of the teacher educators in our study mentioned recent experiences with the National Council for Accreditation of Teacher Education (NCATE) and how the experiences influenced the selection and retention of teachers in their programs. Although accreditation of a program seems to increase the number of teachers receiving state licensure (Allen, 2003), there is little research on whether accreditation equates to effective teaching. Each teacher education program is charged with demonstrating an ability to accomplish mandated goals, and teachers not showing strong commitment to the program or who do not appear to take seriously the rigors of the program often find themselves counseled out; that is, they are encouraged to leave the program through various means. It might seem appropriate simply to raise the qualifications for teachers in these settings; however, again, doing so can have dangerous consequences for increasing the number of capable teachers of color in the profession. Moreover, raising minimum standards on admission criteria, such as standardized test scores, could aggravate the shortage of teachers in this country (Allen, 2003).

Qualitative: Indiana University

There exist some teacher education programs—usually small—that focus on a specific *quality* or qualities in selecting teachers and so develop entrance requirements that seek out these qualities in prospective teachers. The following programs nominated by our teacher educators provide alternatives to the traditional 4-year program based on coursework and fieldwork in close proximity to the college or university. Indiana University maintains several quality-driven programs in its School of Education at Bloomington. One such program, the Cultural Immersion Projects, comprised of the Overseas Project and the American Indian Reservation Project (Indiana University, 2008a), provide student teaching placements in 11 foreign countries and on Navajo Reservations in three states. Participants in the Overseas Project are involved in the local community and provide cultural reports during the placements. The selection process includes meetings to describe the programs in detail and an application process through which students can decide whether they are a good fit with the program's aims.

The American Indian Reservation Project (Indiana University, 2008b) includes specific expectations that, we assume, can be used to select prospective teachers with amenable dispositions. These expectations include the provision of "opportunities for student teachers to live and work in a culturally different setting and to use culturally appropriate and pluralistic learning activities and materials in the classroom." Although no specifics are mentioned, we assume from the description that most of the teachers engaging in this program are not Native Americans but likely represent the demographic trends of teacher education (as discussed earlier).

Qualitative: Teachers College

Teachers College at Columbia University has an Office of Diversity and Community, complete with a Diversity Mission statement:

> To establish Teachers College as an institution that actively attracts, supports and retains diverse students, faculty and staff at all levels, demonstrated through its commitment to social justice, its respectful and vibrant community and its encouragement and support of each individual in the achievement of his or her full potential. (Teachers College, 2008)

This mission spells out specifically that Teachers College wants to rewrite the current demographic profile and select teachers of color and candidates from outside the White, middle-class mainstream.

One teacher educator that we sought for guidance commented on how market needs can help define the qualities a teacher education program desires. In her own program, located in the American Southwest, there is a need for English Language Learner (ELL) educators; culture and language thus become specific factors in selection. Sadly, teacher education in the United States seems to rely on bilingual teachers being born rather than building capacity to educate teachers from a range of backgrounds to teach ELLs (Guerrero, 2003). Thus, to produce bilingual teachers, teacher education programs often rely on selecting teachers with bilingual experiences, competence, or expertise. We should also recognize that heritage bilingual speakers may speak a home language that is not the same as an academic language and will require specific instruction and experience to become effective educators (Sutterby, Ayala, & Morillo, 2005). Thus, as Gay (2000) asserts, similar language and cultural backgrounds do not guarantee pedagogical success in the classroom.

This *quality*-based method of selection is spreading through other programs, such as Clemson's Call Me MISTER program (www.callmemister .clemson.edu) and through more general commitments to multicultural preparation at all levels. We wonder what might occur if all teacher education programs were to be more quality-specific in their selection processes, following the lead of the Call Me MISTER program to produce teachers who are *servant leaders* dedicated to developing dignity and self-respect in their students. What would happen to a college of education that states that it endeavors primarily to produce teachers who hold social activism as a core value, for instance? Would teachers selected for such a program be more effective in classrooms that are growing more racially, ethnically, culturally, economically, and linguistically diverse? What would happen if programs began to recruit teacher candidates from specific populations? In the following section, we describe programs that move beyond just selection and employ specific recruitment approaches.

Teacher Recruitment

The teacher educators who helped us identify promising teacher education programs in this study did not nominate any programs that recruit teachers; the following examples are drawn from our review of the literature. A number of special programs have evolved that recruit prospective teachers from specific populations, similar to examples from the mid-1980s (cf. Post & Woessner, 1987), where teacher educators went into high schools and actively recruited diverse students to become teachers. They set up Future Teacher Clubs, and then worked to get those students into teacher education programs. We elect to highlight the following three programs because they are characterized by several common attributes we believe lead directly to their successful recruiting and placing of teachers. Among the commonalities of the programs described are the explicit goal of supplying teachers to schools in high-need areas; intentional outreach to and recruitment of a specific population of potential teacher candidates; and in two cases monetary, professional, and social support throughout teacher preparation and early career periods.

Recruitment: CAPE

The Council Attracting Prospective Educators (CAPE) is an Ohio program founded as a means to combat the growing disparity between the state's diverse student population and the predominantly White teaching force (Young, 2008). Like the work done by Post and Woessner (1987), the primary goal of the 5-day summer program is to increase diversity in the teaching force by recruiting talented youth from diverse backgrounds and introducing them to teaching as a potential career field (Ohio Department of Education, 2008). The program rotates among university campuses and includes meetings with experienced professionals, participant presentations, and cultural activities. Since 1992, almost half of the CAPE participants have gone on to become teachers (Young, 2008).

Recruitment: INPEACE

The nonprofit Institute for Native Pacific Education and Culture (INPEACE) operates on the Leeward Coast of O'ahu, Hawaii. Here, the student population is two-thirds native Hawaiian, typically scores lowest in the state on standardized tests of achievement, endures 17–20% teacher turnover, and has fewer fully licensed teachers than in urban areas such as Honolulu (Kawakami, 2008). INPEACE recognizes the need to provide the children of the Leeward Coast fully licensed (as opposed to provisionally or emergency-licensed) and dedicated teachers who could fill in the educational and cultural gaps between native children and school practices. In response to this need, INPEACE developed Ka Lama Education Academy (KLEA). The academy aims to recruit and support high school students, educational assistants, long-term substitutes, and other members of the community in education. In addition, through the teacher preparation process the program provides the ongoing support (financial, social, and professional) often needed by community members who are often first-generation college students and possibly not as prepared for college-level work. KLEA is dedicated to supporting teachers by offering counseling and mentorship throughout the processes of recruitment, teacher preparation, induction, and retention. As a result, 91% of the KLEA recruits who have completed the teacher preparation program are teaching on the Leeward Coast and continue to mentor beginning teachers (Kawakami, 2008).

Recruitment: Urban Teacher Pipeline

Whereas CAPE introduces high school students to careers in education and the KLEA recruits members of the community into teaching, the Step to College—Urban Teacher Pipeline at San Francisco State University (SFSU) is a program designed to recruit and prepare urban youth as urban teachers. The program is a two-phased effort based in an Oakland, California, high school that serves predominantly African American and Latino/a youth. Phase One began during students' 10th-grade year (2005–2006 school year). A group of 25 students (11 African American, 14 Latino/a) joined the Step to College program comprised of a 3-year series of courses to provide them with enrichment in critical thinking, academic literacies, technology, and additional college preparatory work (Cesar E. Chavez Institute, 2008). The goal of Phase One is for 100% of program participants to enroll at a 4-year university, whether they pursue education as a major or not.

Phase Two of the Urban Teacher Pipeline constitutes the long-term goal of the program, which is to return urban youth to their communities as teachers. At present, about half of the Step to College students plan to enroll at SFSU to prepare as classroom teachers. At the university, students will matriculate through the urban teacher preparation program as a cohort. Similar to the KLEA, SFSU recognizes the need to support students to ensure the academic, social, and professional success of first-generation college students. Each student is provided a scholarship to the university, a laptop computer, and ongoing mentorship by university faculty (Cesar E. Chavez Institute, 2008). Moreover, participation in regular cohort activities enables students to maintain existing social networks. Participants enroll in courses to prepare them as urban teachers in addition to coursework in their chosen majors. Throughout the program, students work in local schools and, in their junior year, will begin apprenticeships with master teachers. Upon completion of the SFSU Teacher Credential Program, they will return to Oakland as classroom teachers (Duncan-Andrade, 2008).

The special missions of these three programs working directly with community members and high school students may offer models to larger postsecondary institutions concerned with preparing teachers to meet the needs of the rapidly growing numbers of diverse students in American schools. Connections to communities; financial, social, and professional support; and pipelines to specific high-need areas and schools are characteristics of these programs well within the capabilities of institutions with significant financial and human resources.

With the attention to purpose-driven recruitment established, we turn now to ask what happens to these and other teachers when they move into the classroom? To address this question, the next section of this chapter focuses on teacher induction programs and structures designed to support teachers once they have graduated from teacher preparation programs.

Teacher Induction Programs

Whereas all teachers need support, it is especially important to nurture new-to-the-field teachers, who often cite job dissatisfaction as their reason for leaving the profession (Ingersoll, 2001; Johnson, 1990). In addition, turnover rates among new teachers often are statistically higher than the rates experienced by veteran teachers (Ingersoll, 2001, 2003). Contributing factors to this phenomenon are situations in which new teachers are often given the same responsibilities as veteran teachers and are expected to learn and implement a set of established rules, policies, procedures, and ways of behaving that make a particular school a unique work environment (Kardos & Johnson, 2007). Historically, the teaching profession has not provided these teachers with a structured program aimed to facilitate the necessary support, guidance, and orientation needed to succeed (Lortie, 1975; Smith & Ingersoll, 2004; Tyack, 1974). Complicating matters, the majority of teaching is done in isolation from other colleagues (Ingersoll, 2003; Johnson, 1990; Sizer, 1992). Teachers are often left to "sink or swim" in their own classrooms, an experience likened to some researchers as "lost at sea" (Johnson & Birkeland, 2003; Kauffman, Johnson, Kardos, Lui, & Peske, 2002).

In an effort to address the teacher turnover issue, states and school districts developed and implemented teacher induction programs. The overarching goals of new teacher induction programs are to provide new-to-the-field teachers with necessary support, guidance, and orientation into the profession. Teacher induction programs aim to help new teachers move beyond practices of isolation and to provide all participants with the necessary skill set to handle the diverse student populations they serve. Teacher induction programs include at least one of the following components: (a) mentoring, general orientation to both the district and/or school; (b) training on curriculum; and (c) effective teaching practices. Teacher induction programs differ from pre-service teacher training programs because they are designed to assist new teachers who have completed a basic training program.

Teacher induction programs have grown considerably in the last 20 years. During the 1990–1991 academic school year, approximately 40% of teachers new to the profession participated in an induction program (Smith & Ingersoll, 2004). By the 1999–2000 school year, the new teacher induction participation rate had risen to 80%. More recently, states and school districts have invested enormous amounts of money into new teacher induction programs. In 1999, 16 states spent nearly $150 million combined on teacher induction programs (Education Week, 2000). Currently, 25 states require and financially support teacher induction programs that range between $500 and $3,500 per newly inducted teacher annually (Education Week, 2008). It must be noted that of these states, only 19 have established mentor selection criteria, 14 have mentor training criteria, and only 10 have mentor–protégé matching criteria (Education Week, 2008).

Teacher induction programs vary across and within states (Ingersoll & Kralik, 2004; Johnson, Berg, & Donaldson, 2005; Smith & Ingersoll, 2004). Eight states (California, Connecticut, Kentucky, Louisiana, New Jersey, North Carolina, Ohio, and Oklahoma) have statewide designs for their induction programs. An additional 19 states design a new teacher induction program for districts to follow, and within a state each local school district tailors the program to meet both the statewide standards and their specific local needs. Eighteen states provide or require some form of training for mentors; mentors are paid in 12 states, 9 states have set minimum time requirements for interactions between mentors and protégés (new teachers), and 10 states require mentors to observe and provide feedback on at least one classroom lesson instructed by their protégés (Education Week, 2000). Although the logic behind a strategy, that a district-tailored program will provide a better, more appropriate and responsive fit, is seemingly sound, it has led to variability in the scope, length, and rigor—arguably, the quality—of each induction program. For example, some induction programs include only a single meeting, usually held at the beginning of the year, between mentors and protégés whereas other induction programs provide all participants (both mentors and protégés) with release time from their normal teaching schedules to attend weekly scheduled meetings for mentors and protégés (Fideler & Haselkorn, 1999). Given the variety of induction and mentoring programs in place across the United States, we reviewed the mentoring literature with two key questions in mind. First, how is mentoring defined by the field? And, what are the key components of a successful mentor–protégé relationship? It is this relationship, as an integral feature of an effective induction program, that we focus on in the next section.

Mentor–Protégé Relationships

Research suggests that mentoring is often a key component of induction programs and program participants (new teachers) often cite the ability to work with a mentor as a helpful resource (Danielson, 1999; Feiman-Nemser, 1996; Gentry, Denton, & Kurz, 2008). Mentoring refers to the interpersonal relationship between a veteran teacher (mentor) and new teacher (protégé or mentee) (Allen, 2004; Allen, Eby, Poteet, Lentz, & Lima, 2004; Eby, Allen, Evans, Ng, & DuBois, 2008; Kram, 1985; Raggins & Cotton, 1999). Mentoring has to do with the larger issues of career socialization, inspiration, and belief between the mentoring pair. Mentoring relationships should promote excellence and passion for the work of teaching through guidance, protection, support, and networking. Mentoring has a relational and reciprocal nature to it; teachers take an interest in each other as human beings and support each other's professional practice (Vance, 2002). In theory, mentors are close trusted colleagues and guides to protégés. Mentors are supposed to provide their protégés with guidance pertaining to content-specific, pedagogical techniques and classroom management skills. Further, the role of the mentor is to purposefully bring their protégés (new teachers) to a level of professionalism that empowers new teachers to make informed decisions and enrich their content and pedagogical knowledge aimed to improve and expand their teaching modalities. Mentors are supposed to provide their protégés with guidance pertaining to career development (e.g., assigning challenging projects, coaching, advocate for career advancement) and psychosocial roles (e.g., support, role modeling, friendship) (Kram, 1985). Mentoring is a process aimed to mitigate teacher isolation and promote a collegial workplace.

In the current era of accountability in education, it is important to study not only what kinds of induction programs exist but also under what conditions they are beneficial to new teachers. Within the last two decades, several studies have been conducted to investigate and examine the impact of new teacher induction programs on retention (Brown & Wambach, 1987; Charles A. Dana Center, 2002; Gold, 1987; Smith & Ingersoll, 2004), while other studies have tried to measure the extent to which induction programs can serve as a policy lever to improve teacher quality (Klug & Salzman, 1991; Roehrig & Luft, 2006; Schaffer, Stringfield, & Wolfe, 1992). The mentoring and induction literature provide support "for the hypothesis that well-conceived and well-implemented teacher mentoring and induction programs are successful in increasing the job satisfaction, efficacy, and retention of new teachers" (Smith & Ingersoll, 2004). Unfortunately, the majority of teacher induction programs are implemented in localities based solely on intuition and anecdotal evidence (Robbins, 2004), and programs are rarely evaluated (Fideler & Haselkorn, 1999; Ingersoll & Kralik, 2004; Smith, 2007). We conclude this chapter with recommendations drawn from our analyses of the demographics, selection and recruitment practices, and induction processes in teacher education.

Recommendations and Conclusions

Based on our analysis of teacher and teacher candidate demographics, selection and recruitment, and induction, we conclude this chapter with recommendations for transformation. In terms of selection, we encourage all teacher education programs to move beyond the well-entrenched system of quantitative selection and begin to (a) include qualitative factors in their selection process and (b) develop recruitment programs to recruit and support future teachers from the community.

Qualitative Factors

It seems that adding at least some qualitative data to the selection process would not be difficult. A specific essay topic or candidate interview may offer a glimpse beyond the numbers to gauge whether potential teacher candidates' dispositions, attitudes, and goals align with a particular teacher education program's stated mission. To take this step effectively, we believe that each program must define for itself the qualities it wants to see in the teachers it will prepare. These qualities will not and should not be the same for every program in every location. Selecting prospective teachers with a commitment to social action cannot be effective if the teacher education program is not also committed to social action. We doubt that the programs at Indiana University described earlier would still be in existence if that school of education was not committed to the improvement of education for marginalized populations.

Community Recruitment Programs

We believe each teacher education program bears some responsibility for improving education in the local community; it is our job, we believe, to work against an "ivory tower mentality" that often finds the top teacher education programs located alongside struggling public school systems. The pipeline metaphor used by the Urban Teacher Pipeline and SFSU is a model we think has the potential for adaptation to other local situations. Aggressive recruitment from and a mutually beneficial presence in local high schools may help develop a more diverse teaching force that is both pedagogically sound and community relevant.

We propose two recommendations based on our review and analyses of teacher induction: (a) specific care should be taken to match mentors and protégés, and (b) induction programs should be a school-wide effort. The first focuses on the interpersonal relationship between the mentor and the protégé. The second focuses on the shared responsibility of the community to support new teachers.

Matching Process

Mutually rewarding mentoring relationships can provide protégés (new teachers) and mentors (veteran teachers) with the opportunity to learn professionally. The pairing and matching of mentors with protégés need to consider cultural and racial experiences that go beyond subject matter expertise, interest, and teaching philosophy. Learning and developmental opportunities increase in an environment that provides members with trust, commitment, and interpersonal comfort (Noe, 2002). A poor match between mentors and protégés is a common threat to a healthy mentoring relationship. A difference in age, background, interpersonal communication styles (e.g., communicating and providing feedback), personality, interests, and work-related values are all reasons given by protégés with regard to why there was a mentor–protégé mismatch (Eby & Lockwood, 2005). Structural and geographical differences should also be considered when matching mentors and protégés. For example, a poor match may manifest with mentors who may not work in the same school as their protégé, are assigned too many protégés to mentor, or teach in a different content area.

School-Wide Effort

Mentoring is supposed to help the protégé learn and develop professionally, and it is plausible for one to assume that beginning teachers will, at a minimum, develop informal mentoring relationships with other employees. Unlike formal mentoring relationships, informal mentoring relationships are typically not governed by the organization and depend on the mutual and, often, spontaneous identification of both mentors and protégés (Raggins, 2002; Wanberg, Welsh, & Kammeyer-Mueller, 2007). The actual nature of the mentoring experience is of great importance to schools. For starters, schools should provide support and capacity for their mentoring and induction activities. Although mentoring typically reflects a one-on-one relationship, schools can create environments in which healthy mentoring relationships can be pursued. It is unlikely that one mentor will possess the combination of expertise and experience to meet the ubiquitous needs of each new teacher. School leaders should create support networks for beginning teachers within and across the school administration team and veteran teachers to ensure that the beginning teachers are integrated into the school culture and climate. Further, school leaders should develop school-wide professional learning communities that promote the engagement and exchange of content-specific knowledge and pedagogical techniques across teachers with varying experience levels (Johnson & Birkeland, 2003).

In light of the growing racial, cultural, linguistic, and economic disparities among and between teachers and their students, we see a strong need for continued research and innovation across the components of selection, recruitment, and induction in teacher education. Teacher education programs as well as school districts should strive to better understand and to improve their practices. We have argued that it is important for teacher education programs and P–12 school districts to develop strategies and processes that promote the diversification of the teaching force, support and guide teachers into and beyond the induction years, and (hopefully) increase every student's opportunity to learn and achieve at high levels.

References

Allen, M. (2003). *Eight questions on teacher preparation: What does the research say? A summary of the findings.* Denver, CO: Educational Commission of the States.

Allen, M. (2005). *Eight questions on teacher recruitment and retention: What does the research say?* Denver, CO: Educational Commission of the States.

Allen, T. D., Eby, L. T., Poteet, M. L., Lentz, E., & Lima, L. (2004). Career benefits associated with mentoring for protégés: A meta-analysis. *Journal of Applied Psychology, 89,* 127–136.

American Association of Colleges for Teacher Education. (1999). *Teacher education pipeline IV: Schools and departments of education enrollments by race, ethnicity, and gender.* Washington, DC: Author.

Applegate, J. H. (1987). Teacher candidate selection: An overview. *Journal of Teacher Education, 38,* 2–6.

Banks, J. A. (2003). *Teaching strategies for ethnic studies* (7th ed.). Boston: Allyn and Bacon.

Brown, J. G., & Wambach, C. (1987). *Using mentors to increase new teacher retention: The Mentor Teacher Induction Project.* Paper presented at the annual meeting of the American Association of Colleges for Teacher Education, Arlington, VA.

Cesar E. Chavez Institute. (2008). *Research in action: Step to College—The Urban Teacher Pipeline.* Retrieved April 20, 2008, from http://cci.sfsu.edu/taxonomy/term/66

Charles A. Dana Center. (2002). *Texas Beginning Educator Support System: Evaluation report for year three, 2001–02.* Austin: University of Texas, College of Natural Sciences.

Clewell, B. C., & Villegas, A. M. (1999). Creating a nontraditional pipeline for urban teachers: The pathways to teaching careers model. *Journal of Negro Education, 68*(3), 306–317.

Danielson, C. (1999). Mentoring beginning teachers: The case for mentoring. *Teaching and Change, 6*(3), 251–257.

Duncan-Andrade, J. M. R. (2008). *Thug life principles for literacy research: Toward research agendas indignant about suffering and guided by love, purpose, and hope.* Presentation made at National Council of Teachers of English Assembly for Research Mid-Winter Conference, Bloomington, IN.

Eby, L. T. & Lockwood, A. (2005). Protégés' and mentors' reactions to participating in formal mentoring programs: A qualitative investigation. *Journal of Vocational Behavior, 67*(3), 441–458.

Eby, L. T., Allen, T. D., Evans, S. C., Ng, T., & DuBois, D. L. (2008). Does mentoring matter? A multidisciplinary meta-analysis comparing mentored and non-mentored individuals. *Journal of Vocational Behavior, 72*(2), 254–267.

Education Week. (2000, January). Quality counts 2000: Who should teach? *Education Week,* 19. Retrieved February 17, 2010, from http://rc-archive.edweek.org/sreports/qc00/

Education Week. (2008, January). Quality counts 2008: Tapping into teaching? *Education Week, 27*(18). Retrieved February 17, 2010, from www.edweek.org/ew/toc/2008/01/10/index.html

Ehrenberg, R. G., & Brewer, D. J. (1994). Do school and teacher characteristics matter? Evidence from high school and beyond. *Economics of Education Review, 13*(1), 1–17.

Feiman-Nemser, S. (1996). *Mentoring: A critical review.* Washington, DC: ERIC Clearinghouse on Teaching and Teacher Education.

Fideler, E., & Haselkorn, D. (1999). *Learning the ropes: Urban teacher induction programs and practices in the United States.* Belmont, MA: Recruiting New Teachers.

Freeman, D. J., Martin, R. J., Brousseau, B. A., & West, B. B. (1989). Do higher program admission standards alter profiles of entering teacher candidates? *Journal of Teacher Education, 40,* 33–41.

Gay, G. (2000). *Culturally responsive teaching: Theory, research and practice.* New York: Teachers College Press.

Gay, G., & Howard, T. (2000). Multicultural teacher education for the 21st century. *Teacher Educator, 36*(1), 1–16.

Gentry, L. B., Denton, C. A., & Kurz, T. (2008). Technologically based mentoring provided to teachers: A synthesis of the literature. *Journal of Technology and Teacher Education, 16*(3), 339–373.

Gitomer, D. H., Latham, A. S., & Ziomek, R. (1999). *The academic quality of prospective teachers: The impact of admissions and licensure testing.* Princeton, NJ: Educational Testing Service.

Gold, M. (1987). *Retired teachers as consultants to new teachers: A new inservice teacher training model.* Final report. Case 09–87. New York: City University of New York, New York Institute for Research and Development in Occupational Education; Washington, DC: American Association of State Colleges and Universities.

Guerrero, M. D. (2003). We have correct English teachers. Why can't we have correct Spanish teachers? It's not acceptable. *Qualitative Studies in Education, 16*(5), 647–668.

Guyton, E., & Farokhi, E. (1987). Relationships among academic performance, basic skills, subject-matter knowledge, and teaching skills of teacher education graduates. *Journal of Teacher Education, 38,* 37–42.

Haberman, M. (1993). Predicting the success of urban teachers (the Milwaukee trials). *Action in Teacher Education, 15*(3), 1–6.

Haberman, M. (1995). *Star teachers of children in poverty.* West Lafayette, IN: Kappa Delta Pi.

Indiana University. (2008a). *Cultural immersion projects: General eligibility and requirements.* Retrieved March 27, 2008, from http://site.educ.Indiana.edu/Default.aspx?tabid = 4215

Indiana University. (2008b). *Cultural immersion projects: About the American Indian reservation project.* Retrieved March 27, 2008, from http://site.educ.Indiana.edu/Default.aspx?tabid = 4218

Ingersoll, R. (2001, Fall). Teacher turnover and teacher shortages: An organizational analysis. *American Educational Research Journal, 38*(3), 499–504.

Ingersoll, R. (2003). *Who controls teachers' work?* Cambridge, MA: Harvard University Press.

Ingersoll, R., & Kralik, J. (2004). *The impact of mentoring on teacher retention: What the research says.* Denver, CO: Education Commission of the States.

Irvine, J. (2003). *Educating teachers for diversity: Seeing with a cultural eye.* New York: Teachers College Press.

Johnson, S., Berg, J., & Donaldson, M. (2005). *Who stays in teaching and why: A review of the literature on teacher retention.* The Project on the Next Generation of Teachers. Cambridge, MA: Harvard Graduate School of Education.

Johnson, S. M. (1990). *Teachers at work: Achieving success in our schools.* New York: Basic Books.

Johnson, S. M., & Birkeland, S. E. (2003). Pursuing a "sense of success": New teachers explain their career decisions. *American Educational Research Journal, 40*(3), 581–617.

Kardos, S. M., & Johnson, S. M. (2007). On their own and presumed expert: New teachers' experiences with their colleagues. *Teacher College Record, 109*(12), 2083–2106.

Kauffman, D., Johnson, S. M., Kardos, S. M., Liu, E., & Peske, H. G. (2002). "Lost at sea": New teachers' experiences with curriculum and assessment. *Teachers College Record,* 104(2), 273–300.

Kawakami, A. J. (2008). *The Ka Lama Education Academy & Kukuluao Teacher Support System: Community-based teacher recruitment and retention.* Paper presented at the Annual Meeting of the American Association for Colleges of Teacher Education, New Orleans.

Klug, B. J., & Salzman, S. A. (1991). Formal induction vs. informal mentoring: Comparative effects and outcomes. *Teaching and Teacher Education, 7,* 241–251.

Ladson-Billings, G. (1994). *The dreamkeepers: Successful teachers of Black children.* San Francisco: Jossey-Bass.

Lortie, D. (1975). *Schoolteacher: A sociological study.* Chicago: University of Chicago Press.

Mikitovics, A., & Crehan, K. D. (2002). Pre-professional skills test scores as college of education admission criteria. *Journal of Education Research, 95*(4), 215–223.

Milner, H. R. (2006). Preservice teachers' learning about cultural and racial diversity: Implications for urban education. *Urban Education, 41*(4), 343–375.

Milner, H. R., & Howard, T. C. (2004). Black teachers, Black students, Black communities and *Brown*: Perspectives and insights from experts. *Journal of Negro Education, 73*(3).

National Center for Education Statistics (2007a). *Digest of Education Statistics: 2007.* Retrieved November 24, 2008, from http://nces.ed.gov/programs/digest/d07/

National Center for Education Statistics. (2007b). *Public elementary and secondary school student enrollment, high school completions and staff from the common core of data: School year 2005–06.* Retrieved November 24, 2008, from http://nces.ed.gov/pubsearch/pubsinfo.asp?pubid = 2007352

National Center for Education Statistics. (2007c). *Schools and staffing survey.* Retrieved November 24, 2008, from http://nces.ed.gov/surveys/sass/tables/state _2004_18.asp

National Center for Education Statistics. (2008). *Public elementary and secondary school student enrollment and staff from the common core of data: School year 2006–07.* Retrieved November 24, 2008, from http://nces.ed.gov/pubsearch/pubs info.asp?pubid=2009305

Noe, R. A. (2002). *Employee training and development* (2nd ed.). New York: McGraw-Hill Higher Education.

Nunez, M., & Fernandez, M. R. (2006). Collaborative recruitment of diverse teachers for the long haul—TEAMS: Teacher education for the advancement of a multicultural society. *Multicultural Education, 14*(2), 50–56.

Ohio Department of Education. (2008). *Council attracting prospective teachers.* Retrieved February 9, 2008, from www.ode.state.oh.us/GD/Templates/Pages/ODE/ODEDetail.aspx?page=3&TopicRelationID=564&ContentID=5074& Content=45599

Orfield, G. (2001). *Schools more separate: Consequences of a decade of resegregation: The civil rights project.* Cambridge, MA: Harvard University Press.

Post, L. M., & Woessner, H. (1987). Developing a recruitment and retention support system for minority students in teacher education. *Journal of Negro Education, 56,* 203–211.

Raggins, B. R., & Cotton, J. L. (1999). Mentor functions and outcomes: A comparison of men and women in formal and informal mentoring relationships. *Journal of Applied Psychology, 84,* 529–550.

Raggins, B. R. (2002). Understanding diversified mentoring relationships: Definitions, challenges, and strategies. In D. Clutterbuck & B. R. Raggins, (Eds.), *Mentoring and diversity: An international perspective* (pp. 23–53). Woburn, MA: Butterworth Heinemann.

Riggs, I. M., Riggs, M. L., & Sandlin, R. A. (1992, April). *An assessment of selection criteria validity for a teacher education program.* Paper presented at the American Educational Research Association's Annual Meeting, San Francisco, CA.

Robbins, S. (2004). *Organizational behavior* (10th ed.). Upper Saddle River, NJ: Prentice Hall.

Roehrig, G. H., & Luft, J. A. (2006). Does one size fit all? The induction experience of beginning teachers from different teacher preparation programs. *Journal of Research in Science Teaching, 43*(9), 963–985.

Schaffer, E., Stringfield, S., & Wolfe, D. (1992). An innovative beginning teacher induction program: A two-year analysis of classroom interactions. *Journal of Teacher Education, 43*(3), 181–192.

Sizer, T. R. (1992). *Horace's School: Redesigning the American high school.* Boston: Houghton Mifflin.

Sleeter, C. E. (2001). Epistemological diversity in research on preservice teacher preparation for historically underserved children. In W. G. Secada (Ed.), *Review of research in education* (Vol. 6). Washington, DC: AERA.

Smith, T. M. (2007). How do state-level induction and standards-based reform policies affect induction experiences and turnover among new teachers? *American Journal of Education, 113,* 273–309.

Smith, T. M., & Ingersoll, R. M. (2004). What are the effects of induction and mentoring on beginning teacher turnover? *American Educational Research Journal, 41*(3), 681–714.

Sutterby, J. A., Ayala, J., & Morillo, S. (2005). El sendero torcido al español [The twisted path to Spanish]: The development of bilingual teachers' Spanish-language proficiency. *Bilingual Research Journal, 29*(2), 435–452.

Teachers College. (2008). *Office of the vice president for diversity and community.* Retrieved March 27, 2007, from www.tc.edu/diversity

Tyack, D. (1974). *The one best system.* Cambridge, MA: Harvard University Press.

University of Georgia. (2008). *First-year admission criteria.* Retrieved March 27, 2008, from www.admissions.uga.edu/article/admission_information_for_first_year_students.html

University of Wisconsin-Madison. (2008). *Undergraduate admissions: Freshman admissions.* Retrieved March 27, 2008, from www.admissions.wisc.edu/freshman.php

Vance, C. (2002). Mentoring at the edge of chaos, *Creative Nursing, 8*(3), 7.

Villegas, A. M., & Clewell, B. C. (1998). Increasing teacher diversity by tapping the paraprofessional pool. *Theory Into Practice, 37,* 121–130.

Villegas, A. M., & Davis, D. E. (2007). Approaches to diversifying the teaching force: Attending to issues of recruitment, preparation, and retention. *Teacher Education Quarterly, 34*(4), 137–147.

Wanberg, C. R., Welsh, E. T., & Kammeyer-Mueller, J. (2007). Protégé and mentor self-disclosure: Levels and outcomes within formal mentoring dyads in a corporate context. *Journal of Vocational Behavior, 70,* 398–412.

Young, P. (2008). *The Council Attracting Prospective Educators (CAPE) teacher academy: A statewide effort targeting high school students.* Paper presented at the Annual Meeting of the American Association for Colleges of Teacher Education, New Orleans.

Zeichner, K. M., Grant, C., Gay, G., Gillette, M., Valli, L., & Villegas, A. M. (1998). A research informed vision of good practice in multicultural teacher education: Design principles. *Theory Into Practice, 37,* 163–171.

Zumwalt, K., & Craig, E. (2005). Teachers' characteristics: Research on the demographic profile. In M. C. Smith & K. M. Zeichner (Eds.), *Studying teacher education: The report of the AERA panel on research and teacher education* (pp. 111–156). Mahwah, NJ: Lawrence Erlbaum Associates.

PART THREE

ACCOUNTABILITY AND
EVALUATION

5

A MODEST PROPOSAL FOR MAKING TEACHER EDUCATION ACCOUNTABLE

How to Make University-Controlled Teacher
Education and Alternative Certification Programs
Accountable for the Quality of Teachers in Schools
Serving Children and Youth in Poverty

Martin Haberman

The typical explanation of why 15 million children and youth in poverty are not achieving as they should be blames the victims, their families, their ethnicity, and their lack of valuing of and commitment to education. This explanation, however, does not explain why low-income students do achieve in the classrooms of effective (star) teachers who comprise approximately 8% of the teaching force. The need for more effective teachers cannot be met by university-controlled teacher education, which provides continuous rewards to programs and faculty for producing individuals who do not deign to work in challenging schools or who quit or fail if they do. Similarly, the alternative certification programs (AC programs) that provide most of the teachers for the major urban districts serving children and youth in poverty cannot provide sufficient numbers of effective teachers and are continually rewarded for hiring quitters/failures.

This chapter begins by examining the condition of educational failures in poor schools and the rationale for transformation and accountability. Second, it outlines a system for holding university-controlled teacher preparation programs responsible for preparing quality teachers for children and youth in poverty. And third, it continues the discussion with a plan for district-level accountability systems that hold AC programs liable to the children they have been hired to serve. Concomitantly, these two systems are a modest proposal for making teacher education accountable for disenfranchised learners in America's schools.

Educational Transformation and Accountability Deferred

Every 3 years, American schools provide enough dropouts to create a city the size of Chicago (Balfanz & Letgers, 2004). These individuals are unlikely ever to have adequate health care, retirement plans, or jobs that will pay them enough to live in decent housing or in safe neighborhoods. It is likely that their children will attend schools as bad or worse than the ones they attended and will add to the millions of those unprepared to provide for themselves or to participate in a democratic society. Even worse, if such a thing is possible, is the miseducation of even larger numbers of high school pushouts who do not discover until after they graduate as "A" and "B" students that they lack the skills and knowledge either to continue in higher education or to enter the workforce without extensive, expensive reteaching of basic skills and common knowledge.

Our society's inability to prepare 15 million children from diverse, low-income families to function in American society creates personal tragedies on a scale that boggles the mind. Economists agree that our society cannot keep producing and absorbing failure of this magnitude and at this rate—handed down across generations—and still sustain our standard of living or our way of life. Indeed, the evidence is clear that most children will no longer surpass their parents in achieving the American dream. Each subsequent generation will find upward economic mobility more difficult and less attainable. Although most experts point to factors in the world economy to explain this phenomenon, they inevitably get around to the failures in American education as one basic cause of our economic problems. I am convinced that the failure of our schools to educate diverse students in poverty is not merely one cause but the fundamental cause that best explains the decline of prospects for children and youth in poverty and for society at large.

Change agents have attempted to transform failing schools since the end of World War II. After squandering trillions in public and private funds, transformers reach retirement age and inevitably explain their failures as change agents by concluding what most Americans have always known:

"Urban schools can't be changed easily." The truth is that these schools do change every year. They get worse! The 120 major urban districts miseducating 7¹/₂ million diverse, urban students in poverty are all dysfunctional bureaucracies that operate for the benefit of the adults employed in them, and the vendors who supply them, at the rate of half a trillion dollars per year.

Dysfunctional Bureaucracies and District Norms

Nowhere is the dysfunctional nature of the urban school districts more evident than in the conditions of work in their schools and in the size of their central offices. Even the most effective teachers begin to burn out beginning in their fifth year. The power of the mindless bureaucracies to wear down teachers increases for teachers who are the most caring and sensitive. Teachers who empathize with students and the life challenges they face soon realize that the dysfunctional bureaucracies will not permit them to meet the needs of their students. Half of the starry-eyed beginners are gone in 5 years or less.

Ultimately, urban school districts are left with a majority of teachers who are "lifers." These are the strong *in*sensitives who are not worn down by working in dysfunctional systems that destroy children. Lifers make no effort to meet the needs of the students. Lifers are teachers who share an ideology that defines the role of the teacher as a presenter of subject matter. Lifers do not know the difference between teaching and simply telling students stuff. Lifers do not accept accountability or responsibility for motivating students to want to learn. Their ideology is based on the assumption that if students can't listen quietly and follow directions for 5 hours a day, they, their families, or their ethnicity is somehow lacking and at fault.

The following are just a few typical comments that exemplify the lifer's ideology: "I teach those who want to learn; there's nothing I can do with those who don't want to learn." "I'm not a social worker. I'm here to teach. Nutrition, health care, getting them glasses or to a dentist is someone else's problem." "It's up to the parents to raise their kids; I raise mine and they should raise theirs." "If anyone acts up in my class, I show them the door." "If they don't do homework and the parents don't help them, there's nothing I can do." "My job is to teach and theirs is to learn." "If they don't have the basic skills to do the work, they shouldn't have been put in my class." "I wasn't trained in special education. What's all this inclusion stuff? I don't have time to deal with retarded or disturbed kids." "I have my family and a life; I'm out of here at 3:00 on the dot" (Sabir, 2007). Lifers are jobholders who never let their inadequacies as teachers lead them to burn out or quit. Their primary goal is maintaining their health care and retirement benefits and not trying to meet the needs of students they do not respect. In my city, the benefits package for teachers is 61.5% so that a lifer at the top of even a modest salary schedule makes (not "earns") approximately $100,000 annually.

My experience in 260 urban school districts over the last 55 years is that nearly half of the teachers in these urban districts are lifers. They offer what I refer to as the *pedagogy of poverty*. Students come into their rooms. The teacher explains the lesson for the day. The students complete an assignment. The teacher collects it (from those who hand something in) and grades it. Any students interrupting this ritual are removed from the room. Repeated interruptions are cause for suspension. In my city, the number of students enrolled (86,500) equals the annual number of suspensions (86,500, including 180 kindergartners). In one year, more than 26%, or more than 1 in 4 students, was suspended 3 or more days. Lifers experience little or no stress because they are not emotionally engaged in teaching. They are assignment makers. They are able to continue working in the most dysfunctional bureaucracies imaginable without feeling anxious or worn down. Because they have no expectations that their students will learn they are not anxious or stressed out about the lack of student learning. Like students who do not complete assignments or do any homework, lifers take nothing home with them. They do not plan because "teaching" is simply assigning the next few pages in the text. Like the students who have been conditioned simply to show up each day, lifers show up each day and go through the rituals of teaching.

In the major urban districts, there are as many employees supposedly helping the teaching–learning process who work outside of classrooms as there are teachers working inside of classrooms. Several of the major districts have ratios of between 1:1 and 2:1 of employees who work outside of classrooms to teachers who work inside of classrooms . . . and this does not count bus drivers. In almost every major urban district, the schools have become the largest employer. In my city, the schools employ more than 12,300, but teachers comprise fewer than half this number. I don't know of a major urban area in which the school system is not the single largest employer in its city.

The dysfunctional nature of urban school districts is evident to any objective observer. Consider merely a few examples. As enrollments decline, budgets continue to rise. Fewer than half the students graduate from school districts that serve diverse students in poverty. Students labeled as having handicapping conditions comprise 20% or more and graduate at a higher rate (roughly 75%) than African American students (less than 47%) and Latino students (around 40%). According to the 2008 report of the Schott Foundation, only 19% of African American students in Indianapolis graduated. In Detroit, this number is 20%; in Norfolk, Virginia, 27%; and in Rochester, New York, 29% (Schott Foundation, 2008). Half of the beginning teachers quit or fail in 5 years or less. Private foundations in these urban areas no longer award grant funds to their local school districts because they don't trust how the districts will spend their money. In my city, if the number of students is divided into the total school budget, there is more than $14,500 per year per student at the start of the school year. When the school principals are asked how much they actually receive from central office to operate their schools, however, elementary principals receive about $6,000 per student per year and high school principals receive an estimated $8,000 per student. Given that there is more than double the number of elementary than high school students, this means that for the district as a whole, less than $0.50 of every dollar is spent on the actual education of students *in* schools and classrooms. More than $0.50 of every dollar disappears before it ever reaches the schools.

The culture of these dysfunctional school districts is one in which process is infinitely more important than product. How things are done takes precedence over any outcomes. Procedures and processes are valued whereas results are ignored with impunity. The staff showing up and being there is more important than what is done, and what is done is almost always and entirely process. This is especially true for central office staff engaged in planning, preparation, gathering of resources, reorganization of staff, assigning functions, preparing interim and final reports, and engaging in endless communication activities. Getting ready for committee meetings, holding committee meetings, and following up with committee notes and subsequent agendas comprise more than half of the "working" time of central office personnel. These endless procedures become the "work" of supervisory and administrative staff who are never evaluated on the stated outcomes of the organization (i.e., student learning) but on the procedures they engage in as "leadership" staff. Whenever I ask central office functionaries if they are busy, they prove how busy they are by taking out their appointment books. "Here, look at my meeting calendar. I don't have a minute to myself." Nowhere has the substitution of committee meetings and paperwork for doing anything useful been as highly developed by supervisors and administrators as they have in dysfunctional urban school districts.

The history of these dysfunctional bureaucracies shows clearly that they have deflected and co-opted all change efforts. Like strains of viruses, they only grow stronger and more resistant as they respond to the latest "antibiotics" of a new curriculum, a new textbook series, a new form of scheduling, different staffing arrangements, or a new computer program. These school systems survive and grow more resistant regardless of the mountains of data collected documenting their failures and the enormous amount of national, state, and local treasure injected into them. If it is not possible to change these systems, then what good would it do to make them accountable?

The Rationale for Transformation

There are two benefits for holding school districts accountable. First, if the growth of these dysfunctional districts can be slowed, then the numbers of dropouts and miseducated graduates will be decreased. It would be no small benefit to drop the number of human tragedies (i.e., dropouts and graduates with no skills) from millions to thousands. Second, if these districts were to be broken down into hundreds of smaller, accountable ones, more resources would be spent inside schools and classrooms on teaching and learning rather than on supporting the metastasizing central offices. By spending these funds inside rather than outside of classrooms, it is more likely that more students would learn more. Within even the worst of these districts there are individual schools where students do learn. Establishing a system of accountability would make it possible to unyoke effective schools from their dysfunctional bureaucracies and thereby increase their number. For genuine change to occur, the unit of analysis must be the school building not the school district! Sixty years of trying (and failing) to scale up the success of individual schools to the district level should have led more change agents and transformers to the inescapable fact that what causes individual schools to be successful cannot be scaled up to make all schools in a dysfunctional district successful.

As soon as there is an effort to replicate what a few effective schools have done (i.e., scale up), more resources are pumped into the district for the replication effort to be disseminated. The dysfunctional bureaucracy then sucks up and appropriates more than $0.50 of every new dollar of any new resources for staff and services other than teachers and classrooms. When the dysfunctional bureaucracy tries to improve reading, it does so by hiring hundreds of reading coaches who work *outside* of classrooms as coaches. If the parents win a lawsuit to improve the education of students with special needs, then the system hires hundreds of supervisors, coaches, and mentors to work *outside* of classrooms to help teachers apply new inclusion strategies. If the goal is improved safety, the system hires hundreds of safety aides and/ or pays the local police department for overtime to patrol *outside* of middle and high schools. Regardless of the initiative, supervisors, administrators, coaches, clerical staff, guidance counselors, safety personnel, and all who work *outside* of classrooms are hired to scale-up these initiatives.

The result is always the same: more funds spent for more jobs outside of classrooms than on teaching and learning inside of classrooms. In any of these initiatives, if the resources were to be invested in more classroom teachers, class size could be cut in half or even thirds and more learning, more safety, more guidance, and more of every other putative improvement could be initiated. Lowering class size and hiring more competent, accountable teachers to work more closely with individual students can best improve every desirable function that has ever been tried or can be imagined. On the other hand, no amount of funds invested outside of classrooms can close the achievement gaps based on income, race, gender, and special needs.

Unfortunately, in the real world the reverse occurs. When budgets are cut in these dysfunctional bureaucracies, more classroom teachers rather than any other category of employee are fired. The skyrocketing costs of fuel and health care have required all the urban districts to cut back. The greatest number of jobs cut in these dysfunctional bureaucracies has been of nontenured teachers and teachers in "frill" areas such as art, music, and physical education. Urban districts across America have typically absorbed increases in the cost of energy, health care, and inflation by doing away with the art and music curricula.

The caveat in hiring more teachers rather than those who work outside of classrooms is the need to start identifying and hiring real teachers rather than more lifers. There would be no benefit to cutting class size so that lifers can have the even greater, in-depth influence that naturally accrues in smaller classes with more intensive individual contact. Cutting class size but maintaining the present number of lifers would simply worsen the present pandemic of miseducation.

If we are not misled by the hyperbolic goals stated by these dysfunctional bureaucracies and look at what these urban school districts actually accomplish, it is clear that their primary goal is job development for their communities—and they perform that function quite successfully. Every urban school superintendent has anecdotal data exemplifying the difficulty of trying to close a high school that has been a dropout factory in his or her district for 25 years or more. A high school that has been graduating less than half of its students, with fewer than 10% of its students able to pass state-mandated tests, cannot be closed because parents and community members demand that these schools be kept open. Naïve analysts frequently talk about the need to organize urban parents and community to demand that urban school districts stop miseducating their children. This admonition fails to recognize that the parents and community have a greater goal than their children's education and feel they must protect these failing districts.

The dysfunctional urban school bureaucracies are typically the largest employers in their cities. Parents and community members work in food services, on maintenance staffs, as safety aides, as teaching assistants and paraprofessionals, as clerical staff, and as translators, in addition to serving as teachers, principals, and central office staff. Bus companies also typically employ parents and community members. Urban school districts are also the largest employers of members of minority ethnic groups. Parents and community are not about to threaten to close or even downsize the very systems that provide them their livelihood, even when these systems are miseducating their children. As a result, parents and community in even the worst of the dysfunctional bureaucracies (i.e., Washington, DC, New Orleans, St. Louis, Milwaukee, Newark, Cleveland, Baltimore, and so forth) resist demanding the breakup of their school systems, or even making them more accountable, because that would lead to downsizing staff. It is an anomaly to note the growing number of parents employed in these districts who enroll their children in charter, voucher, and private schools but who remain staunch supporters of the dysfunctional bureaucracies that employ them.

What parents and community demand in place of closing failing schools is expanding services for children in these schools because that translates into more jobs. In effect, the dysfunctional urban school bureaucracies hold the parents and community as employed hostages who must support and main-tain the very systems working against the educational interests of their own children. This explains why in even the worst-of-the-worst districts the par-ents and community always demand "improvement" (read "expansion") of the system rather than alternatives that might decentralize or downsize even the most egregious, debilitating burnout factories and dysfunctional central offices that are not held accountable for student achievement and teacher quality.

A Syllogism of Accountability

Nothing works without accountability. Not holding universities responsible for the teachers and principals they graduate and dub "competent" and not holding school districts responsible for the educators they hire as "fully qualified" explains why 15 million diverse children and youth in poverty wander in an educational wasteland taught by quitter/failure teachers and led by incompetent principals.

In the vernacular, accountability connotes more than some vague notion of being answerable or responsible. Accountability means that there are clear, specific, real consequences for performance. Holding someone accountable infers that an individual's performance is rewarded or punished in tangible ways. Positive performance leads to rewards such as promotion, greater responsibility, or a raise in salary. Negative performance results in no salary increase, demotion, or even dismissal. When an institution or organization is held accountable, it too is recognized and rewarded in tangible ways for achieving its stated objectives; expanded missions, greater authority, and increased budgets are the most common forms of reward. Accountable organizations or institutions that do not meet their stated objectives experience cutbacks in personnel, decreased authority, and budget cuts. Accountability means that failing individuals or organizations are not allowed to continue to damage their clients indefinitely. There must be consequences for failure before an individual or an organization can be described as accountable. On the basis of this definition, such terms as "accountable school districts," "accountable teachers," "accountable central offices," "accountable teacher education programs," "accountable school hiring departments," or "accountable education professors" are all oxymorons.

The syllogism is as follows: Schools improve when there are more effective teachers and principals. Universities and alternative certification can improve the quality of the teachers and principals they prepare only if they are made accountable. Therefore, the way to improve the schools is to make the universities and AC programs that prepare teachers and principals accountable by rewarding or punishing them on the basis of how well the teachers and principals they prepare actually function in the schools.

Making Universities Accountable for the Teachers They Prepare

No school can be better than its teachers. But even effective teachers can be ground down and burned out by incompetent school principals. Getting teachers who are knowledgeable and able to make learning relevant for children and youth and principals who can create the conditions of work for such teachers should be the job of those who prepare educators and those who hire them. The history of the last 60 years of educational decline for children and youth in poverty makes it clear that the systems for preparing and selecting educators must be made more effective. The surest means for increasing school effectiveness is to make organizations and individuals responsible for preparation and hiring directly and transparently accountable.

Typically, accountability schemes are limited to the public schools that select and hire teachers and principals. The criterion of accountability, however, must also be applied to the schools of education in universities and to the alternative certification programs that prepare educators. Why is it that universities and alternative certification programs are not held accountable? Is it possible to make universities accountable for those they pronounce "fully qualified"?

Universities are even less accountable than are public schools for the benefits they claim their services provide graduates and society. Schools of education, ensconced as they are in the bosom of universities, are as protected as the other colleges that train professionals. Schools of education are not required to make any follow-up assessments of how well their graduates perform in the real world. The criterion universities use to prove the value of their programs is simply the increased number of doctors, lawyers, engineers, dentists, accountants, nurses, veterinarians, social workers, and teachers they graduate.

The University of California System, the State University of New York, and the University of Wisconsin System, the three largest university systems in the United States, recently congratulated themselves in a 2008 "accountability" report. They evaluated themselves using the following criteria: increased graduation rates, undergraduates taking fewer courses and thus saving money, using more technology and distance learning, and attracting more low-income students and students of color. In addition, graduate schools were evaluated on the basis of the amount of external grants they secured for their institutions and the number of faculty publications. The public is supposed to assume that these criteria are somehow connected to whether graduates actually take jobs in their chosen fields and perform effectively. But universities do not evaluate themselves on whether their graduates, in any profession, function effectively after graduation.

Based on any lack of follow-up assessment of their graduates' performance it would seem more appropriate to regard universities as having zero accountability, but the situation is even worse. In the case of all the professional schools and especially of schools of education, there is actually negative accountability. Many graduates never take jobs, and many of those who do quit, fail or leave their profession after brief periods.

In Wisconsin, for example, it is typical for as many as two thirds of the teacher graduates in a given year never to take teaching jobs. Most of the available teaching jobs are in districts serving diverse students in poverty. Of the 10% of graduates who deign to take jobs in the "challenging" schools where there are vacancies, half are gone in 5 years or less. Meanwhile the budgets of the universities and the schools of education that prepared these teachers grow in size every year without exception or interruption. The education professors who train these teachers receive salary increases and promotions regardless of the number of their graduates who take jobs, quit, or fail. Receiving continuous, uninterrupted institutional and individual rewards when substantial numbers of certified graduates do not take jobs, quit, or fail does not simply reflect zero accountability. It is an institutionalized system for rewarding failure and might more accurately be described as negative accountability because neither the declining number of graduates who take jobs nor the poorer quality of their performance as teachers interrupts the rewards, which continue to accrue. As an increasing number of graduates with the imprimatur of the university never take jobs, and quit or fail if they do take them, those responsible for their preparation receive uninterrupted rewards in terms of increased budgets, higher salaries, and promotions.

In my own institution, there has not been a systematic assessment of the effectiveness of the basic teacher education program since the institution was founded more than a century ago as a teachers college. Imagine, not one ever! In my own city, my university has prepared more than half of the teachers with initial certification or a master's degree and no one raises the issue with us of why the teachers we send the schools aren't more effective. When the public is concerned with the quality of the schools they inevitably focus on the school district. They never stop to consider where all the ineffective teachers and principals came from. The result is predictable: a continuous flow of teachers who do not take jobs or who are unable to improve the learning of students in the urban schools if they do.

The following critical dimensions refer to four of the dysfunctional components of university-based teacher education and explain what might be done to make these programs more accountable.

The Faculty

Teachers of teachers are faculty with doctorates in the various specialties offered in schools of education: for example, educational psychology, research and assessment, guidance, school administration, exceptional education, early childhood, and the various subsets of curriculum such as language arts, math, science, social studies, and the arts. These individuals are hired as faculty on the basis of having completed their respective doctoral programs, not because they themselves were outstanding teachers. None of the doctoral programs they completed ever required them to prove they had been outstanding teachers, or even satisfactory ones, as an admission requirement into their doctoral programs. In almost every case, the programs of doctoral study do not even require the applicants to have been certified educators. Indeed, the more prestigious the school of education the less likely the faculty is to have had successful teaching experience for any sustained period and the more likely they will be education professors who pursue careers as researchers and writers with no teaching experience at all. This is a systemic, historic pattern, not a simple "oversight," and raises some obvious questions. How can people who might not have been good teachers, or who might never have taught at all, develop the courses and set the requirements that others must fulfill to become effective teachers?

Even more puzzling, "How can these experience-free individuals teach others to teach?" Specifically, how can those who have never taught diverse students in urban poverty teach others to succeed in dysfunctional bureaucracies? The typical retort to this charge that the education faculty is incompetent, or at least inappropriate, is an interesting dodge, to wit: "The faculty teaches the basic courses. There are field staff made up of current or former teachers who teach the actual 'how to do it' in field work and student teaching." The faculty claims to offer "basic" knowledge in their courses and to leave the implementation of the knowledge they offer to supervising and cooperating teachers with a great deal of classroom experience. The problem with this explanation is that faculty free of successful teaching experiences in real-world schools cannot offer any "basic" knowledge that is useful. It is not useful to teach methods of teaching courses without being able to make those methods applicable to the real world. It is not useful to teach child development without teaching how that development influences the day-to-day work of the teacher. It is not useful to teach about curriculum, in any content area, without teaching the specific strategies for offering instruction of that content. It is not useful to teach basic knowledge about learning without teaching the specific ways in which teachers can elicit learning from real students in actual school classrooms. It is not useful to teach "basic" knowledge about children's normal and atypical behavior without giving specific, concrete instruction of what teachers must do to organize, manage, and discipline students with and without special needs.

This question of whether faculty without deep and insightful personal experience as effective classroom teachers can offer any "basic" knowledge of teaching and learning is only a debatable issue among education faculty who must justify their existence as university faculty. For those afflicted with common sense, Will Rogers the cowboy philosopher, got to the heart of the matter: "You can't teach what you don't know about places you ain't never been." I don't know of a single school of education faculty that could function as effective teachers in an urban school district serving diverse students in poverty for even 1 month. Neither would I want them even trying to teach children and youth who are most in need of competent teachers.

The solution to this problem is straightforward. In addition to having completed doctoral study, education faculty should be able to produce a verifiable record that they were effective teachers of diverse children or youth in dysfunctional urban or rural districts that typically miseducate 15 million children in poverty. Further, they should prove that their period of teaching service was for a substantial period, such as 5 years or longer. Typically, applicants for beginning positions on education faculties get their jobs by discussing the areas of research they plan to pursue by reviewing their doctoral dissertations. Observing would-be faculty giving a lesson and interacting with children and youth in a local school serving diverse students in poverty should replace this hiring procedure. Those aspiring to faculty positions in schools of education should demonstrate the applicability of the basic concepts they will be teaching in their courses, should they be hired.

Faculty in schools of education should not be allowed to continue acting as analogues of liberal arts professors who can justify their teaching as generally liberating without having to show that the knowledge they pass on to students can be used in daily life or in the practice of a specific profession. Until education faculty start demonstrating that their knowledge base derives from life in real schools and is applicable in even the dysfunctional systems where graduates may teach, teacher education will remain preparation for the best of all nonexistent worlds. Sabbaticals for education faculty should require them to actually teach for a semester or a year in a challenging school situation rather than pursue some arcane topic of interest and value to only the five or six other education professors they meet at annual conferences or write articles with. These solutions would transform educational faculty from "professors" to teacher educators.

Making these changes requires no institutional changes in the university and could be readily implemented without additional funds. Making these changes does not require the approval of education faculty but does require university administrators with vision, courage, and even common sense. The objective of these suggested changes is to get the education professors to start acting as if the children and youth in schools are their clients, not the college students majoring in education. So long as teacher educators are allowed to pretend that their university appointments define their clients as college students preparing to teach and not the children and youth in schools, accountability cannot be realized. Implementing these suggestions is a necessary but not sufficient condition for making education faculty and schools of education more accountable. But it's just a start.

The Knowledge Base

The second condition that must be changed to make schools of education and education faculty more accountable deals more directly with the knowledge base offered in teacher education programs. From observations in classrooms it quickly becomes clear to any rational observer that life in classrooms involves a set of ritualized behaviors performed by teachers who operate on the basis of craft experience not on any theory or research. Over three centuries, these behaviors have become the rites, ceremonies, and customs of school teaching. In effect, what certified teachers, that is, individuals with 2 years of professional coursework (elementary level), or 1 year of professional coursework (secondary level), call "teaching" is no different from what people with no education courses do when they are simply dumped into classrooms with no formal training; I call these rituals the *pedagogy of poverty versus real teaching*. The following acts, with no requirement that any learning is taking place, are considered prima facie evidence that teaching is going on:

- Giving information
- Giving directions
- Making assignments
- Reviewing assignments
- Asking questions
- Monitoring seatwork

- Assigning homework
- Reviewing homework
- Settling disputes
- Punishing noncompliance
- Marking papers
- Giving tests
- Reviewing tests
- Giving grades

These rituals are performed thoughtlessly on the assumption that they have intrinsic value. Everyone and anyone who has been to school can replicate these same acts whether they are children playing school or they are hired as teachers without having taken any formal preparation. It is not necessary to take education courses to learn these behaviors. They are the acts of people called "teachers" that all high school graduates recall seeing repeated daily for 13 years during their own school experiences The pedagogy of poverty is so powerful that even certified teachers recall and perform these behaviors learned during their own school experiences rather than the idealistic behaviors taught them in education courses (Haberman, 1991).

The solution to this is straightforward. To substantiate the claim that the schools of education offer a knowledge base in their coursework three things must occur. The education faculty in schools of education must be able to state (write) this agreed-upon knowledge base, demonstrate that it is being learned in the courses they teach, and show that if graduates implement this knowledge base in their subsequent teaching they will be effective teachers. To do this, the behaviors and functions of what constitutes effective instruction in the real world must first be identified. What specific functions do teachers perform that result in diverse students in poverty truly learning? Educational research has identified a very limited number of these effective behaviors. The next step is even more problematic because it requires justifying the claim that there are concepts and theories that undergird and support these effective teacher functions and behaviors. If it is all craft knowledge, it can be learned on the job and there is no need for pre-service education courses. To justify one education course the following must be demonstrated:

1. Basic knowledge, that is, the theory and research undergirding effective teacher behaviors, exists.
2. This basic knowledge can be taught and learned in education courses.

3. The learners of such knowledge can apply it in real-world settings.
4. The application of this basic knowledge improves children's learning.

There is not sufficient research and development within the knowledge base of teacher education to establish that these four things can be accomplished within programs—not enough to fill one 3-credit education course. Developing 30 credits of coursework (secondary programs) that meets these four criteria, or 60 credits of such coursework (elementary programs) will require decades of research and development. The fact that the validation of what schools of education claim as their "knowledge base" has never been demonstrated in nearly two centuries of normal schools, teachers' colleges, and schools of education leads to the reasonable assumption that it does not exist. What effective teachers demonstrate is neither theory nor research: It is craft knowledge learned through practice. Further, it is a craft knowledge that can be learned only by individuals who hold a particular ideology regarding the nature of child development, the nature of learning, and the role of schooling for all children and youth in a free society.

On what basis can we continue to pretend that education professors who could not, themselves, be effective teachers in dysfunctional bureaucracies serving low-income, diverse students be the source of a relevant, useful "knowledge base"? On what basis can we pretend that teacher education programs that are never evaluated in terms of their graduates' effectiveness with children and youth in poverty are anything other than self-serving enterprises? Despite these realities, it is most likely that the public perception that schools of education can prepare teachers who can teach all children will continue. Those who know better will continue to foster this assumption because schools of education provide too much income to colleges and universities to call a halt to their activities regardless of how fatuous education courses are. As a result, the 5000 plus education faculty nationwide will continue to offer an idiosyncratic, widely diverse set of personal preferences passed off as "basic knowledge" for teachers and the 50 states will continue to accredit their programs. To call a halt to this monstrous hoax the state departments of education would have some serious explaining to do regarding their own raison d'être.

The solution to this problem requires transforming teacher preparation programs in schools of education to function as the research and development arm of public school teaching. The syllabi of any course required for certification would have to state the concepts and theories (i.e., basic knowledge) that students are expected to learn. In addition to these complete and transparent syllabi, there must be supportive documents for state accreditation that include the research and development showing that effective teachers in the real world use these concepts and theories. It would be understood by both faculty and students that these course syllabi would be subject to constant change and revision as more effective classroom teacher behaviors are identified and translated into concepts taught in education courses. What is taught future teachers would be in a constant state of becoming more valid and reliable in predicting and effecting learning in schools. This solution would change present assumptions 180 degrees. The pretense that there is already an existing knowledge base that explains and predicts the behavior of effective teachers of diverse students in poverty and that current education faculty know this knowledge base must be abandoned.

At present, we have some rudimentary knowledge to explain the behavior of effective teachers in diverse settings, but it is far from substantial or complete and the few researchers who hold this limited knowledge have no impact whatever on the "things" 5000 education professors choose to teach in their courses. Rather than beginning with the experts, a useful knowledge base should be developed from analyses of what effective teachers do. Supporting concepts and theories would be developed from the ground up (classrooms), not from the top down in doctoral seminars for wannabe education faculty taught by current education faculty. Developing a real-world knowledge base would not by itself lead to greater accountability in schools of education. It, too, is a necessary but not sufficient condition.

Field Work, Student Teaching, and Internships

It is in these fieldwork experiences that the would-be teacher is supposed to practice the "basic knowledge" she or he has been taught in the school of education coursework. These forms of practice in schools are the heart of the university claim that its preparation is useful and relevant. Unfortunately, what happens when students are placed in schools to practice is that they do not apply any "basic knowledge" from the coursework they have completed. They merely become skillful at imitating the mindless rituals and ceremonies of their cooperating teachers, who will grade them and give them references (Pintrich, 1990). In the real world, the primary goal of student teachers is to get along with their cooperating teachers. If there should be any conflict between the "basic knowledge" gained in coursework and the rituals of their cooperating teachers, student teachers have no choice but to follow the practices of their cooperating teachers.

For example, if the education faculty teaches strategies of cooperative learning but the schools where neophytes student teach are required to use only direct instruction, student teachers have no choice but to follow the directives of the schools in which they are placed and practice only direct instruction. If the university faculty advocates whole language learning but the schools use phonics as the required method for teaching reading, student teachers will practice teaching reading using phonics and ignore the faculty and their coursework. There are also conflicts between education course and state laws. Twenty-two states still allow corporal punishment; no school of education offers "methods of hitting kids without leaving marks." Do the schools of education in these 22 states place their student teachers in only districts that do not use corporal punishment? Certainly not! They go along with the school district policies and programs. Student teachers observe kids being hit on a regular basis by school staff in these states.

Schools of education need places for more than half a million student teachers every year. In many cases, one school of education may place thousands of student teachers in a single year. It is not logistically possible to find enough placements for this number of student teachers nationwide every year in only classrooms of outstandingly effective teachers because such teachers comprise approximately 8% of the teaching force. As a result, more than 90% of student teachers reinforce the pedagogy of poverty that they themselves experienced as school children and that their cooperating teachers mentor them in during student teaching. To deny the fact that student teachers practice what they see in schools rather than any "basic knowledge" taught in education courses requires a dangerously high level of naïvety or a deliberate effort to avoid reality.

The dilemma for schools of education that sincerely try to prepare future teachers for the 15 million diverse students in poverty is that, on the one hand, students can learn to teach only by gaining practice and experience in real classrooms with real teachers in real schools. On the other hand, the urban schools are dysfunctional bureaucracies in which *half* or more of the teachers are burnouts and lifers offering the pedagogy of poverty. Where, then, should neophytes practice and with whom? The fact that so many graduates never take teaching jobs might well reflect their good judgment in understanding that they have not been adequately prepared to work in dysfunctional bureaucracies as much as it reflects a lack of willingness to work with diverse students in poverty.

The antidote to the present system of creating nonteachers, quitter/failure teachers, or those trained to be increasingly skillful in offering the pedagogy of poverty, is to develop a theory of school learning that neophytes could learn and actually practice. Am I really saying that there is presently no theory of school learning in either the "basic knowledge" taught in coursework or in what practicing teachers actually do? Precisely so! I recently examined the four most widely used texts sold to faculty and students in schools of education. They carry titles such as *Principles of Learning for Teachers*, *Introduction to Educational Psychology*, and *Learning in Classrooms*. Every accredited program of teacher education in the country requires at least one such course to teach neophytes the "basic knowledge" of how school learning occurs.

Unfortunately, I found no connection anywhere in these texts between the endless lists of behaviors they recommend to future teachers and any theory of learning. Each of these volumes exceeded 300 pages. Because controlling the classroom is the biggest problem beginning teachers face, I looked up the words *classroom management* and *discipline* in the books' indexes and found a total of two pages devoted to these topics of the more than 1200 contained in these volumes. These two pages consisted of do's and don'ts with no connection to any theory of learning. This is noteworthy because the three volumes contained literally hundreds of admonitions of precisely what teachers should do in teaching various content, which are simply lists of teacher behaviors with no connection to any theory or research that would justify their use. The reason for this is simple; expert advice regarding what future teachers should do is not connected to any theory of learning or to any reality of life in school classrooms.

Each of the volumes had separate sections with a few pages devoted to a total of six "theories" of learning that no teacher I have ever met would know how to implement, assuming such theories exist in more than the "expert" writers' minds. The theories presented bore the following titles: radical constructivism, information processing, cognitive connectivism, social constructivism, situated cognition, and socioculturalism. I read the description of these "theories" carefully. They neither explain nor predict how learning occurs in schools, nor do they offer anything approaching a coherent explanation of how learning occurs in life. If there actually were a "learning theory" called situated cognition (or any of the other meaningless titles the authors invented), what would teachers do to implement it? When I ask practicing teachers, including effective ones, about these six theories they express lack of knowledge and confusion and dismiss them as irrelevant to anything they do.

In the process of observing classrooms for half a century (5000 plus observations), I have collected volumes of the teacher talk that goes on in classrooms. Two thirds of what happens in classrooms is talk; two thirds of that talk is the teacher talking; and two thirds of teacher talk is giving directions. Following are just a few typical teacher comments one can hear in a classroom. There are comments made by effective teachers as well as by quitters and failures.

"Jerome, for the last 3 days you haven't handed in any work. What's going on?"

"Okay. When you finish page 65 answer the questions and leave your paper on my desk."

"Whatever isn't finished in class is your homework for tonight."

"Lina, we've spoken about this before. I'm going to have to call home."

"Don't interrupt, Kyle. Let her figure it out for herself."

"I'm not calling on anyone out of their seat or anyone who has already had a turn."

"Today we're going to pick up the story from where Robin wakes up in the woods. Who remembers what he was doing in the woods?"

"Who knows the difference between 'ensure' and 'insure'?"

"Okay. That's how it's done. I want you to do the next three examples just like I did mine. I will be coming around to help anyone who needs help."

"We're not leaving the room until everyone shows me they're ready."

"What did you find the most exciting part of the story, Alexandria?"

"Who would like to read next?"

"This is a good piece of writing. Please copy it over, include my corrections, and hand it back in."

"On your blank map of Africa fill in as many countries and rivers as you can."

"That's a good idea, Preston. Is it your idea or your team's suggestion?"

"If you don't have a book, look on with Eric."

"You've been sitting here for 5 minutes. Why don't you get started?"

"When you come back tomorrow we'll pick up with page 32. I will ask you the causes of the war."

"If you've finished, please check your work before you hand it in."

Do these statements and the thousands more like them indicate that teachers are implementing any theory of learning? What is the likelihood that the teachers who make statements like these are being guided in terms of "radical constructivism," "information processing theory," "cognitive constructivism," "social constuctivism," "situated cognition," or "socioculturalism"?

What is the likelihood that these "theories" could provide teacher statements that would enable teachers to manage a classroom in the real world?

The solution is to stop the pretense that there is an agreed-upon body of knowledge that includes any theory of school learning. The specific functions and behaviors of effective teachers need to continue to be compiled and expanded and then taught to neophytes. This cannot be done in university courses. It requires on-the-job mentoring by outstanding teachers and coaches. The time, effort, and money that goes into course work that cannot be justified in terms of its usefulness needs to be devoted to actually practicing, that is, replicating the behaviors of effective teachers. As with the previous solutions, this remarkable achievement would still be a necessary but not a sufficient condition for making university-controlled teacher education accountable.

Selection of Students Into Teacher Education

Practicing the behaviors of effective teachers (assuming we knew how to transfer them from star teachers to quitter/failures) would still not constitute adequate teacher preparation. Effective teacher behaviors only become effective if they are the actions of teachers who hold a specific ideology regarding the nature of students, the nature of teaching, the nature of learning, and the nature of societal and community influences on school curriculum.

In the absence of this ideology the neophyte would be set merely to imitate actions, which would become new rituals and which would have no impact on students. The very same teacher acts, when undergirded by the effective teacher's ideology, does cause learning in children and youth. What is an example of this ideology? Effective teachers explain their students' success on the basis of effort not ability. Failure/quitter teachers explain student success on the basis of ability. As a result of this belief, effective teachers spend their time generating effort. Quitter/failure teachers who attribute success in school to ability think in terms of tracking and grading practices, not in terms of what they have to do to generate effort. This is merely one example of the need to know the ideology of effective teachers. Not buying into this ideology and trying merely to mimic teacher behaviors lead to ritualistic behavior akin to the pedagogy of poverty described previously.

The need for future teachers to share the ideology held by effective teachers creates an insurmountable problem for schools of education. The criteria used in colleges and universities for admission to teacher education programs are grade point average, faculty references, and students' statements of purpose. Just as there is no agreement among education professors on what constitutes "basic knowledge" and no agreement on what constitutes a theory of school learning, there is no agreed-upon ideology that those presenting themselves for admission into university training programs must possess. Even more daunting is the naïve assumption that college students who do not already possess the ideology of effective teachers can be taught this ideology by taking education courses. The several hundred articles and studies in teacher education that I have read as an editor and reviewer all claim that their particular course has changed their students' ideology in some way. I have never reviewed a single article from an education professor whose course failed to change his or her students' ideology. Unfortunately, this remarkable record of "evidence" that education courses transform future teachers' ideology is not substantiated by behavior, let alone subsequent behavior as a teacher. Graduates of teacher education programs practice the same pedagogy of poverty as do experienced teachers in dysfunctional school systems.

The solution to this problem is to admit that GPA, faculty references, and students' statements of "why I would like to be a teacher" have no predictive validity. Indeed, a good case can be made that these admission criteria systematically admit more graduates who are potential quitter/failures than effective teachers. In effect, the present system may well be highly predictive at selecting the very population of future teachers most likely never to take jobs in challenging schools or to quit or fail if they do. My interview (the Star Teacher Selection Interview) is used to select and hire teachers in more than 260 urban districts. The interview assesses the degree to which a prospective teacher's ideology is closer to that of a star teacher or to that of a quitter/failure. Whereas the interview is readily adopted by school districts in the process of hiring, it has been less widely adopted by schools of education. Too many potential education majors would fail the interview, not be admitted, and thus seriously decrease the budgets of schools of education. The ultimate value to be preserved, however, is not the maintenance of schools of education budgets; it is selecting future teachers with the ideology that is absolutely essential to teaching children and youth in poverty. As with the preceding components, changing the selection criteria for admission to teacher education programs is a necessary but not sufficient condition for making these programs relevant and effective in the real world.

Training for Students With Special Needs

The dysfunctional school districts have disproportionately high and increasing numbers of students with special needs. In my city, the number of such students, including those in the pipeline to be tested, is now more than 20% of the student body and growing. In some districts, the percentages are even higher. This means that future teachers in a class of 30 or more children might have 6 to 8 special needs students. This problem is exacerbated by continuous judicial reviews by courts at every level, of the precise responsibilities schools and teachers have to provide these students with the education they need and deserve. Without controlling class size there is no way to implement an effective inclusion program, which explains why no major urban district has one.

The goal for changing "business as usual" at the university level must be the highest priority for changing the state of teacher education. In the following section, I share the first system for how to make this happen.

System I: Making Schools of Education Accountable and How to Do It

We must begin by recognizing that these conditions are likely to continue characterizing schools of education well into the future (i.e., a faculty comprised primarily of individuals who were never themselves effective teachers in dysfunctional school districts miseducating diverse children in poverty; a preparation program of coursework without a relevant, agreed-upon knowledge base that can be connected to raising student achievement; a system of field work and student teaching that replicates the pedagogy of poverty practiced in currently failing schools; and a system of selecting future teachers based on irrelevant, nonpredictive criteria). Continued failure to produce effective teachers for the poor is a reasonable assumption because the history of teacher education beginning with the first teacher-preparing program in 1823 indicates that these conditions are endemic and continually worsen. Teacher education's historic and deepening failures are not only tolerated but also rewarded in university budgets because they are the cash cow providing students for not only education courses but also for liberal arts courses that cannot generate sufficient numbers of their own students. Were it not for education majors being required to take liberal arts courses, several departments in these universities would not have sufficient majors to sustain themselves, and without a liberal arts college it would not be possible to maintain a "university."

Because this systemic failure is rewarded for not changing itself, the solution lies in creating a system of accountability. There must cease to be budgetary rewards for continuous failure based on input criteria and budgetary rewards for improved output. The surest way to achieve such accountability is by changing the criteria used to determine school of education budgets. The current system that rewards universities for maintaining and expanding schools of education and the number of education majors should be replaced by a system based on the effectiveness of education graduates as teachers. How might this be accomplished? Instead of basing the budgets of schools of education on the number of their students and how many college credits these students take (input criteria), the budget should be based on outcomes. How many education graduates take jobs in schools serving students in poverty? How many graduates stay in these positions for 3 years? How well do the children and youth in the classes of these graduates learn? Currently, university budgets are based on generating student credit hours, that is, the number of students multiplied by the number of credits they take. Budgeting on this basis has resulted in schools of education seeking increasing numbers of students and requiring them to take more courses. If the budget is based on how many students take how many courses, it is in the self-interest of university administrators and their faculties to expand enrollment and the number of required courses.

In some states, the legislature has attempted to thwart this gaming of the system by capping school of education budgets based on increased student enrollment. In these states, the legislatures have said, in effect, "your budget is fixed. You may accept more students if you choose, but your budget will not be increased beyond its present level." In Texas, for example, the legislature tried to cap school of education budgets by limiting the state support to a fixed number of education credits (18). Universities sidestepped this cap on the number of education courses the state would support by offering education courses under different titles in the liberal arts and fine arts colleges.

State attempts to limit the growth of education majors and their requirements have simply not been effective. The reason various states have not been effective at controlling increases in education majors and school of education budgets is that they have thus far still remained focused on input criteria and fallen into the trap of being gamed by the universities and their faculties. Even when caps are placed on the number of students and the number of required courses, faculty still game the budgets with summer appointments. The faculty is appointed on the basis of a 9-month academic year. Education faculty are rewarded with additional 15% to 20% salary increases by having summer school appointments. By making more courses "required," students are more likely to be forced to attend summer schools, thus providing faculty with annual rather than academic appointments. This added income also accrues to faculty retirement and sick leave benefits and reaches substantial amounts when extended over a 30- or 40-year career (I have several *thousand* days of sick leave). This incentive system has nothing do with being accountable for the competence of graduates. It is driven entirely by faculty self-interest and based on a budget that pays off for maximizing student numbers and required courses. No matter how few graduates take jobs, how short their period of service, or how ineffective their teaching, the school of education budgets continue to increase.

The economic strains on state budgets in future require that this system of rewarding irrelevance and failure must end. It is inevitable that budgets of schools of education will eventually all be based on output criteria. An accountable budgeting formula should be composed of the following factors. The first factor (X) in the budgeting formula should represent the number of graduates who take jobs teaching (in my own state, nearly two thirds of certified university graduates do not even take teaching jobs because the jobs are in the "challenging" schools). This factor should be weighted by the number of graduates who take teaching jobs in schools serving a majority of students on free lunch. The second factor in the formula (Y) should be based on whether the graduates teach for 3 years. For graduates who have taught less than 3 years, this factor has a weight of zero. For graduates who teach longer than 3 years, an annual credit of $1,000 is added to the school of education budget for every year they stay in teaching and provide evidence of their students' learning. The third factor represented in the formula (Z) should be determined by children's learning in the classes of the graduates. In school districts using mandated achievement tests, these scores are used. However, school districts do not use tests in every grade and in every subject area in which teachers teach. A state-approved system based on work sampling must be developed for districts serving students in poverty to evaluate all teachers' effectiveness. State Departments of Education must develop and provide school districts with a system of specific criteria and rubrics showing how to use work samples to demonstrate student learning in every subject area and grade level. This system of using work samples as assessments of students' achievement should also be used with students having special needs in all specializations in which the schools of education are accredited to certify special education teachers.

The level of budgetary state support for schools of education can be computed on a 3-year cycle for every school of education accredited in the particular state. Because it requires 3 years to determine whether graduates have stayed in teaching and their impact on the learning of their students, a particular school of education's present budget would represent a 3-year lag so as to include the number of graduates who took jobs, the income level of the students in their schools, how long they stayed, and how well their students have achieved.

To begin the process a benchmark fixing the current level of state support would be established on the basis of how well the particular school of education has met the X, Y, and Z criteria over the last 3 years. Each subsequent budget for education schools reflects the X, Y, and Z factors of the preceding 3 years and determines whether to increase or decrease state support to the particular school of education. This is a value-added system providing budgetary rewards and punishments for each individual school of education based on whether the benchmark of the first year is met or surpassed in each succeeding year. There is a direct relationship between state government and the schools of education that requires colleges and universities not to interfere with this process of making schools of education accountable. Universities would not be allowed to add or subtract from state funds allocated to schools of education for teacher certification programs. Universities are free to fund other programs offered by schools of education (e.g., doctoral programs) as they see fit.

Finally and foremost, this system allows a linkage between state-supported K–12 education and the preparation of teachers. Universities are free to continue to prepare teachers for the best of all nonexistent worlds or graduates who never teach, quit, or fail, but they won't receive ever-increasing state budgets for doing so. Indeed, their budgets will shrink to reflect their actual contribution to the staffing in challenging schools and the learning of students in those schools.

Instituting a system of accountability can cause schools of education to raise new kinds of questions—questions they have never raised before in setting their policies. For example, in hiring new faculty the emphasis shifts from examining candidates' doctoral dissertations to whether candidates have demonstrated any know-how and effectiveness in teaching children in poverty in dysfunctional school districts for a sustained period of time. The present focus in schools of education on which faculty teaches which courses shifts to publicly defending the content of those courses as representing a theoretic and research knowledge base that actually leads to children in poverty learning more. The nature of field work shifts from giving every student teacher an "A" for getting along with their cooperating teacher to having student teachers actually practice instructional behaviors that have a research connection to how children in poverty can best learn. Finally, holding schools of education accountable causes them to shift admitting future teachers on the basis of traditional university criteria (i.e., GPA, letters of reference, and an essay on "why I want to teach") to examining applicants' beliefs and predispositions, which can predict how they will function with diverse children and youth in poverty. Using this form of accountability as the basis of its support for schools of education, the state will be able to answer the age-old question, "Do the university-based teacher preparation programs offered by the schools of education have any redeeming social significance?"

Were a state to try to establish such a system of accountability for schools of education, it can be predicted that university administrators and faculty would respond with a myriad of reasons why a budget based on results could not work, is not fair, and should not be applied to them. Maintaining the current system of budgeting based on input criteria with no accountability for the quality of graduates' performance is the ultimate value to be preserved for universities, for schools of education, and for education faculty who benefit, without interruption, from their failures. These problems of input performance, as opposed to output performance, are exacerbated on the local level.

System II: Making School Districts Accountable for Teachers and Principals They Hire

Making AC programs more accountable should be simpler to accomplish because the school districts themselves hire teachers and can more directly assess their effectiveness, but this is not the case (Beuchler, 1992). Although there is no direct state support to school districts offering AC programs, there is a built-in system of continuous reward for failure that comes from the school districts themselves. The budgets of the departments of human resources in school districts that hire teachers are based on how many teachers they need to hire in a given year. As a result, the greater the teacher shortage and the higher the teacher turnover in a particular district, the busier these departments are. In effect, the poorer job they do at hiring teachers who will stay and be effective, the more the departments of human services can protect their own jobs and even demand the expansion of their departments. The salaries of the directors of these departments of human resources are determined by how many employees they have and the total budgets of their departments. It is clearly in these directors' self-interests to have as many employees as possible, and there is no surer way to keep more hiring officials busy than to maintain present systems of hiring teachers who are quitter/failures. Like the other employees of school districts, those who hire teachers receive salary increases every year regardless of the performances of those they hire. In all the major urban districts the human resources departments and all those employed in them, benefit every year with salary raises despite the fact that half of the teachers they hire leave in 5 years or less and those who stay do not raise student achievement.

In some of these dysfunctional urban districts, teachers are hired without ever having to speak with another human being. They are hired on the basis of their scores on recorded telephone interviews that have no predictive validity in connecting to subsequent teacher effectiveness. Up to 10 forms of written documentation, including a criminal records check, a tuberculosis test, references, college transcripts, and trite statements of why the teacher applicant wants to teach in the district, are also collected. It is only *after* candidates are hired that they are interviewed by a school principal for placement in a particular school. If the principal does not select them, they are used as permanent substitutes because they have already been hired by the district and signed a teaching contract. As new schools are opened or reorganized, teachers who no principal has accepted are simply placed in these schools before new principals are assigned.

This procedure of not having a face-to-face interview before hiring a teacher is unheard of in even the most humble jobs. It would not be possible to secure a job in a car wash or as part-time help cleaning toilets in a bus terminal without having to speak to another human being. The practice of hiring teachers using only paper credentials and scores on recorded telephone interviews is an egregious, scandalous practice ensuring that a continuous flow of quitter/failures is inflicted on children and youth in need of effective teachers. When asked why they use telephone rather than personal interviews, the typical explanation is that they are too busy to spend a half hour or more on interviews given the large number of teachers they need to hire. No one ever stops the idiotic assembly line to ask the commonsense question: "Do you think that if you hired teachers who stayed and were effective you would not be so very busy hiring more teachers?"

Most of the dysfunctional urban school districts do speak face-to-face with candidates prior to hiring but do not do any better at selection. School hiring officials do not know what to ask applicants or how to evaluate candidates' responses. The most common questions asked teacher applicants are,

"Why do you want to teach?" "When did you decide to become a teacher?" "What is your philosophy of education?" and "Why do you want to teach in this district?" Even the least able, most foolish, most incompetent applicant has sufficient self-interest as a job seeker to know the "correct" responses to these inanities. To wit, "I want to teach because I love children." "I've wanted to teach since I was a little girl and played school." "My philosophy of education is that all children can learn." And "I want to teach in this district because I want to contribute to serving children and youth in poverty." Given that these are the most frequently asked questions, it is not surprising that the urban school districts of America have an unbroken record of recruiting, selecting, and hiring quitter/failure teachers.

In the 120 major urban districts serving 7½ million students in poverty, the departments of human resources are all very busy constantly hiring teachers. A conservative estimate is that more than $2.7 billion is spent annually by school districts strapped for funds to continue to hire the wrong people (Alliance for Education, 2004). Reasonable people might raise the question of why these dysfunctional districts are willing to spend this much on hiring when they are under such budget constraints. Major urban districts are not able to pay the benefits packages they have negotiated over the years with teacher unions. In my own city, for example, the benefits package is 61.5% and there is a $2.2 billion debt hanging over the district for future retirees. In a cynical but refreshingly honest moment, a school board member announced, "We are dependent on teacher turnover to keep actual payments to teachers for salary and benefits down and keep this system functionally solvent" (Barsuk, 2008). In other words, to not become insolvent the district must hire teachers who will not stay long and run up the district's retirement benefits because the district cannot even pay the obligations it has already encumbered. No better example can be found to explain systemic dysfunction: The financial solvency of the district requires hiring teachers who will leave. This churn of teachers coming and going results in children and youth in these districts who attend school for the entire 13 years that includes more than a full year of substitute teachers, incompetent teachers in the process of leaving, and insensitive lifers who offer the pedagogy of poverty.

The means of making AC programs more accountable is straightforward and requires fewer changes to implement than changing the basis on which schools of education receive state funding. The present system in the school districts' departments of human services is to involve several individuals in the hiring process. One employee checks references, college transcripts, and

GPAs. Another might check the results of telephone or in-person interviews. At the point of hiring a teacher candidate, several different employees of the department have been involved in compiling the applicant's folder. Who precisely makes the decision to hire a particular teacher is unclear because three, four, or more people were involved in compiling the applicant's folder. This is not an accidental or serendipitous circumstance. The employees of the human service departments know very well the danger of allowing their own work to be clearly tied to the hiring of specific teachers. It is in their interests to keep the hiring process murky and to involve several employees with each applicant so that no one can be held responsible as the sole or final decision maker.

The solution to this problem is clear. There must be specific employees in the departments of human services who can be held accountable for hiring specific teachers. The director of this department is technically responsible for making the final decision on all new hires; however, there are some subordinates who recommend to the directors that candidate X has met the hiring criteria and should be hired. In sum, the director and the specific subordinate(s) can and should be identified and held accountable for the hiring of every teacher offered a position in the district.

But even these changes are not sufficient for making the school district accountable for hiring teachers new to the district. The final step is a system in which any final hiring decision is made by a particular principal willing to have the particular teacher candidate as a teacher in his or her school. We cannot hold principals accountable for student learning until and unless they have control over the teachers assigned to their schools. What this means in practice is that we must be able to identify *specific individuals* in the human resource departments of school districts who make the recommendations to hire *specific teachers and specific school principals* who then hire *specific teachers* into their particular schools. Establishing such clear lines of decision making regarding who recommended which teachers for hire can be put in place without additional funding. It is a change begging to be made and readily implemented. The track records of the hiring officials regarding which teachers they recommend be hired, how well those teachers actually perform, and how long they remain teaching in the district can be easily compiled. The annual salaries of *everyone* who does the hiring should include decreases as well as increases based on how well a particular hiring official has selected teachers who are effective and who stay.

If the number of quitters/failures selected by a hiring official is more than 10%, then that human services director and that school principal should be replaced. Holding school districts accountable for who they hire is something a naïve public already expects and would be shocked to learn is actively being prevented by school districts that continually reward hiring officials for recruiting and selecting failures. The fact that AC programs are offered by the school districts removes their age-old rationalization that they cannot be held responsible for the low quality of those prepared to teach by universities.

Valid interview instruments can predict teacher effectiveness and staying power. State departments of education must require that school districts use these instruments with *all* teacher applicants, whether they are graduates of university-based teacher education programs or AC programs and whether applicants are new teachers or simply new to the district. Connecting annual raises to human services directors and school principals to the effectiveness of the teachers they hire is something that any school district can mandate in one day without costing the districts a penny. Indeed, they would save the district the $15,000 it presently costs to continually recruit and hire quitters/failures. The key decision points for holding universities and school districts accountable for the preparation and licensing of teachers are in the state legislatures and state departments of education. State legislatures control their state department budgets, appointments, and staffing and also control state support to universities and school districts. If state legislators genuinely seek to improve the schooling of children in poverty, they must understand that getting more effective teachers is the best way—indeed, the only way.

The Bottom Line for Accountability in Teacher Education

The failure of our schools to educate diverse students in poverty is not merely one cause but the fundamental cause that best explains the decline of prospects for children and youth in poverty and for society at large. Present systems of teacher preparation and selection will never stop rewarding themselves for producing failures/quitters until their budgets reflect results rather than procedures. The best hope of getting more effective teachers from university teacher preparation programs is to base such programs' budgets on the number of their graduates who serve in challenging schools and those teachers' effectiveness with children and youth. At the district level, the salaries of hiring officials should be based on how well these officials identify and retain quality teachers. The two accountability systems explained in this chapter for university-controlled teacher education and AC programs can lower current costs in the process of identifying quality teachers in high-needs schools.

Accountability in teacher education requires a concerted university–district effort and serves as the primary indicator of teacher success and accountability. This is a modest proposal for holding colleges of education and school districts accountable for teacher education—with transformational implications.

References

Alliance for Education. (2004). *Tapping the potential: Retaining and developing high quality new teachers.* Washington, DC: Author.

Balfanz, R., & Letgers, N. (2004). *Locating the dropout crisis.* Baltimore: Johns Hopkins University.

Barsuk, A. T. (2008, October 14). Benefit payments hanging over Milwaukee public schools. *Milwaukee Journal Sentinel,* 8.

Beuchler, M. (1992). Alternative certification for teachers. *Policy Bulletin, 17.* Bloomington, IN: Indiana Education Policy Center.

Haberman, M. (1991, December). The pedagogy of poverty versus good teaching. *KAPPAN.*

Pintrich, P. R. (1990). Implications of psychological research on student learning and college teaching for teacher education. In R. W. Houston (Ed.), *Handbook of research on teacher education: A project of the Association of Teacher Educators* (pp. 315–327). New York: Macmillan.

Sabir, M. (2007). *The impact of conditions of work in urban schools on outstanding African American and European American teachers.* Ph.D. dissertation, University of Wisconsin Milwaukee, Milwaukee, WI.

Schott Foundation. (2008). *Given half a chance.* Cambridge, MA: Author.

6

HIGH-STAKES ACCOUNTABILITY AND TEACHER QUALITY
Coping With Contradictions

Jennifer King Rice

High-stakes accountability has been part of the education policy landscape for many years. Throughout the 1980s and 1990s, states throughout the country increasingly developed testing and accountability policies to monitor school performance. As a result of these efforts, states implemented policies to encourage higher levels of student achievement (Olson, 2006). The federal No Child Left Behind (NCLB) Act of 2001 shifted this state trend to the national level by requiring states to monitor student achievement as a condition of federal compensatory education funding.

The NCLB legislation specified teacher quality as a key ingredient for improving student performance. Public perceptions as well as a growing body of research supported this emphasis on teacher quality. As the accountability movement was sweeping the nation, the evidence base documenting the importance of teacher quality continued to grow more persuasive (Darling-Hammond, 1996, 2000; Hanushek, 1992; Rivkin, Hanushek & Kain, 2005; Sanders, 1998; Sanders & Rivers, 1996). Regardless of the empirical approach, researchers from a variety of disciplinary perspectives confirmed

The author recognizes research support from MetLife Foundation and the Economic Policy Institute and acknowledges the contributions of Chris Rollke, Tammy Kolbe, Dina Sparks, Allison Clarke, and Lauren Duff.

conventional wisdom that teachers are the most important school resource provided to students. In her analysis of teacher preparation and student achievement across states, Darling-Hammond (1996, 2000) reports that measures of teacher preparation and certification are more strongly related to student achievement than other kinds of educational investments, including reduced class sizes, overall spending on education, and teacher salaries.[1]

Using a very different conception of teacher quality,[2] Rivkin, Hanushek, and Kain (2005) identify teacher quality as the most important school-related factor influencing student achievement. They conclude from their analysis of 400,000 students in 3000 schools that although school quality is an important determinant of student achievement, the most important predictor is teacher quality. In comparison, class size, teacher education, and teacher experience play a small role.

Hanushek (1992) estimates that the difference between having a good teacher and having a bad teacher can exceed one grade-level equivalent in annual achievement growth. Likewise, Sanders (1998) and Sanders and Rivers (1996) argue that the single most important factor affecting student achievement is teachers, and the effects of teachers on student achievement are both additive and cumulative.[3] Further, they contend that lower-achieving students are the most likely to benefit from increases in teacher effectiveness. Taken together, these multiple sources of evidence—albeit different in nature—all imply that quality teachers are a critical determinant of student achievement.

Acknowledging teacher quality as one of the most powerful strategies available for boosting student achievement, NCLB emphasizes raising the quality of the teacher workforce as a necessary requirement for improving student achievement and narrowing the achievement gap. NCLB's highly qualified teacher provision reflects the assumptions that qualified teachers are quality teachers, that states and districts have the capacity to staff all schools with qualified teachers, and that doing so will promote higher levels of student achievement.

Drawing on findings from a set of multilevel case studies of teacher policy in three states, this chapter considers how, despite the rhetoric around improving teacher quality, NCLB actually may undermine efforts to staff all schools with high-quality teachers. Evidence from the case studies suggests that despite its stated goals, NCLB and other high-stakes accountability policies may exacerbate the staffing challenges in districts that have an inadequate supply of qualified teachers and chronically low-performing schools.

The case study data suggest three explanations for this problematic consequence of the law, and each has important implications for policy. First, NCLB prioritizes measures of teacher qualifications over matters of teacher quality, resulting in some schools bypassing candidates deemed to be of high quality to hire teachers with the documented qualifications required by the law. Second, some teachers who meet the highly qualified standards are not high quality, given the contextual factors of the school. Third, the emphasis of NCLB on standardization and a narrow set of performance measures often repels teachers from low-performing schools. The findings from this relatively small sample of administrators, principals, and teachers ($n = $ 111) give rise to several key considerations for education policy and future research efforts.

In the next section, I describe NCLB's requirements for highly qualified teachers, and I review the empirical evidence that is available to support those policies. In the section that follows, I present the case study data and methods used to understand how states, districts, and schools approach teacher policy in the broader context of NCLB. I then report findings from the case studies that illustrate how NCLB may actually undermine efforts to improve teacher quality. I conclude with a discussion of implications for future policy and research.

NCLB's Highly Qualified Teacher Requirements: The Policy and the Evidence

A starting point for understanding the contradictions between NCLB and the realization of high-quality teachers for all students involves understanding the nature of the federal requirements and assessing those requirements in light of the available empirical evidence.

Highly Qualified Teachers: The Policy

The No Child Left Behind legislation clearly specifies expectations for teachers assigned to the core academic subjects including English, reading or language arts, mathematics, science, foreign languages, civics and government, economics, arts, history, and geography. In general, the legislation defines a highly qualified teacher as one who has a bachelor's degree, full state certification and licensure, and content knowledge in each subject taught.[4] How a teacher demonstrates his or her content knowledge is somewhat different by grade level and for new and existing teachers. At all levels of education (elementary, middle, and secondary), new teachers much have a bachelor's degree, hold full state certification, and demonstrate subject knowledge and teaching skills. The demonstration of subject knowledge varies by grade level. For elementary school teachers, this may consist of state-required certification or licensing tests or some other more general test such as PRAXIS. For middle and secondary school teachers, subject matter knowledge may be demonstrated using state-designed or -approved subject matter tests or by having an academic major, graduate degree, or advance degree in the subject area taught. Experienced teachers may either meet the grade-level requirements for new teachers or demonstrate competency in all subjects taught using a high objective uniform state standard of evaluation (HOUSSE) developed by their respective state educational agency. Because the act calls for *all* teachers of the core academic subjects (teaching in Title I programs or elsewhere) to be highly qualified by the end of the academic school year 2005–2006, the transitional HOUSSE provisions have become far less relevant than they were when the law was first adopted.

In addition to demonstrating that all teachers in core academic subjects are highly qualified, the law also obliges states to ensure that poor and minority children are not taught in greater proportions than other children by inexperienced or underqualified teachers. NCLB's "teacher equity" requirements direct states to develop and implement equity plans that ensure that low-income and minority children, as well as students in schools that have failed to meet their adequate yearly progress (AYP) targets for student achievement under the law, are not disproportionately taught by teachers who are less experienced, who are not highly qualified, or who teach "out-of-field" (Goe, 2006; Peske, Crawford, & Pick, 2006). In doing so, NCLB's highly qualified teacher provisions responded not only to deficiencies in the overall qualifications of the teacher workforce, but also to the serious inequities in the distribution of qualified teachers across and within states, districts, and schools.

While NCLB established new federal guidelines for the minimum qualifications a teacher must have to teach, responsibility for implementing these guidelines primarily falls to the states. To be eligible for Title I funds, each state must establish its own definition for a highly qualified teacher that is consistent with federal guidelines. The law provides flexibility in how states might accomplish this task. For instance, states retain broad authority for teacher licensure and certification, one of the key components of the highly qualified teacher designation. In addition, states may develop and administer their own tests of teachers' subject matter knowledge and establish a state-specific approach for determining whether experienced teachers are highly qualified. Local school districts and their teachers also bear some responsibility for implementing the law's highly qualified teacher definition. Districts may no longer hire teachers who do not meet the state requirements of a highly qualified teacher or employ existing teachers who have not demonstrated competency through their state's HOUSSE requirements (Kolbe & Rice, in press).

No Child Left Behind (ESEA, Title II) provides federal funding to states and districts for activities that strengthen teacher quality in all schools, especially those with a high proportion of children in poverty. Specifically, Title II of ESEA "provides funding to assist states and local school systems prepare, recruit and retain a highly qualified teaching force" (U.S. Department of Education, 2002b). As described on the Department of Education website, the vast majority of Title II funds is allocated to the Improving Teacher Quality State Grants program. This program recognizes that communities nationwide face a variety of needs when it comes to teacher quality; consequently, the law gives schools and districts a great deal of flexibility in how the money is spent and holds them accountable for the proper and effective use of the funds. Specifically, the funds can be used to support a wide array of activities, including interventions for teacher professional development, so long as the activities are grounded in scientifically based research. In addition to the state grants program, Title II includes funding for other teacher quality–related grant programs. Several of these programs support alternative routes to traditional teacher preparation. Examples include the Transition to Teaching program and Troops to Teachers. No Child Left Behind also emphasizes ongoing teacher professional development and allows districts to pool Title I and other professional development federal formula funds.

Each state that receives Title II funds must develop a plan that establishes annual, measurable objectives for each local school district and school to ensure that they meet the highly qualified teacher requirement. Further, principals of schools that receive funds under Title II must report annually on the school's compliance with the highly qualified teacher requirement, and districts are required to make this information available to the public. Further, school districts are required to report to the state each year on progress in meeting the requirement that all teachers be highly qualified.

Throughout the NCLB legislation is a heavy emphasis on practices that are grounded in research evidence. As described in a U.S. Department of Education (2002b) presentation on NCLB implementation: "All activities and uses of funds must be grounded in scientifically based research and must focus on improving student academic achievement." The next section examines the strength of the research base for the highly qualified teacher requirements in NCLB.

Highly Qualified Teachers: The Evidence

To the extent that research can identify a set of teacher qualifications that are consistently related to teacher performance, those qualifications *should* be used as a floor for teacher employment. In other words, these criteria would set the bar for a "minimally qualified teacher." Beyond those basic qualifications, district and school administrators should be free to take into consideration contextually relevant factors to select the highest quality teachers available to them.

This argument implies an important distinction between teacher quality and teacher qualifications. In most basic terms, *teacher quality* is a teacher's ability to realize desired outcomes (i.e., to effectively educate his or her students).[5] This implies a wide range of outcomes that reflect the broad goals of public education: to produce individuals who can contribute to the economic, political, civic, social, and cultural institutions in our society. We expect high school graduates to have acquired a wide range of competencies, skills, and personal qualities that "contribute to a successful life and a well-functioning society" (Rychen & Salganik, 2003, p. 3). However, measuring the effectiveness of education investments, including teachers, has typically focused on a narrow set of indicators driven, in large part, by the quantity, quality, and accessibility of available data. In the current policy context of high-stakes accountability, the dominant measures of school and teacher performance are student test scores.

Measures of teacher quality are limited in that they typically focus on a narrow set of outcomes, are not widely trusted by teachers, are often contextually dependent, and are retrospective based on what a teacher has done. Consequently, teacher hiring and, in most cases, compensation policies have relied heavily on *teacher qualifications* such as experience, degrees, and certification as proxies for teacher quality (Odden & Kelly, 2002). However, empirical research has not found these qualifications to be strong predictors of teacher effectiveness (Goldhaber, 2007; Rice, 2003). Even when they are statistically significant predictors of teacher performance, they explain only a small proportion of the variability in student achievement attributable to variation in teacher quality.

Several researchers have reviewed the empirical literature on the impact of teacher qualifications on student performance. Some of these reviews focus on quantitative production function studies and find predominately inconsistent and inconclusive evidence on the relationship between teacher qualifications and student performance (Hanushek, 1997; Wayne & Youngs, 2003). For instance, Hanushek's (1997) review of the literature found that 86% of the estimates of the impact of a teacher's education program on student performance were statistically insignificant. For teacher experience and teacher test scores, the percentages of statistically insignificant estimates were reported to be 66% and 54%, respectively. Among the statistically significant estimates, the number of positive estimates consistently exceeds the number of negative estimates for each qualification included in the review. However, the number of statistically insignificant estimates swamps the positive estimates in all cases. Although Hanushek's review has been criticized on methodological grounds and for its inclusion of only production function studies (a narrow subset of the available empirical evidence on teacher qualifications),[6] more comprehensive reviews tell only a slightly better story and help explain some of the consistencies. Rice's (2003) review of the empirical evidence on teacher qualification includes studies using a wide range of analytic methods, teacher qualifications, and outcome measures. Teacher qualifications were grouped into five categories: (a) experience, (b) education program and degree, (c) certification, (d) coursework, and (e) test scores. Key findings from the study are summarized in Table 1.

Although this review reinforces the importance of teachers in producing desired education outcomes, it also reveals the large gaps in our knowledge base. The study finds that many current teacher hiring and compensation policies are based on thin or no empirical evidence, and that policy and research focused on teacher quality must acknowledge the complexity of defining, measuring, monitoring, and enhancing teacher quality.

So, although teacher qualifications may have something to do with teacher quality, other more elusive teacher characteristics may be more important predictors of teacher effectiveness. Further, these teacher characteristics may well vary for different kinds of students and school communities. Because teacher quality involves context-specific criteria related to a teacher's potential to be effective in a particular school and teaching assignment, compared to teacher qualifications that are more widely applicable across school settings, it follows that externally imposed minimum qualifications are easier to legislate.

TABLE 1
Summary of Findings on the Impact of Teacher Qualifications

Teacher Qualifications	Key Findings
Years of experience	*Experience* matters during the first several years of teaching; after 5 to 7 years, more experience doesn't lead to higher teacher effectiveness.
Preparation program and degree	The evidence is mixed regarding the degree to which *teacher education programs* contribute to teachers' knowledge.
	Evidence suggests a modest positive effect of *institutional selectivity* on student performance at the elementary level and a positive effect at the high school level.
	Studies of *extended teacher education* programs reveal positive effects on entry into the profession and retention rates but no clear impact on teacher performance.
	Studies of *advanced degrees* have found a modest positive effect of subject-specific advanced degrees on student achievement (only for high school math and science).
Certification	Evidence suggests a positive effect of teacher certification only in studies that measure *subject-specific certification*. Research has demonstrated a positive effect of certified teachers on high school mathematics achievement when the certification is in mathematics. This subject-specific teacher certification effect is less obvious in other high school subject areas and is zero or even negative in elementary-level math and reading.
	Studies of *emergency or alternative route teacher certification* have shown little clear impact on student performance in high school mathematics and science, relative to teachers acquiring certification through standard channels.
Coursework	*Coursework in both pedagogy and content areas* has a positive impact on student achievement. Pedagogical coursework matters at all grade levels, and coursework in content areas is most apparent at the secondary level.
	Field experiences tend to be disconnected from other components of teacher education programs. Despite this, studies suggest positive effects in terms of opportunities to learn the profession and reduced anxiety among new teachers.
Test scores	Research suggests that some *test scores* predict teacher performance and desired educational outcomes. In particular, tests that assess the impact of literacy levels or verbal abilities of teachers tend to show positive effects.

Source: Rice, J. K. (2003). *Teacher quality: Understanding the effectiveness of teacher attributes.* Washington, DC: Economic Policy Institute.

However, to accept a set of federal- or state-specified teacher qualifications as a legitimate floor for teacher employment decisions, we must assume that requirements such as certification and subject-matter competency are specified in ways that have been empirically shown to predict teacher performance. Otherwise, these qualification requirements limit the supply of teachers available to schools for no good reason. As noted previously, research on the relationship between teacher qualifications and teacher effectiveness has been plagued by inconsistent and inconclusive findings. Even in cases where the measures are more consistently related to student performance, the effect size is small and the outcome measure is narrow. These findings suggest that the qualification versus quality balance in NCLB may need to be recalibrated.

Data and Methods

This study is part of a broader program of research designed to understand the policies, practices, and resources needed to staff all schools with high-quality teachers (see Rice, Roellke, & Sparks, 2006).[7] Data for the analysis come from multilevel case studies of teacher policy in three states: Maryland, New York, and Connecticut.

Site Selection and Data Collection Processes

Using a nested case study design, we examined teachers in schools, schools in districts, and districts in states. We purposefully selected the states, districts, and schools for this study. The sites chosen for this study are not intended to be nationally representative but provide interesting contexts to begin to develop a better understanding of the complexity of teacher policy across levels of the education system and to test our policy typology. The three states are all located on the eastern seaboard and reflect variability in education context and teacher policy climate. For instance, we were particularly interested in the large county-based school district context in Maryland, the high-profile legal challenges surrounding the adequacy of education in New York State, and the high salary context of the neighboring state of Connecticut. Also important, we had strong connections with policymakers in these three states and so had good access to data and essential professional connections to aid in recruiting state, district, and school administrators to participate in the intensive data collection required in this study.

In each state, we identified two districts based on guidance provided by members of our expert panel composed of national experts from teacher and administrator organizations,[8] recommendations from state officials, document review of policies, and analysis of data on teacher staffing. In two states (Maryland and Connecticut), we chose neighboring districts that compete for the same pool of teachers. Within each district, we selected up to three schools based on district recommendations and extant data on teacher staffing patterns.[9] In all cases, our goal was to identify districts and schools that face teacher staffing challenges but that are perceived by leaders in the system as employing interesting or promising strategies.

Four sources of data inform the analysis: (a) documents providing information on teacher recruitment and retention policies and investments in those policies at the state, district, and school levels; (b) extant data on teacher staffing patterns in the selected schools and districts; (c) interviews with state, district, and school administrators about their views of the teacher quality challenge and the kinds of investments they are making in policies to staff schools with quality teachers; and (d) focus groups with teachers in selected schools to understand the critical issues related to their decisions about where to work and to assess their perceptions of the impact of policies and practices on teacher recruitment and retention. Throughout the data collection process, we made adequate provisions to protect the privacy of the subjects and to maintain the confidentiality of identifiable information.[10]

In addition to taking field notes, when possible, we audiotaped the interviews and focus groups. In cases where interview respondents declined the request to be taped, we took careful and extensive notes to document responses during the interviews. Willingness to be taped was a requirement for participation in the focus groups. Immediately following the interviews and focus groups, we transcribed the proceedings and organized our data into a typology for each site. In some cases, it was not clear exactly where a particular policy fit in the typology and some policies legitimately fit in several places. For instance, an induction program for new teachers can be considered both a recruitment and a retention tool. Decisions about where to place policies in the typology were made based on evidence from the interviews and documents. We then used the typologies to construct a case profile for each state (see Rice et al., 2006).

Our data collection activities included a number of checks for bias and error. We used open-ended, semistructured interview protocols, took detailed notes during our interviews, promptly transcribed and edited the interviews, and followed up with respondents for clarification as needed (Patton, 1990). We cross-checked information using multiple sources of data from each site, including multiple interviews and public documents. In addition, we offered study participants the opportunity to review the case profiles, and several members of our research team reviewed each typology and case profile for accuracy, clarity, and consistency.

Descriptions of the Case Study Sites

This section provides a brief overview of the state, district, and school sites included in our study.[11] Table 2 summarizes key characteristics of our sites. All data are from the 2004–2005 academic year, unless otherwise noted. The three states in our study—Maryland, New York, and Connecticut—reflect a range of characteristics of interest in this study. All three states face teacher shortages and staffing issues but differ in the specific circumstances surrounding those challenges. Maryland is home to more than 56,000 teachers across 24 large and often diverse county-based school districts. Maryland ranks 12th among the states in average teacher salary. Comparatively, New York is quite large with more than 217,000 public school teachers employed by 700 school districts. On average, teacher salary in the state of New York ranks 6th in the nation. Connecticut is home to 42,000 teachers across 166 districts. With a 20-year history of emphasizing teacher quality, Connecticut's average teacher salary ranks first in the nation.[12] The "neighboring" status of Connecticut and New York is of interest because these states may compete for the same pool of teachers. Taken together, these three states provide an opportunity to test our typology against an array of teacher policies across sites with different problems and perspectives on how to staff all schools and classrooms with high-quality teachers.

Maryland Sites

We selected two large, neighboring districts in the Washington, DC, metropolitan area of Maryland: Montgomery County Public Schools (MCPS) and the Prince Georges County Public Schools (PGCPS). Each district faces challenges associated with serving a diverse community—rural and urban, high and low poverty—and as neighboring districts they often compete for the same teacher candidates. The districts are comparable in size, both ranking in the top 20 school districts in the nation; each operates about 200 schools and enrolls almost 140,000 students. In the 2004–2005 academic year, MCPS had 18 Title I schools. More than 36% of enrolled students qualified for free and reduced meals (FARMS) and about 3% were classified as English language learners (ELLs) (MCPS, 2005). MCPS teacher compensation averaged $40,542 for beginning teachers and reached a maximum

TABLE 2
Description of Multilevel Case Study Sample

State Characteristics	Maryland	New York	Connecticut
Number of districts	24	700	166
Number of teachers	56,149	217,000	42,000
National teacher salary rank[a]	12th	6th	1st

District Characteristics	Montgomery	Prince Georges	NYC Region 9	New Haven	Westport
Number of schools in district	197	205	179	49	8
Enrollment (2004–2005 SY)	139,393	136,095	105,768	20,759	5,306
Number of Title 1 schools	18	65	141	26	0
% of FARMS students	36.4%	46.4%	66.0%	69.0%	1.3%
Number (and %) of English language learners	12,843 (3.2%)	7,064 (4.4%)	13,842 (13.1%)	2,142 (10.4%)	81 (1.5%)
Beginning average teacher salary	$40,542	$38,307	$42,512	$38,053	$39,974
Maximum average teacher salary	$90,529	$80,774	$93,416	$79,912	$88,762
Per-pupil expenditures	$10,974	$8,403	$11,786[b]	$13,104	$14,073
Total number of schools included in sample	3	2	4	2	2
Elementary	2	1	0	1	0
Middle	1	1	1	0	1
Secondary	0	0	3	1	1

[a] National rank for *average* teacher salary.
[b] This is 2003–2004 information. NYC Department of Education does not currently have more current information available.

Source: Rice, J. K., Roellke, C. F., & Sparks, D. (2006). *Piecing together the teacher policy landscape: A multi-level case study findings from three states.* Research report. Washington, DC: Economic Policy Institute.

average of $90,529 for veteran teachers with advanced degrees. Teacher salaries combined with other classroom expenditures resulted in a $10,974 per pupil expenditure for the academic year 2004–2005 (MSDE, 2005). We sampled three schools within MCPS: two Title I elementary schools and one middle school.

In 2004–2005, PGCPS included 65 Title I schools, which is consistent with the relatively high proportion of FARMS students (46.4%) enrolled in the district. PGCPS serves 7,064 ELL students, just over 4% of PGCPS students. Teacher compensation in PGCPS is slightly lower than the neighboring MCPS. The average beginning teacher salary is $38,307, and the average salary of a veteran teacher with an advanced degree is $80,774. Per-pupil expenditures are lower in PGCPS than in MCPS—the district spends $8,403 per pupil, which is $2,571 less than the per-pupil expenditure in neighboring MCPS. We sampled two schools in PGCPS, a Title I elementary school and a middle school.

New York Sites

Incorporating four administrative units, New York City's Region 9 spans lower Manhattan north to 59th Street, stretches through the Upper East Side and East Harlem, and crosses into the South Bronx. We further narrowed our inquiry to a specific network of schools located in Manhattan and the Bronx. Region 9 includes 179 schools that serve more than 105,000 students, including 141 Title I schools. Sixty-six percent of students in Region 9 qualify for FARMS and nearly 14,000, or 13.1%, are ELL students. Student performance within the region also is quite varied because the area includes pockets of both the highest and lowest academic achievement in the state. Teacher salaries range from an average beginning salary of $42,512 to a maximum salary of $93,416. In 2004–2005, the per-pupil expenditure in the district averaged $11,786. We sampled four schools within Region 9: (a) a high school in East Harlem; (b) a middle/high school located in the Chelsea section of Manhattan; (c) a high school on the Upper East Side; and (d) a high school in the Bronx.

Connecticut Sites

We selected two neighboring and highly contrasting districts in Connecticut, the New Haven Public Schools (NHPS) and the Westport Public Schools (WPS). Similar to the districts selected in Maryland, our Connecticut districts are neighboring jurisdictions that vary in terms of student characteristics and resource levels. The New Haven Public School system includes 49 schools, including 26 Title I schools. Of the 20,759 students enrolled in the district, 69% are eligible for FARMS and 10.4% are ELL students. Teacher compensation in NHPS is the lowest among the districts in our study. The average beginning teacher salary is $38,053, and the average maximum salary is $79,912. In 2004–2005, NHPS spent $13,104 per pupil. We sampled two schools within the NHPS: one intradistrict magnet elementary/middle school; and one intradistrict magnet high school. The magnet elementary/middle school was identified by NHPS district officials as an appropriate site to study because of its chronic teacher supply challenges. As a contrasting example, NHPS district officials suggested the magnet high school for its ability to attract teacher candidates relative to other high schools in the district.

The Westport Public School System is the smallest district in our case study with only eight schools serving 5306 students in 2004–2005. WPS did not operate a Title I school in the study year, and less than 2% of its students qualified for either FARMS or ELL services. Average teacher salaries in the district range from $39,974 for beginner teachers to $88,762 for veteran teachers with an advanced degree. In 2004–2005, per-pupil expenditures were $14,073. We sampled two schools within WPS: the comprehensive high school within the district, and a middle school within the district.

Findings: NCLB and Teacher Quality

Evidence suggests that despite its stated goals, NCLB and other high-stakes accountability policies may exacerbate the staffing challenges in districts that have an inadequate supply of qualified teachers and chronically low-performing schools.[13] Our case study data suggest three explanations for this problematic consequence of the law, and each has important implications for policy. First, NCLB prioritizes measures of teacher qualifications over matters of teacher quality, resulting in some schools bypassing candidates deemed to be of high quality to hire teachers with the documented qualifications required by the law. Second, some teachers who meet the highly qualified standard are not high quality, given the contextual factors of the school. Third, the emphasis of NCLB on standardization and a narrow set of performance measures often repels teachers from low-performing schools.

Prioritizing Qualifications Over Quality

The federal government's highly qualified teacher standard assumes that a college degree, state certification, and subject matter expertise—regardless of the state, district, or school in which a teacher works—constitute the set of qualifications needed to raise student achievement and close achievement gaps. The law's emphasis on this set of teacher qualifications, however, has not been without controversy. The empirical literature studying the relationship between teacher qualifications and student achievement has found that these qualifications are, at best, weak predictors of teacher performance.

The importance of distinguishing between teacher quality and teacher qualifications was apparent in the districts and schools in our case studies. In particular, we found that the highly qualified teacher requirement prioritizes qualifications over quality and effectiveness, and this emphasis on qualifications was most dramatic and had the most profound effects in low-performing and difficult-to-staff schools and districts. We found that more attractive districts with a surplus of qualified teachers had the luxury of emphasizing policies that enhance *teacher quality* (i.e., effectiveness) based on internally determined criteria that take into consideration the strengths and needs of the school community. In contrast, districts with an undersupply of qualified teachers were forced to focus on externally imposed *teacher qualifications* (e.g., federal and state criteria), paying little attention to other teacher characteristics that might be more likely to improve student performance.

In many cases, the principals and teachers in the schools we studied made it clear that they hired teachers based on highly qualified teacher requirements of No Child Left Behind, when they would have preferred other candidates who, by their assessment, better met the needs of the school. These findings suggest that districts and schools that can hire from a surplus of teachers have a tremendous advantage over their difficult-to-staff counterparts because they have the luxury of focusing on effectiveness rather than on basic-level staffing issues. In other words, these surplus districts can focus their efforts on policies that will yield the highest quality teachers in terms of effectiveness, whereas schools and districts that face shortages are limited to hiring practices that will help staff schools with teachers who meet a set of externally imposed qualifications that are not strong predictors of effectiveness.

Several principals in our sample, particularly those working in the most disadvantaged schools, expressed great frustration with the NCLB highly qualified teacher requirement. A local instructional superintendent in the New York City Public Schools commented on this challenge that is particularly salient in the most difficult-to-staff schools:

> So we are directed by the state and the city to hire only highly qualified teachers. The problem is that in District 7—which is demographically high

poverty, lots of projects, poor working environment—it's very hard to attract highly qualified teachers. . . . Our principals go to job fairs. . . . When we tell them we're District 7, they don't even drop an application off to us. . . . We can't be extremely selective *about who we hire simply because we don't attract personnel here in District 7.*

In some cases, school officials found themselves hiring teachers who had all the credentials needed to be designated highly qualified, but who were considered by principals to be less effective than others who did not meet the qualifications specified in federal requirements and state policy. As a result, these principals found themselves turning away some of the "best candidates" for their open positions in favor of less-promising teachers who met the highly qualified teacher requirements. As described by an assistant principal in a Maryland Title I elementary school:

We were only allowed to interview HQ [highly qualified] teachers. We did get a lot of calls from people who were already documented in personnel, but they had not received a HQ rating or they hadn't gone through the process. We were very interested in some of them, but they were not eligible to come to our school because they did not meet the requirements of highly qualified. . . . Sometimes they seemed as if they would be good matches for us, but they didn't have the rating. . . . I remember one we were particularly interested in because of her skill set, but she was not going to be rated as highly qualified until she had more paper requirements met.

Our findings suggest that the impact of NCLB on teacher quality will be limited until all schools and school districts have an adequate supply of qualified teachers. State and district policymakers need to adopt more targeted policies that will improve the distribution of qualified teachers across schools within their boundaries. For instance, policies that provide substantial incentives for teachers to accept positions in difficult-to-staff schools and teaching assignments are needed, and more research is required to identify how large those incentives need to be. Our data suggest that these incentives need to be more substantial than the common $1,000 to $3,000 signing bonuses that we observed, and that they need to be sustained to retain those teachers over time. Further, given the high proportion of inexperienced teachers in low-performing schools, resources should also be allocated in ways that attract more experienced and accomplished teachers. For example, states could provide large incentives to teachers who have earned National

Board Certification to work in economically and educationally disadvantaged schools. However, in most of the contexts we studied, state rewards for National Board Certification were not differentiated by the nature of the teaching assignment.

When Highly Qualified Is Not High Quality

A second issue that undermines the goals of NCLB is that highly qualified teachers are not always high-quality teachers, and this disconnect is particularly apparent in some types of schools and teaching assignments. NCLB and other policies that define standards for teacher hiring must consider the context in which the teachers will be teaching. In many cases, we spoke with teachers who, despite meeting the highly qualified teacher requirements, felt ill prepared to teach the diversity of students in low-performing schools. In some cases, this was because of language differences. In other cases, the students simply needed more instruction and remediation than the teachers had been prepared to give. This lack of context-specific preparation suggests that having the highly qualified teacher designation is insufficient to be a high-quality teacher in some schools and in some teaching assignments.

A veteran elementary teacher in a Maryland Title I school described the insufficient preparation of novice teachers entering the challenging teaching environment:

> There is a disconnect between the teacher prep program and the real world. They are naïve and come into, especially a Title I school, and don't understand the societal issues that impact the classroom. . . . The gap between teacher education and what is going on in the school has increased over the years.

A novice teacher in Maryland commented on her specific teaching assignment:

> I wasn't prepared to teach a class where none of [the kids] can speak English. That is the one thing I struggle with. These kids were not on a second grade level when they came to school. I teach a second grade curriculum, but the kids are not on a second grade level. They are very behind.

One piece of this puzzle is teacher preparation. We talked with many teachers who completed quick-entry alternative certification programs (AC programs) and, upon completion, felt unprepared for their teaching assignments. This is not to say that AC programs are bad. In fact, research has found some to have had a positive effect on urban school systems (Johnson, Birkeland, & Peske, 2005). Neither do we mean to suggest that traditional university-based teacher preparation is necessarily good. In fact, many of these programs are not tailored to the needs of teachers headed to struggling schools. Regardless of the source and type of their preparation, novice teachers entering these schools may need site-specific training, induction, and professional development that will prepare them to be effective in the particular environments in which they are teaching. Researchers and policymakers should work toward identifying and investing in high-quality, site-specific training for teachers working in particularly challenging environments.

In addition to adequate preparation specific to the students and communities they are serving, teachers with particularly challenging teaching assignments may need reduced teaching loads for class preparation or sabbaticals to provide the time they need for additional training. Given the hefty costs associated with these policies, research is needed to understand the effects of these sorts of highly targeted investments. In all cases, teachers in challenging schools need strong administrators and mentor teachers who can provide ongoing support to help them be effective. However, we know little about what makes principals effective or how to invest in the recruitment, distribution, and retention of good principals.

In sum, our case studies suggest that highly qualified teachers working in low-performing, high-intensity schools need additional resources to be high-quality teachers. Such provisions, including site-specific induction and professional development, sabbaticals, reduced teaching loads, and supportive master teachers and principals, may have the potential to offset more difficult assignments with workplace conditions that attract well-prepared teachers to these schools, make them more effective in their teaching assignments, and retain them in those positions over time.

A Broader Understanding of Professionalism and Performance

A third concern about NCLB is that high-stakes accountability policies, in general, often drive good teachers away from low-performing schools, exacerbating the staffing challenges in these schools. Many teachers in our focus groups expressed great frustration with the high degree of standardization that has resulted from high-stakes accountability policies. Several argued that the implementation of uniform curricula has damaged the professionalism of teaching. One school principal in Maryland explains:

> The teaching profession in the Title I world today is not the creative venture it used to be. There is still a little bit of latitude, but it is not nearly the latitude that was once allowed in previous years.

Putting aside questions surrounding the impact of such policies on equity and efficiency in public education, these sorts of threats to the autonomy and professionalism of teachers cause many to reconsider their career choices and may make the profession less attractive to potential teachers. This concern was expressed by a high school mathematics teacher in Connecticut:

> What makes people want to teach is going to get lost, and the whole concept that we have to create end products and everybody has to be in the same box. They're trying to force fit this and then when it doesn't work, the blame comes back on us.

Adding to the difficulty, low-performing schools face greater challenges than do other schools in meeting performance standards. High-stakes accountability policies, such as NCLB, that hold teachers accountable for outcomes that are well beyond their control undermine staffing low-performing schools with qualified, let alone quality, teachers. Several teachers from urban schools in our sample described their frustration. A pre-kindergarten teacher in a Maryland Title I school commented,

> You feel like you've done well and then someone tells you that you've not done enough. . . . I felt so thrilled with my kids' progress, and then someone told me it wasn't good enough; I was devastated. My kids will be able to write their name next year and they are telling me that's not good enough.

The ultimate effect of high-stakes accountability, according to many teachers we spoke with, is high attrition in low-performing schools. One Maryland middle school teacher captured this well:

> The biggest factor in my mind for retaining teachers is NCLB and standardized testing and its effect on each teacher and classroom. When the school doesn't have the means to increase the scores, then teachers' jobs are in jeopardy and teachers are discouraged. Teachers will go elsewhere or go to schools where meeting the tests are easier and don't have to worry about outside factors, whether it's in other states or other districts because the tests are less rigorous.

High-stakes accountability policies are not inherently bad. In fact, equity demands that we hold schools accountable. However, to the extent that these policies drive good teachers away from low-performing schools, we have a serious problem. High-stakes accountability policies need to be designed in ways that draw the best teachers to the most challenging schools, provide support to help teachers be as effective as possible, and reward those teachers for staying there. This implies not only a greater targeting of resources to support teachers in those environments (as described earlier), but also a broader understanding and assessment of teacher quality. High-stakes accountability policies, such as NCLB, must consider a broader set of indicators, beyond student achievement test scores, to monitor teacher and school performance. We found that the heavy reliance on the narrow set of outcomes captured by standardized testing is very frustrating to teachers and often discourages them from remaining in low-performing schools. A broader set of measures (including, but not limited to, principal, peer, and parent evaluations and multiple measures of teachers' knowledge of students and teaching) may capture the many ways that effective teachers have an impact on students.

Discussion: Coping With the Contradictions

Taken together, the evidence from existing empirical studies of the impact of teacher qualifications on student performance coupled with findings from the case studies of teacher policy across levels of the system in three states reveals that NCLB may affect teacher quality in ways that directly contradict the rhetoric in the legislation. Three factors help explain how NCLB may detract from teacher quality, particularly in chronically low-performing schools: (a) the emphasis on measures of teacher qualifications over matters of teacher quality; (b) the fact that some teachers who meet the highly quali-fied standard are not high quality, given the contextual factors of the school; and (c) the emphasis of NCLB on standardization and a narrow set of per-formance measures.

Although national data show that most teachers (82.0%) who teach in NCLB-defined core academic subject areas meet the federal definition of a highly qualified teacher, disparities continue to exist in the distribution of these teachers (Kolbe & Rice, in press). Teachers in high-minority and high-poverty schools are more likely to be "underqualified" than are their peers in low-minority and low-poverty schools. Teachers in high-minority, high-poverty urban and rural schools are less likely to meet the highly qualified teacher requirements, and students in these schools are also less likely to be taught by an "experienced" teacher.

One concern with NCLB's highly qualified teacher requirements is that state policy responses often mask important variations in teacher quality across schools, districts, and states. Because all teachers must meet the federal requirements, many states no longer distinguish among different paths to certification that might be associated with quality, making it difficult for researchers to assess and document the incidence and distribution of teachers taking different pathways into the profession.

Several important implications follow from these findings. First, a striking and consistent finding from the case studies involves the distribution of qualified teachers so that all schools—rich and poor, high achieving and low achieving—can select from a surplus of qualified teachers. Considerations of quality and fit should not be reserved only for the advantaged and high-performing districts that enjoy a surplus of qualified teacher candidates from which to choose. Stronger incentives and better working conditions need to be employed to attract more qualified principals and teachers to low-performing schools.

Second, the case study findings indicate that teacher preparation, induction, and professional development need to be tailored to specific kinds of schools. Current teacher preparation and professional development are inadequate and insufficient for challenging environments. The lack of context-specific preparation suggests that having the highly qualified teacher designation is insufficient to be a high-quality teacher in some schools. Further, the heavy reliance on quick-entry (and often low-quality) AC programs in difficult-to-staff districts is problematic. The case studies reveal a consistent tension between the effort to increase standards in teacher preparation with the need to create a large enough supply of highly qualified teachers to staff classrooms. Opportunities to improve the staffing of shortage areas include (a) better information to educate prospective teacher candidates about the state-specific job market so that they make informed decisions about their field of expertise; (b) high-quality, grow-your-own alternative teacher certification programs that draw from uncertified local school staff and provide the teacher education components identified by research to be important; and (c) targeted economic incentives to support teacher candidates and reward highly qualified teachers willing to teach in geographic and subject shortage areas.

Third, the case studies and the empirical evidence suggest that a broader set of outcome measures should be developed and used to monitor teacher and school performance. While an expert panel of researchers and educators should be convened to construct these measures, it seems plausible that *teacher effectiveness* should be based on peer and principal evaluations as well as student achievement measures (e.g., value added). *School performance* measures should include not only achievement test scores but also dropout rates and college attendance rates. *Principal performance* measures should include school performance measures as well as teacher evaluations. Broader measures such as these recognize the complexity of the task and hold teachers, principals, and schools accountable for multiple outcomes using multiple sources of data.

These findings pave the way for future research. In particular, we need better information on the role of financial incentives and improved working conditions in making chronically low performing schools more attractive to high-quality teachers. Further, more information is needed on how best to target policies and resources to meet the differential needs of all schools. Finally, we need better evidence on the effectiveness of supply-side policies such as alternative teacher certification programs and "grow-your own" teacher efforts. In the end, if we really want to staff all schools with quality teachers, policy efforts must be guided by empirical evidence on how best to invest limited resources.

Notes

1. Of course, to the degree that reduced class sizes, overall educational spending, and teacher salaries are related to teacher quality, these can be viewed as investments in teacher quality, albeit indirect.

2. Rivkin, Hanushek, and Kain (2005) identify teachers as a major determinant of student performance, but they do not describe teacher quality in terms of specific qualifications and characteristics. They show strong, systematic differences in expected achievement gains related to different teachers using a variance-components model. In contrast, Darling-Hammond (1996, 2000) equates teacher quality with specific qualifications.

3. The Sanders and Rivers results regarding the cumulative effects of teachers assume that a student is exposed to a very strong teacher or a very weak teacher for several years in a row. Arguably, this is an implausible condition because many students are likely to have a very good teacher or a very bad teacher at some point in their academic career, but few are likely to have the very best or the very worst teachers for multiple years in a row.

4. For more detailed federal guidelines on the highly qualified teacher requirements, see U.S. Department of Education (2002a).

5. This distinction relies heavily on the argument constructed in Rice (2008).

6. See Hedges, Laine, and Greenwald (1994a, 1994b) and Krueger (2002) for discussions of the methodological weaknesses of the Hanushek reviews.

7. Because this is part of a broader study, this description of data and methods is shared in several other publications including Rice, Roellke, Sparks, and Kolbe (2009) and Rice and Roellke (in press).

8. Our expert panel consisted of seven individuals representing national teacher, administrator, and education policy organizations. This group met twice during the course of this study to participate in discussions about the teacher staffing problem, provide guidance on site selection, and offer suggestions on our research questions and study design.

9. The New York context is a bit different from the others. We selected Region 9 of New York City as our district, and four schools in four different subdistricts within Region 9.

10. Each participant in the study signed an informed consent agreement that describes the study goals and methods and their role in providing data for the study. We assigned each participant an identification code so that the researchers could attribute responses to specific individuals without using participant names. Individuals' names and other identifiable information were not used in written transcripts, coded data, or written reports or papers describing the study or its findings. However, because we identify the states and districts used in the study, it may be possible to identify participating district and state administrators, given the public nature of their positions. Whereas teachers and principals provided personal information on their decisions about where to work and their perceptions of state, district, and school policies, the information provided by district and state administrators is more public in nature (i.e., describing public policies and investments in them).

11. For a more detailed description of our sites, including the completed case profiles, see Rice, Roellke, and Sparks (2006).

12. In 1986, Connecticut adopted a comprehensive policy approach to teacher quality with the statewide Educational Enhancement Act (EEA). The first stage of teacher quality enhancement under the EEA involved making teacher salaries comparable to those in fields requiring similar levels of education and training.

13. This section draws heavily from Rice (2008).

References

Darling-Hammond, L. (1996). *Teacher quality and student achievement: A review of state policy evidence.* Unpublished manuscript.

Darling-Hammond, L. (2000). Teacher quality and student achievement: A review of state policy evidence. *Education Policy Analysis Archives, 8*(1).

Goe, L. (2006). *Revising the equitable distribution component in your state's plan for highly qualified teacher.* Washington, DC: National Comprehensive Center for Teacher Quality.

Goldhaber, D. (2007). Teachers matter, but effective teacher quality policies are elusive: Hints from research for creating a more productive teacher workforce. In H. Ladd & E. Fiske (Eds.), *Handbook of research on education finance and policy.* Princeton, NJ: Erlbaum.

Hanushek, E. A. (1992). The trade-off between child quantity and quality. *Journal of Political Economy, 100*, 84–117.

Hanushek, E. A. (1997). Assessing the effects of school resources on student achievement: An update. *Education Evaluation and Policy Analysis, 19*(2), 141–164.

Hedges, L. V., Laine, R. D., & Greenwald, R. (1994a). Does money matter? A meta-analysis of studies of the effects of differential school inputs on student outcomes. *Educational Researcher, 23*(3), 5–14.

Hedges, L. V., Laine, R. D., & Greenwald, R. (1994b). Money does matter somewhere: A reply to Hanushek. *Educational Researcher, 23*(4), 9–10.

Johnson, S. M., Birkeland, S. E., & Peske, H. G. (2005). *A difficult balance: Incentives and quality control in alternative certification programs.* Boston, MA: Project on the Next Generation of Teachers. Harvard Graduate School of Education.

Kolbe, T., & Rice, J. K. (in press). Are we there yet? The distribution of highly qualified teachers post-NCLB. In J. K. Rice & C. F. Roellke (Eds.), *High-stakes accountability: Implications for resources and capacity.* Greenwich, CT: Information Age Publishing.

Krueger, A. (2002). Understanding the magnitude and effect of class size on student achievement. In L. Mishel & R. Rothstein (Eds.), *The class size debate.* Washington, DC: Economic Policy Institute.

Maryland State Department of Education. (2005). *Professional salary schedules: Maryland public schools.* Baltimore, MD: Division of Accountability and Assessment.

Montgomery County Public School. (2005). *Our call to action: Pursuit of excellence. The strategic plan for Montgomery County Public Schools 2004–2009.* Rockville, MD: Office of the Superintendent of Schools.

Odden, A. & Kelley, C. (2002). *Paying teachers for what they know and do: New and smarter compensation strategies to improve schools.* Thousand Oaks, CA: Corwin.

Olson, L. (2006). A decade of effort. *Education Week, Quality Counts 2006*, 8–16.

Patton, M. Q. (1990). *Qualitative evaluation and research methods.* (Rev. ed.). Newbury Park, CA: Sage.

Peske, H. G., Crawford, C., & Pick, B. (2006). *Missing the mark: An Education Trust analysis of teacher-equity plans.* Washington, DC: Education Trust.

Rice, J. K. (2003). *Teacher quality: Understanding the effectiveness of teacher attributes.* Washington, DC: Economic Policy Institute.

Rice, J. K. (2008). From highly qualified to high quality: An imperative for policy and research to recast the teacher mold. *Education Finance and Policy, 3*(2), 151–165.

Rice, J. K., & Roellke, C. F. (in press). Struggling to improve teacher quality in difficult-to-staff schools: NCLB and teacher policy. In J. K. Rice & C. F. Roellke (Eds.), *High-stakes accountability: Implications for resources and capacity.* Greenwich, CT: Information Age Publishing.

Rice, J. K., Roellke, C. F., & Sparks, D. (2006). *Piecing together the teacher policy landscape: A multi-level case study findings from three states.* Research report. Washington, DC: Economic Policy Institute.

Rice, J. K., Roellke, C .F., Sparks, D., & Kolbe, T. (2009). Piecing together the teacher policy landscape: A policy-problem typology. *Teachers College Record, 111*(2), 511–546.

Rivkin, S., Hanushek, E. A., & Kain, J. F. (2005). Teachers, schools and academic achievement. *Econometrica, 73*(2), 417–458.

Rychen, D. S., & Salganik, L. (2003). *Key competencies for a successful life and a well-functioning society.* Toronto: Hogrefe & Huber.

Sanders, W. L. (1998). Value-added assessment. *School Administrator, 55*(11), 24–32.

Sanders, W. L., & Rivers, J. C. (1996). *Cumulative and residual effects of teachers on future academic achievement.* Knoxville, TN: University of Tennessee. Value-Added Research and Assessment Center.

U.S. Department of Education. (2002a). *No Child Left Behind: A desktop reference.* Washington, DC: Author.

U.S. Department of Education. (2002b, October). Presentation at the Student Achievement and School Accountability Conference, Washington, DC.

Wayne, A. J., & Youngs, P. (2003). Teacher characteristics and student achievement gains: A review. *Review of Educational Research, 73*(1), 89–122.

7

MEETING THE CHALLENGE OF HIGH-STAKES TESTING

Toward a Culturally Relevant Assessment Literacy

Kris Sloan

I n this chapter, I describe my efforts to develop strategies to help pre-service teachers maintain high-quality, equitable classroom instruction in the face of the pressures related to high-stakes testing. Specifically, I describe my efforts to develop in pre-service teachers a *culturally relevant assessment literacy (CRAL)* that better equips them to face the challenges of the current context posed by the expanded uses of high-stakes testing. The importance of such work is magnified given a review of the available teacher education literature. It seems clear that teacher education programs are not adequately preparing pre-service teachers for the realities and rigors, both personally and professionally, of teaching in an era of intensified test-centric accountability. Given that high-stakes testing has increased in importance, not properly preparing teachers to deal with the rigors and intricacies of standardized assessment and the resulting assessment data is, as Popham (2004) ominously warns, a prescription not only for failure, but for professional suicide for teachers.

In the current historical moment in the U.S. educational systems, high-stakes standardized tests—such as those advanced by the No Child Left Behind Act of 2001—are the primary engine of educational accountability, indeed of educational reform. There has been a proliferation of discourse, within the popular media and the educational literature, addressing both the perils and promises of such tests in terms of improving the overall quality of public education and communicating to the public the overall quality of public schools (see, for example, Sloan, 2004, 2007; Steele, 2004; Sunderman, Tracey, Kim, & Orfield, 2004). The available teacher education literature, however, reveals little about strategies teacher educators employ to prepare pre-service teachers for the personal and professional rigors of teaching *with* such tests.

Increasingly, teachers are confronted with standardized, high-stakes instruments as the principal indicator of students' proficiency in a content area as detailed in state standards. Moreover, teachers are presented with a veritable mountain of testing data from which they are expected to formulate instructional plans that target these specific state standards. More and more, however, teachers are not asked to formulate their own instructional plans of actions based on "the data" (Sloan, 2006). Instead, district and school administrators provide teachers with curriculum or lesson plans that teachers are expected to follow closely. Given that accountability and high-stakes testing will be with us for a long time into the foreseeable future, not properly preparing teachers to cope with standardized assessment and the resulting assessment data is a prescription for professional suicide (Popham, 2004).

In my own research, I find that far too many pre-service teachers report feeling both anxious and unprepared to teach in an era dominated by standardized high-stakes testing. In this chapter, I report on my efforts to develop strategies to help pre-service teachers maintain high-quality, equitable classroom instruction in the face of the pressures related to high-stakes testing. I intend for the culturally relevant assessment literacy (CRAL) to better equip pre-service teachers to face the challenges of expanded use of high-stakes testing. The chapter begins by offering a definition of the knowledge and skills that make up assessment literacy and a review of the teacher education literature related to assessment literacy.

The Need for Assessment Literacy

For James Popham (2004), *assessment literacy* ranks as one of education's most trendy educational phrases, but also one of its most glaring needs. Given the current educational milieu, Popham reasons that assessment literacy and educational accountability are "joined at the hip—or should be" (p. 82). Webb (2002) defines *assessment literacy* as the knowledge of: (a) the state-mandated instruments used for assessing what students know and can do, (b) the types of results these instruments yield, and (c) processes by which the results of these instruments can improve student learning and program effectiveness. However, a wider reading of the assessment literacy literature presents definitions that go far beyond knowledge of "state-mandated instruments" or drawing on data from these instruments to improve student learning and program effectiveness. A wider reading of this literature offers educators classroom-level strategies to gather evidence of student learning and their own teaching effectiveness. Even more, this literature offers teachers strategies to gather clear evidence of student learning that they can then use to challenge the inadequate, perhaps even misleading results from high-stakes standardized tests.

The term *assessment literacy* also includes the following teacher skill sets:

- The ability to define clear learning goals as the basis for developing methods to validly and reliably assess student learning
- The ability to use a mix of assessment techniques to gather evidence of student learning
- The ability to analyze student achievement data—both quantitative and qualitative data—and make good inferences from the data gathered
- The ability to provide appropriate and effective feedback to the learner
- The ability to craft appropriate instructional adaptations to facilitate student improvement based on analyses of student assessments
- The ability to involve students in the assessment process and to communicate to them the results in effective ways
- An ability to motivate students to perform well on assessments (Black, Harrison, Lee, Marshall, & William, 2003; Chappuis, Stiggins, Arter, & Chappuis, 2004; Stiggins, 2002)

The glaring need for bolstering these assessment literacy–related skills of pre-service teachers surfaced in my own research with pre-service teachers.

I now briefly describe the educational research, including my own, concerning pre-service teachers and high-stakes testing. Next, I give a detailed description of my efforts to bolster in pre-service teachers' knowledge and skills related to assessment literacy and what I came to call a culturally relevant assessment literacy (CRAL).

The Current Teacher Education Context

Although there has been a proliferation of discourse concerning the effects of test-based systems of accountability on in-service teachers and their teaching practices, there is a relative paucity of literature concerning the effects on teacher education in general and pre-service teachers in particular (see, for example, McNeil, 2000; Sloan, 2007; Smith, 1991; Sunderman et al., 2004). What little literature that exists to inform the field of teacher education seems to parallel the mostly critical literature concerning the effects of accountability and high-stakes testing on teachers and their practices.

In her research of pre-service teachers, Flores (2001) concludes that test-centric systems of accountability negatively affect pre-service teachers' work during their field placements. Through analyses of classroom observations and these pre-service teachers' field journals, Flores reports that pre-service teachers focused excessively on "the basics," emphasized rote learning, engaged in test-explicit instruction, and promoted an English-only curriculum. Moreover, Flores reports that these pre-service teachers expressed disillusionment with the teaching profession because of what they perceived as an overemphasis on testing.

In their self-described "qualitative study," Flores and Clark (2003) provide 18 undergraduate pre-service teachers, 10 in-service teachers, and 30 public school students a forum to express their views about high-stakes testing. The authors report that six themes emerged through their threaded e-mail discussions with both pre- and in-service teachers:

1. Teachers were not against accountability; however, they viewed assessment as distinct from high-stakes testing.
2. Teachers posited that an overemphasis on results from high-stakes tests led to an unbalanced curriculum and inappropriate instructional decisions.
3. Teachers suggested that excessive pressure was placed on particular grade levels that were "tested grades."
4. Teachers were having second thoughts about pursuing or remaining in the teaching profession because of the impact of high-stakes testing on the educational environment.
5. Teachers proposed that results of high-stakes tests alone should not be used to make decisions for promotion or retention of students.
6. Teachers observed that an emphasis on testing affects students negatively, manifested as physical, psychological, or emotional symptoms (Flores & Clark, 2003, p. 8).

For the most part, the findings from these two studies of pre-service teachers mirrors the parallel literature concerning the effects of such tests on classroom teachers and their teaching practices (see, for example, Hoffman, Assaf, Pennington, & Paris, 2001; Jones et al., 1999; McNeil, 2000; McNeil & Valenzuela, 2000; Sloan, 2004; Smith, 1991).

My own research, which includes more than 300 pre-service teachers at a major research university in the Southwest, reveals that pre-service teachers are well schooled in the critiques and limitations of high-stakes standardized tests (Sloan, 2006, 2007). Pre-service teachers in my research doubted whether high-stakes tests positively motivate teachers to teach better or that such tests positively influence student learning. In addition, more than 80% of the pre-service teachers surveyed "strongly agreed" that high-stakes tests lead to teachers "putting too much pressure on students." Not only did more than 80% of the pre-service teachers in my research perceive that high-stakes tests produced negative outcomes for teachers and students, but less than 30% of them reported believing that high-stakes tests were a "valid measurement" of student learning, teacher quality, or school quality. Only 3% of the 300 pre-service teachers surveyed believed that teachers should be terminated from their teaching positions for low student scores on state-mandated high-stakes tests.

It is extremely important to point out, however, that even though a majority of these pre-service teachers held mostly negative views about high-stakes tests and doubted the overall accuracy and validity of such tests, there was strong support for the general notion of educational accountability. More than two thirds of those pre-service teachers surveyed in my research agreed that teachers should be held accountable for the academic achievement of all students. These findings mirror numerous surveys of teachers that demonstrate that although teachers question current accountability policy's overreliance on high-stakes tests, they support the notion of educational accountability (see, for example, Hoffman et al., 2001; Jones et al., 1999; Sunderman et al., 2004). In the words of one senior-level middle school education pre-service teacher that I surveyed, "I agree that teachers should be held accountable for actually teaching the students, but I do not think that high-stakes testing is the way to go about it."

The most disturbing finding of my research with pre-service teachers involved their reported lack of preparedness to teach in an era of test-centric educational accountability. More than one third (35%) of the 148 graduating seniors perceived themselves to be unprepared to teach in an atmosphere where high-stakes testing predominates. An even higher percentage (45%) of elementary education pre-service teachers reported being unprepared.

Responding to an open-ended question about their overall level of prepared-ness, one senior-level secondary education pre-service teacher wrote, "We mostly just received the negative aspects of the testing, kind of leaves a feel-ing of hopelessness." Another senior-level elementary education pre-service teacher reported, "I don't necessarily feel prepared. I feel like we have just been told that the high-stakes tests are bad . . . they make teachers have to teach to tests. Yet, we still have to administer the tests and I don't feel prepared to do so."

Thirty-seven percent (115) of the 300 pre-service teachers surveyed pro-vided written responses to the following open-ended question: "What other comments do you wish to make about your general level of preparedness to teach under conditions of educational accountability?" Fifty-five percent (64) of the respondents to this question reported that they were unprepared to teach under conditions of test-centric accountability. One senior-level elementary education pre-service teacher wrote: "I don't feel like the classes I have taken so far have prepared me well enough to feel confident about teaching under these conditions. I really think it will take experience for me to feel comfortable." A middle-grades education pre-service teacher wrote, "I feel inadequate, unknowledgeable, unprepared." Another secondary edu-cation pre-service teacher wrote, "I am graduating this year and I am not prepared enough. That makes me nervous!"

Ten of the respondents reported feelings of stress over the prospects of teaching in an environment dominated by high-stakes tests. For example, one senior-level elementary education pre-service teacher wrote, "I am a little stressed because of the stress I have seen my mentor teachers under and also the students during my field experiences." A secondary education pre-service teacher responded, "There is not enough space for me to list all of the concerns I have about teaching in such a pressured environment." One ele-mentary education pre-service teacher reported that she hopes to avoid these pressures related to high-stakes testing by teaching in a nontested grade: "I don't want to teach the grades that take [the state test]."

In response to this same open-ended question ("What other comments do you wish to make about your general level of preparedness to teach under conditions of educational accountability?"), numerous pre-service teachers directed their comments at their teacher education program, making pleas for more explicit course content on accountability and high-stakes tests. For example, one secondary education pre-service teacher wrote: "This [senior-level] course is really the first class that has talked about the issues concerning accountability and high stakes testing. This is such a big issue. I do not understand why it is not addressed in other courses." Another elementary education pre-service teacher wrote, "When such a large part of what we will be teaching will center around tests . . . , it is a shame we do not have a class that prepares us more on how to prepare our students for this test." This same senior pre-service teacher continued, "I feel somewhat knowledge-able about [the state's high-stakes test]. However, in the classes I have taken, we have talked about classroom assessments but not high-stakes testing."

Not surprisingly, there is a strong relationship between these pre-service teachers' perceived level of preparedness to teach in the current educational context and their reported levels of apprehension or nervousness (Sloan, 2006). More than two thirds of the 300 pre-service teachers reported feeling apprehensive or nervous about high-stakes testing. Nearly three fourths of pre-service teachers reported feeling apprehensive or nervous about their abilities to prepare their future students for the state's high-stakes instrument.

A positive correlation is also found between the pre-service teachers' general attitudes and perceptions concerning high-stakes tests and their per-ceived levels of preparedness to teach in the current context (Sloan, 2006). In other words, if the pre-service teachers reported that they believed them-selves to be prepared to handle the rigors and pressures of high-stakes testing, they tended to have more positive attitudes and perceptions about such testing.

What might teacher educators garner from these research findings to inform their own efforts to transform teacher education programs? One clear implication of the research on pre-service teachers cited earlier, including my own, is the need for teacher educators to bolster course content related to assessment literacy. Another clear implication of this research is the need for teacher educators to bolster course content that offers their graduates specific strategies to offset the potential deleterious effects of high-stakes testing pro-grams, especially those on low-income students of color (see, for example, Hilliard, 2000; McNeil, 2000; Valencia, Valenzuela, Sloan, & Foley, 2002).

I now move to a discussion of course content related to assessment liter-acy that my colleagues and I have developed for our teacher education pro-grams. We developed this content specifically to bolster in pre-service teachers the knowledge and skills necessary to teach effectively *with*, and if necessary, *around* and *against* high-stakes tests in ways that preserve high-quality, equitable classroom instruction.

The Nuts and Bolts of Assessment

My initial efforts were focused on bolstering my professional knowledge as well as that of my teacher education colleagues. To this end, I worked with a group of teacher educators who organized a professional development workshop titled "Teaching and Learning With Data." In this all-day workshop, teacher educators reviewed the intricacies of the state's high-stakes standardized instrument and developed strategies to help pre-service teachers more systematically read and interpret the resulting testing data. The leaders of the workshop presented us with item-level testing data for individual students and for whole classes. As a group, we drew on these data to categorize errors, or conduct an error analysis. Based on these analyses of errors, we formulated tentative instructional plans to target individual students' and a whole class's weaknesses relative to the curriculum standards assessed on the test.

Although the purpose of this professional development workshop was to help teacher educators better prepare future teachers for teaching in educational environments heavily influenced by high-stakes testing, there was still the question of addressing the needs and concerns of the soon-to-be graduating seniors. To more specifically target these senior-level pre-service teachers, the teacher education faculty developed a web-based mini-course targeting professional knowledge from the "Teaching and Learning With Data" workshop. Upon completion of this web-based mini-course, the teacher education department awarded pre-service teachers a "certification" that could be added to their official transcript of study. After these initial efforts, the department chair made the web-based mini-course on assessment literacy a requirement for all pre-service teachers in the semester prior to their student teaching.

I believe that these initial efforts to develop pre-service teachers' knowledge and skills related to assessment literacy were crucial in terms of helping them to maintain high-quality classroom instruction in the current policy milieu. Although knowledge about the construct, or the "nuts and bolts" of state high-stakes instruments, and skills related to interpreting and analyzing test data are all important, I came to see them as wholly insufficient. Whereas such knowledge and skills may help teachers teach *with* high-stakes tests, teachers may also need knowledge and skills to help them, when necessary, teach *against* and *around* high-stakes tests to maintain high-quality, equitable classroom instruction.

Toward a Culturally Relevant Assessment Literacy

To assist pre-service teachers in maintaining a pedagogical commitment not only to educational quality but educational equity through their assessment practices, I attempted to expand and enrich the concept of assessment literacy. To do this, I turned to the rich literature related to culturally relevant pedagogy (see, for example, Gay, 2000; Ladson-Billings, 1992; Ladson-Billings & Tate, 1995). I take *culturally relevant pedagogy* to mean educational efforts that establish the social, cultural, political, and racial relevance of what is to be learned and the ways it might be applied. Culturally relevant pedagogy seeks to develop in students, in this case pre-service teachers, a critical, and when called for, an oppositional stance to what Apple (1993/2000) calls "official knowledge." Culturally relevant pedagogy represents an effort to help students understand what racism is, how it functions, both at an individual and systemic level, and what they can do to work against it (Ladson-Billings, 1995).

Over the past 2 years at my new teacher education institution, I have developed course content and a range of instructional strategies to enhance pre-service teachers' culturally relevant assessment literacy (CRAL). In a course titled "Learning Processes and Evaluation," I devote 9 hours of instructional time to issues related to CRAL. To enhance the importance of this content to the pre-service teachers—and to connect this effort to an ongoing "value-added" teacher knowledge campaign at my current institution[1]—I situate these 9 hours in a workshop setting.

Over the course of the workshop, pre-service teachers engage in a series of activities that target the assessment literacy skill sets described previously. The students

- List the purposes of classroom observations
- Describe differences between *assessment* and *evaluation*
- Distinguish between formative assessment, summative assessment, and different types of standardized tests
- Describe the limitations, or the possible biases, of standardized assessments
- Identify conditions under which students might experience stereotype threat and create assessment and evaluation conditions that reduce the likelihood of its occurrence
- Develop holistic assessment/evaluation classroom strategies, including self-assessment strategies, that recognize and honor a range of

learning styles, or ways of knowing or demonstrating understanding of curriculum standards

- Evaluate/score a written essay using a rubric
- Identify and create valid and reliable assessment/evaluation items that are as free of bias as possible
- Describe current accountability-related policies as they relate to determining student learning, teacher effectiveness, and school quality

Each of the workshop activities targeting these skills is couched in terms of culturally relevant pedagogy. In other words, none of these skills are presumed to be racially, culturally, or linguistically "neutral," or free from bias. I emphasize that for these assessment literacy–related skills to be culturally relevant requires a constant and sustained attention on issues of educational equity.

One workshop activity involves the development of authentic or performance assessments and the use of rubrics to evaluate students' performance. I first give students a story written by a fourth-grade student based on a prompt used in the state's fourth-grade writing test. I give each pre-service teacher the "6 + 1 Trait" scoring rubric developed by the Northwest Regional Educational Laboratory (NWREL)[2] and ask them to evaluate the student's story. I then group the students and ask them to compare and contrast their scoring of the student essay using the rubric. Each group is required to come to a single score and defend that single score against the scores of the other groups. I then divide the class groups according to content area and certification level. Starting with the state curriculum, each group is charged with selecting a common curriculum objective and creating a student performance that explicitly targets that curriculum objective. The group then creates a rubric that evaluates that student performance. Most important, each group creates examples of what an "A," "C," and "failing" student performance might look or sound like and why.

Another significant aspect of the 9-hour workshop involves developing an ability to identify and create valid and reliable test or quiz items. Such an ability is of increasing importance given the fact that more often than not "benchmark" assessments given to students to evaluate their progress, or their teachers' effectiveness, are created and scored at the school or district level. Often, the school- and district-level administrators who create and score these benchmark tests do not have solid backgrounds in psychometrics; thus, the likelihood of these assessments lacking reliability or validity is increased (Haladyna, 2002; Popham, 2004). Developing a test-writing skill set not only helps teachers better assess and evaluate their own students through in-class formative assessments but helps them better defend themselves against faulty assumptions or conclusions about the knowledge and skills of their students or their teaching based on unreliable or invalid locally created assessment instruments.

After differentiating between the definitions of reliability and validity, I present students with a series of guidelines on how to create high-quality supply or fill-in-the-blank items, true/false questions, multiple-choice items, and essay prompts. Guidelines for higher quality supply items, for example, include locating the blank at or near the end of a statement. For a higher quality true/false item, I advise pre-service teachers to avoid definitive qualifiers such as "always" and "never" and to phrase items succinctly (e.g., "Relative to their body weights, birds eat more per day than cats do" instead of "Birds eat more than cats"). To create higher quality multiple-choice items, I advise them to keep the possible answer choices similar in length, feasible, and grammatically consistent. To create higher quality essay prompts, I advise them to indicate clearly the task they expect students to perform or the content they expect students to target. For example, rather than "Discuss what you learned about the British Parliament and the U.S. Congress," a higher-quality, more valid essay prompt is: "Describe two major differences and one similarity between the British Parliament and the U.S. Congress."

After presenting these guidelines and reviewing specific examples, I present each pre-service teacher with test and quiz items I have collected from local sources, including local district benchmark assessments, items from past state high-stakes tests, or "release tests," and items from textbooks and workbooks used in the local districts. Students review these items to find prompts and items that they believe to be of high quality and those they believe to be lacking in quality, thus raising issues of reliability and validity. To conclude this part of the workshop, I group the pre-service teachers by content area or by certification level. I ask the groups to agree on a "big idea" found in the state curriculum around which a unit of study could plausibly be created. I then ask the groups to create a summative assessment that includes three high-quality supply items, three multiple-choice items, three true/false items, and three essay prompts. Students then share these summative assessments with the other groups, who proceed to evaluate the overall quality of the questions based on the guidelines provided earlier.

The CRAL workshop then moves to Claude Steele's (2003) work on stereotype threat. By drawing on Steele's seminal research, I demonstrate to pre-service teachers the ways "traditional" assessment and evaluation practices and the settings for these practices can inadvertently undermine the performances of students of color. Steele defines *stereotype threat* this way: "the threat of being viewed through the lens of a negative stereotype, or the fear of doing something that would inadvertently confirm that stereotype" (p. iii). Steele clearly demonstrates through his research that students of color tend to perform below their "true" abilities, especially in "testing situations," because of the added pressures they place on themselves not to inadvertently confirm historically negative stereotypes concerning their learning abilities, aptitudes, or intelligence.

After reviewing the definition of stereotype threat, I re-create the scenarios in Steele's research that clearly demonstrate the effect of this threat. To parallel the stereotype threat in Steele's work, I draw on issues of race and issues of gender, first-language, and presumed mathematical ability. Because my current institution is a designated Hispanic-Serving Institution,[3] there is a high percentage of Hispanic students whose first or home language is Spanish.

After a brief intermission in the workshop, I distribute a test booklet and inform the class that I am their proctor for the mathematics portion of the Graduate Record Examination (GRE). I add that this exam will determine whether they are "smart enough" to attend graduate school. As Steele astutely notes, the framing of this test in such a way is enough to activate the stereotype threat for specific identity groups. A class discussion immediately ensues about the assumptions, indeed stereotypes related to gender and mathematical ability. Typically, the conversation quickly moves to issues of race and the language of the test. Whereas the males in the class often report that they do not experience any anxiety or stress over the prospect of taking the mathematics portion of the GRE, which determines whether they are "smart enough" to be accepted to graduate school, the females do. Moreover, the Hispanic students whose first language is Spanish tend to add that because the exam is in English, they are even more anxious about the prospects of not being seen as "smart enough" to go to graduate school. Further, because these are mostly high-achieving students who tend to care deeply about performing well in class, as Steele reasons, they are even more vulnerable to stereotype threat.

Not surprisingly, Steele's work and his clear descriptions of the effects of stereotype threats on students' "true abilities" captivate most pre-service teachers. This is especially true when they are presented with parallel situations where the stereotype threat may connect to their own identity. To

conclude this portion of the workshop, I paraphrase specific recommendations Steele (2004) offers to deal with, even ameliorate, stereotype threat in
relation to assessment and evaluation practices and settings:

1. As much as possible, replace terms such as *intelligence, ability,* and
   aptitude in our educational lexicon when talking about tests, assessments, and evaluations with such terms as *skill level* and *educational
   readiness.* As Steele states, "These terms say no more than we know,
   and thus keep us self-conscious about assuming more than we know"
   (Steele, 2004).
2. Discourage the use of norm-referenced tests in favor of criterion-
   referenced tests, which are based on specific curriculum standards.
3. Develop and use multiple, low-stakes, formative, curriculum-based
   assessments and avoid the use of single-sitting, summative, high-
   stakes tests—including for use in college, graduate school, and professional school admissions (Steele, 2004).

The CRAL workshop then moves to what James Popham (2004) charac-
terizes as the "viscera" of the state's high-stakes standardized instrument.
Drawing on information about the state's high-stakes instrument made available by the state educational agency, I discuss with the pre-service teachers
the relationship between the state curriculum, the state standards, and the
state's high-stakes standardized instrument. In particular, I help the pre-
service teachers distinguish between a criterion-referenced test and a norm-
referenced test, such as the GRE or the Stanford Achievement Test, or SAT-9.

Again, I group the pre-service teachers by content area or certification
level and ask them to take a portion of the state's high-stakes test that corresponds to their content area or certification level. Even though most of the
pre-service teachers have taken this test when they themselves were in public
school, and even though this is only a class learning activity, this activity
tends to produce in them high levels of nervousness and anxiety. At this
point, I introduce to them specific strategies they can employ to reduce test
anxiety of their future students. These strategies include tips about nutrition,
rest, specific prompts, and even breathing techniques that help test-takers
relax and focus on the task at hand.

After they take a portion of the state's high-stakes test we "score" the
tests. I present them with data sheets used by a local school district to chart
individual student performance by objective. In particular, I make note of
the number (and percentage) of questions students need to answer correctly

to "pass" the state test, or what is referred to as the "cut score." We then discuss the politics and equity-related issues surrounding the establishment of cut scores, which are rarely a focus of public or media scrutiny (McNeil, 2005). In particular, I emphasize that cut scores are not psychometrically, or "scientifically," determined, but rather are the result of a subjective and, in the end, a political process. I then show them a historical timeline of cut scores to demonstrate the ways politics, both state and national, can influence the overall pass rates of public school students as much or more than do schools or teachers (McNeil, 2005).

We conclude the CRAL workshop by reviewing and analyzing item-level testing data. Over the years, I have gathered from local school districts a variety of grade levels and content area spreadsheets that provide item-level analysis of students' performances on the state test. Based on these spreadsheets, I ask pre-service teachers to make inferences about the various strengths and weakness of the class relative to the curriculum standards. I also ask them to review the actual questions students miss most or the specific test objectives that they seem to struggle with most. This error-analysis activity also includes identifying patterns of errors with the specific questions to determine why or how students selected the incorrect response. These conversations also involve strategies to determine whether a particular question may potentially mislead students or perhaps may be invalid. If, for example, the spreadsheet shows that many students selected the same incorrect response, I ask pre-service teachers to analyze the question and speculate why so many students select the same incorrect response. At the conclusion of this error-analysis activity, I ask each pre-service teacher to formulate a plausible instructional response based on his or her inferences.

Over the past 2 years, I have presented this teacher education workshop three times. To this point, the pre-service teachers have been highly receptive. Workshop and course evaluations reveal that students have been concerned with issues of high-stakes testing and thus are appreciative of opportunities to be exposed to the workings of such tests. Still left to be done, however, is follow-up research on our recent teacher education graduates to determine whether the content and activities of this assessment literacy workshop achieves its desired ends. Are our graduates more prepared to teach *with, around,* or perhaps *against* high-stakes tests in ways that maintain high-quality, equitable classroom instruction as a result of successfully completing this assessment literacy workshop? Might such a workshop positively influence teacher retention rates of our teacher graduates? These are the questions I will ask as I move forward with these efforts to transform teacher education in an era dominated by high-stakes standardized testing.

Recommendations

To prepare pre-service teachers for the rigors, both personally and professionally, of teaching *with*, and if necessary *around* or *against*, high-stakes standardized tests, I offer the following recommendations for teacher preparation programs. First, teacher preparation programs must bolster or revise current course content to target more explicitly and meaningfully concepts related to assessment and evaluation. Ideally, all teacher preparation programs could bolster and revise this content in a standalone course focused only on assessment and evaluation. In programs where such standalone courses on assessment and evaluation do not currently exist, I recommend that one be created. In programs where issues of assessment and evaluation are integrated across a range of methods courses, I strongly recommend clearer coordination between courses to ensure that this important content is covered as comprehensively as possible.

Second, teacher preparation programs must provide extended opportunities for pre-service teachers to dig meaningfully into the viscera of educational testing (Popham, 2004). Content related to assessment and evaluation must reach beyond classroom assessments or the creation of rubrics to include the nuts and bolts of standardized testing. Guided opportunities with such content can demonstrate to teachers that the complex statistical world of standardized testing is *not* beyond their comprehension.

Third, to help teachers develop and maintain a professional commitment to educational quality and educational equity, teacher education programs must promote culturally relevant assessment and evaluation practices. It is not enough to understand the ways certain forms of assessment and evaluation are biased against specific student populations. Whereas developing a critical stance *against* such forms of assessment and evaluation is important, it is perhaps more important to be able to present valid and reliable alternatives.

Conclusion

In this chapter, I offer an operational definition of assessment literacy by naming and describing the knowledge and skills that make up assessment literacy. This is followed by a comprehensive review of the teacher education literature related to assessment literacy. I then describe my efforts to develop pre-service teachers' assessment literacy to help them maintain high-quality, equitable classroom instruction in the face of the pressures, indeed the high stakes, related to high-stakes testing. Specifically, I describe my efforts to develop in pre-service teachers a culturally relevant assessment literacy that can better equip them to face the challenges of the current context posed by the expanded uses of high-stakes testing. The importance of such work is magnified, given a review of the available literature on these topics. It seems clear that teacher education programs are not adequately preparing pre-service teachers for the realities and rigors of teaching in an era of intensified test-centric accountability. High-stakes testing has increased in importance. Not properly preparing teachers to deal with its rigors and intricacies is a prescription for professional suicide.

Notes

1. This project was connected to a larger effort by the teacher education faculty to create a series of Pre-Service Professional Education (PPE) Certificates. These PPE Certificates were designed to model state Continuing Professional Education (CPE) credit requirements for public school teachers to maintain their certification. Through this project, each teacher educator in the program selected a topic or content to highlight that they believed was the most crucial to our pre-service teachers' future success as classroom teachers. Whereas other teacher educators selected issues of "questioning," "tutoring," and "student grouping," I selected the topic of "assessment literacy."

2. Copies of the rubric can be found at the NWREL website: http://www.nwrel.org/assessment

3. The U.S. Department of Education defines this term: "A Hispanic-Serving Institution (HSI) is defined as a non-profit institution that has at least 25% Hispanic full-time equivalent (FTE) enrollment. This Title V Program helps eligible institutions of higher education (IHEs) enhance and expand their capacity to serve Hispanic and low-income students by providing funds to improve and strengthen the academic quality, institutional stability, management, and fiscal capabilities of eligible institutions" (http://www.ed.gov/programs/idueshsi/index.html)

References

Apple, M. (1993/2000). *Official knowledge: Democratic education in conservative age.* New York: Routledge.
Black, P., Harrison, C., Lee, C., Marshall, B., & William, D. (2003). *Assessment for learning: Putting it into practice.* Berkshire, England: Open University Press.

Chappuis, S., Stiggins, R., Arter, A., & Chappuis, J. (2004). *Assessment for learning: An action guide for school leaders*. Portland, OR: Assessment Training Institute.

Flores, B. B. (2001). The miracle of TAAS: Urban reality or legend? Implications for teacher preparation. *Journal of the Texas Association for Bilingual Education, 6*(1), 11–22.

Flores, B. B., & Clark, E. R. (2003). Texas voices speak out about high-stakes testing: Pre-service teachers, teachers, and students. *Current Issues in Education, 6*(3). Retrieved May 2, 2008, from http://cie.ed.asu.edu/volume6/number3/

Gay, G. (2000). *Culturally responsive teaching: Theory, research, & practice*. New York: Teachers College Press.

Haladyna, T. M. (2002). *Essentials of standardized achievement testing: Validity and accountability*. Boston: Allyn and Bacon.

Hilliard, A. G., III. (2000). Excellence in education versus high-stakes standardized testing. *Journal of Teacher Education, 51*(4), 293–304.

Hoffman, J. V., Assaf, L., Pennington, J., & Paris, S. G. (2001). High stakes testing in reading: Today in Texas, tomorrow? *Reading Teacher, 54*(5), 482–492.

Jones, G., Jones, B. D., Hardin, B., Chapman, L., Yarbough, T., & Davis, M. (1999). The impact of high-stakes testing on teachers and students in North Carolina. *Phi Delta Kappan, 81*(3), 199–203.

Ladson-Billings, G. (1992). Culturally relevant teaching: The key to making multicultural education work. In C. Grant (Ed.), *Research and multicultural education: From the margins to the mainstream* (pp. 106–121). London: Falmer.

Ladson-Billings, G. (1995). Making mathematics meaningful in multicultural contexts. In W. Secada, E. Fennema, & L. Byrd Adajian (Eds.), *New directions for equity in mathematics education* (pp. 126–145). Cambridge, UK: Cambridge University Press.

Ladson-Billings, G., & Tate, W. F. (1995). Toward a theory of culturally relevant pedagogy. *American Educational Research Journal, 35*(3), 465–491.

McNeil, L. (2000). *Contradictions of school reform: Educational costs of standardized testing*. New York: Routledge.

McNeil, L. (2005). Faking equity: High-stakes testing and the education of Latino youth. In A. Valenzuela (Ed.), *Leaving children behind: How "Texas-style" accountability fails Latino youth* (pp. 57–112). New York: SUNY Press.

McNeil, L., & Valenzuela, A. (2000). Harmful effects of the TAAS system of testing in Texas: Beneath the accountability rhetoric. In M. Kornhaber, G. Orfield, & M. Kurlandar (Eds.), *Raising standards or raising barriers? Inequity and high-stakes testing in public education* (pp. 89–123). New York: Century Foundation.

Popham, J. (2004). All about accountability: Why assessment illiteracy is professional suicide. *Educational Leadership, 62*(1), 82–83.

Sloan, K. (2004). Between the inputs and outputs: Assessing the effects of high stakes accountability on educational quality. In A. Valenzuela (Ed.), *Leaving children behind: How "Texas-style" accountability fails Latino youth* (pp. 153–178). New York: SUNY Press.

Sloan, K. (2006, April). *Teacher education and accountability: Developing assessment literacy in pre-service teachers.* Paper presented at the annual meeting of the American Educational Research Association, San Francisco, CA.

Sloan, K. (2007). Teacher identity and agency in school worlds: Beyond the all-good/all-bad discourse on accountability-explicit curriculum policies. *Curriculum Inquiry, 36*(2), 119–152.

Smith, M. L. (1991). Put to the test: The effects of external testing on teachers. *Educational Researcher, 20*(5), 8–11.

Steele, C. (2003). Stereotype threat and African-American student achievement. In T. Perry, C. Steele, & A. Hilliard III. (Eds.), *Young, gifted, and Black: Promoting high achievement among African-American students* (pp. 109–130). Boston: Beacon Press.

Steele, C. (2004, May 3). Not just a test. *The Nation.* Retrieved April 15, 2008, from http://www.thenation.com/doc.mhtml?i = 20040503&s = steele

Stiggins, R. (2002). Assessment crisis: The absence of assessment for learning. *Phi Delta Kappan, 83*(10), 758–765.

Sunderman, G. L., Tracey, C. A., Kim, J., & Orfield, G. (2004). *Listening to teachers: Classroom realities and No Child Left Behind.* Cambridge, MA: Civil Rights Project, Harvard University.

Valencia, R., Valenzuela, A., Sloan, K., & Foley, D. (2002). Let's treat the causes, not the symptoms: Equity and accountability in Texas. *Phi Delta Kappan, 83*(4), 318–321, 326.

Webb, N. L. (2002, April). *Assessment literacy in a standards-based urban education setting.* Paper presented at the American Educational Research Association Annual Meeting in New Orleans, Louisiana.

PART FOUR

TRANSFORMING
TEACHER EDUCATION

8

WHEN POLICIES
MEET PRACTICE

Leaving No Teacher Behind

Jeanita W. Richardson

If you're going to play the game properly, you'd
better know every rule.

    Barbara Jordan, *The Life 101 Quote Book*

E ducation is one of the few professions where external bodies significantly affect practice. The governance and funding structures guiding
public education leave significant decisions to legislators and not
teachers and administrators. In the wake of policies such as No Child Left
Behind (NCLB), teachers and administrators are forced to conform their
practices to suit legislation that to date has done little to live up to its cre-
ators' promise. It seems intuitively unwise to develop educational reforms
without a comprehensive understanding of the world of K–12 educators.
However, corrective actions articulated in statute often place the blame for
student underperformance largely on teachers rather than recognizing that
learning and performance are the results of complex factors within and external to schools (Richardson, 2007, 2008). Furthermore, some variables, such
as exposure to environmental toxins, general health, malnutrition, and housing quality, affect the learning readiness of children and are beyond the
control of school-based personnel (Richardson, 2008). In this chapter, I suggest that as the words of Barbara Jordan admonish, active engagement of
teachers in the policy-making process would be facilitated if they were more
familiar with the governing bodies and rules that dictate practice.

That being said, the reality is that contemporary accountability criteria have shifted classroom practice from a private exchange between teachers and students to fodder for front-page print. This shift has been orchestrated largely by the political bodies with the authority to dictate the rules of teacher practice. Failure to understand formal and informal public policy pathways not only relegates teachers to voiceless implementers of legislative edicts, but also hinders advocacy on behalf of the students they serve. This chapter attempts to mitigate this knowledge gap by deconstructing the roles of federal, state, and local bodies that regulate public K–12 education in the United States.

Teachers at the Nexus of Policy and Accountability

Historically, teachers, with the exception of their unions, have attempted to stay out of the political arena and have concentrated their efforts on pedagogy and discipline-specific content. However, intrusive policies, such as No Child Left Behind (NCLB), breach not only the academic freedom of teachers and districts, but also create pressures to "teach to the test." It is time, particularly given the impending reauthorization of NCLB, for teachers to become more knowledgeable about the education policies and politics because they affect much of what happens during the school day.

At its root, pressures relative to school accountability show movement toward more top-down control of schools. The idea appears to be that public officials (either elected or appointed) believe promotion of student achievement can be legislated through sanctions, distribution of school data (e.g., test scores), student demographic information, and teacher credentials (Moe, 2003). Yet, 20 years of standards-based reform has done little to obliterate the achievement gaps experienced by some children, which hints at the inadequacy of the law alone to ensure outcome parity (Gregorian, 2004). For example, high school dropout rates in the 50 largest cities in the United States average 58% (Swanson, 2008). Embedded in aggregated dropout figures is the overrepresentation of Native Americans, African Americans, and Hispanics (relative to their proportion of the total school-aged population) among students who drop out of school (Swanson, 2008). Between 1992 and 2005, there has been little measurable change in the reading achievement gaps between Whites and Blacks and Whites and Hispanics in both the fourth and eighth grades even as general raw test scores rise. Fourth graders in the highest poverty schools continue to score lower on National Assessment of Educational Progress (NAEP) mathematics tests than those in the lowest poverty schools. For 13-year-olds, overall trends in reading achievement have remained flat for 20 years (U.S. Department of Education National Center for Education Statistics, 2006).

In short, many children and teachers are being left behind, as exhibited by findings of the National Center for Educational Statistics. To change the ways in which teachers are engaged, or more appropriately not engaged, in the policy development process requires alterations in professional thinking about advocacy. As aptly put by one high school literacy curriculum specialist:

> Educators need to be advocates. The majority of our days and lives are spent working in schools. We know schools. We know what works. We can talk about class size or the need for books in a way that no one else can. We're traveling in hard times—budget cuts and top-down decision making take education out of the hands of teachers and [put it] into the pockets of corporate publishers and politicians. In the past 20 years, we have witnessed an erosion of teachers' rights. We can't stand idly by while public education is dismantled. (National Council of Teachers of English, 2005)

The remainder of this chapter is devoted to facilitating an understanding of the comprehensive governance and funding schema of public K–12 education in general and the rationale for participating in the reauthorization of NCLB in particular. It is also appropriate to share the impact of NCLB on a novice teacher's classroom life so that members of the public (including unwitting politicians and educators) who are unfamiliar with "educational policy rules" receive a reality check from unconscious policy that silences its stakeholders.

Policy, Politics, and U.S. Public K–12 Education

Most of America's children attend publicly funded K–12 schools. In the academic year 2002–2003, there were 14,465 public school districts and 95,615 schools. Of the 48.2 million students served, 4.1 million (8.5%) were limited in their English proficiency and 6.4 million (13.4%) were served by federally supported programs for people with disabilities. Nearly 52% of U.S. public school students attend suburban schools, 31% attend urban schools, and 17% are enrolled in schools considered rural (U.S. Department of Education National Center for Education Statistics, 2004). Regardless of location, sources of educational policies originate at the federal, state, and local levels concurrently.

At this juncture, it is germane to make a distinction between the terms *policy* and *politics* because both are applicable to the educational governance lexicon. *Politics* refers to decisions determining who receives which resources, when and how they are delivered, and why the object or target for resources is worthy of investment (Colmers, 2002). Schools and, by inference, teachers are subject to politics by virtue of the fact that they are at the mercy of federal, state, and locally elected and appointed officials who determine the distribution of funds and attention. *Policies* (public, organizational, and budgetary) are the collective actions and inactions of decision-making bodies designed to address social priorities such as public education (Dunn, 1994). The policy process is often depicted as a dynamic process and includes problem definition, policy formulation, adoption, implementation, evaluation, and a redefinition of the problem.

At each of the stages reflected in Figure 1, stakeholders can influence decisions. Teachers in particular are clearly a stakeholder group in terms of educational policy, even if they are not actively engaged by politicians in the policy formulation and adoption stages. They are, however, heavily relied upon to implement many education-based laws and rules, such as No Child Left Behind (2001) and the Individuals With Disabilities Education Acts (2004). Furthermore, they are also held accountable for compliance in assessment mechanisms established in statute.

Problem definition is the process by which a social issue becomes the focus of formal intervention. The issue's rise to prominence is both contextual and relevant to historical, political, and economic contexts. Once it is deemed worthy of statutory status, a bill is formulated by decision makers. Congress and state legislatures have committee and floor processes through which bills become laws. This process, through enactment, is captured in the policy adoption stage. Implementation of the law ensues, followed by an evaluation of successes, shortcomings, and failures of the statute. The law is then reconsidered as generally prompted by public opinion, changing priorities, or time limits in the original language.

Included in Figure 1 is a specific example of NCLB, which was actually not a new law but the reauthorization (problem redefinition) of the Elementary and Secondary Education Act. Congress, through its process, advanced the revised bill (formulation) heavily influenced by the George W. Bush administration. Once the bill was passed into law (adoption), the U.S. Department of Education established the compliance rules and submitted them to the states to further articulate rules and regulations. Rules and regulations imposed on, for example, timing the types of testing and teacher

FIGURE 1
Cyclical Nature of Policy

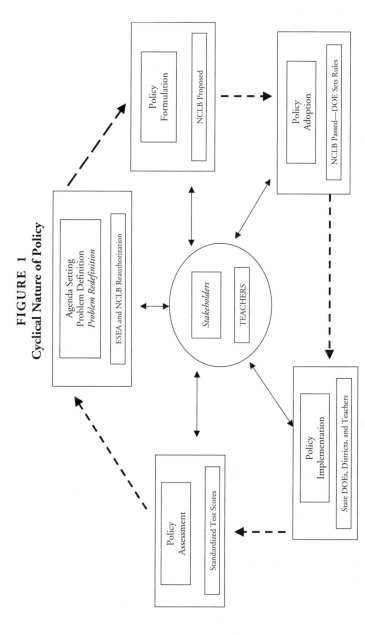

Source: Adapted from: Dunn, W. N. (1994). *Public policy analysis: An introduction.* Upper Saddle River, NJ: Prentice Hall.

licensure criteria (implementation) are measured (assessed) through standardized test scores of both children and teachers. The impending reauthorization of NCLB (problem redefinition) will at least theoretically be informed by evaluations of the shortcomings and successes of the law.

Federal Government's Role in Education

Contrary to popular opinion, a "right" to a publicly funded education is never mentioned in the U.S. Constitution. Public education is principally governed by each state. On average, only 6–10% of public school budgets are supported with federal funds. Federal legislative bodies and agencies do, however, influence schools through incentive programs that tie funding to certain programs or practices.

Though public education is never mentioned, the Tenth Amendment to the Constitution relegates the responsibility for schooling to the states in the verbiage "powers not delegated to the United States by the Constitution nor prohibited by it to the states are reserved to the states respectively or to the people" (Jones, 2001; Valente & Valente, 2005). As a result, each of the 50 state constitutions articulate the creation and structure of public education systems within their respective jurisdictions, none of which are identical (Valente & Valente, 2005).

Even though the federal government does not have direct jurisdiction over the operation of schools, it does operate as a "silent junior partner" (Earley, 2000). The role of the federal government in public education evolved more as a gatekeeper of civil rights and liberties as a function of the Fourteenth Amendment. For example, the Fourteenth Amendment protects citizens against infringement of their constitutional liberties by school officials and provides equal protection under the law, to include children (often summarized as antidiscrimination laws) (Valente & Valente, 2005).

Federal influence pervades schools because of the subsidies made available to states and districts in compliance with federal priorities and laws (Valente & Valente, 2005). Examples of the fiscal influence of the federal government on schools tied to legislation are the No Child Left Behind Act (2001) and the Individuals With Disabilities Act (2004). States in receipt of (or wishing to receive) federal funds must comply with federally imposed conditions. Noncompliance supplies grounds for the federal government to restrict distribution or demand repayment of fiscal resources.

The influence of the President of the United States on schools tends to be both direct and indirect. The direct function is tied to the approval or veto power on legislation and budgets submitted by Congress. In addition, numerous indirect pathways allow for insertion of the president's priorities into educational policy. For example, appointments to key positions, such as the Secretary of Education and the Secretary of the Interior (the agency overseeing Native American education), ensure that like-minded individuals carry out priorities. Presidents influence educational systems through executive orders, tending to direct services and functions of various federal administrative agencies or departments of the executive branch. Finally, speeches (often referred to as the "bully pulpit") also can influence educational systems (Richardson, 2006).

Congress (the House of Representatives and the Senate) exerts its authority by tying standards to funding. For example, some federal funds are available only to schools in compliance with various legislated acts, such as the Civil Rights Act of 1964 and the Individuals With Disabilities Education Act (IDEA) of 2004. In this way, Congress can directly affect aspects of school operations. Federal agencies such as the Department of Education are charged with ensuring the enforcement of legislated mandates through the establishment of regulations. As such, its policy departments and departments of research provide valuable information concerning the compliance status of educational institutions at all levels in the nation (Wirt & Kirst, 2001).

The Department of Education is also responsible for policy development, program oversight and evaluation, and research. On a regular basis, the Secretary of Education reports to Congress the progress and ongoing challenges of educating American's children. New knowledge creation is most often funded through a competitive grant process when prospective projects align with federal priorities. The Department of Education also is the depository of volumes of statistical data generated by and about educational institutions, their students, and faculty. Other federal agencies are required to provide technical assistance to ensure that states and divisions meet federal education-related guidelines. An example of technical assistance is the Office of Civil Rights assisting school districts' development of desegregation plans (Wirt & Kirst, 2001).

You can see from this overview, the principal influence of the federal government on public education systems is tied directly to funding. As a result, it becomes important to grasp how much money states risk losing or gaining as a function of compliance to fully comprehend why school districts are reallocating resources and personnel to meet criteria set forth in NCLB and IDEA.

The fiscal influence of the federal government can be divided into six categories: (a) general aid, (b) differential funding, (c) regulations, (d) promotion of new knowledge, (e) support of services, and (f) moral persuasion.

General aid refers to "no-strings" money dispersed to states or localities. To date, Congress has never approved general aid in the form of a legislative bill. Differential funding is aid earmarked for specified projects or services such as those noted in NCLB and IDEA. The federal government can also regulate school practice or behaviors contrary to federal law, such as discrimination on the basis of race or gender (Wirt & Kirst, 2001).

Figure 2 depicts the average percentage distribution of school systems' budgets that were supplied by federal, state, and local resources in the 2002–2003 academic year. Of the $440.3 billion spent in elementary and secondary education in the school year 2002–2003, only 8.4% came from federal coffers. Forty-nine percent of school budgets were supplied by state sources, and nearly 43% came from localities. The primary source of local monies is real estate taxes, and state sources come from various tax assessments and in some cases lottery proceeds. Thus, proportionately, the federal contribution to school districts is comparatively minimal. However, in districts where the needs of students exceed resources, 8% is too much to risk losing (Richardson, 2006).

Figure 3 shows the average distribution of the $389.9 billion spent on educational services other than capital. The greatest percentage of school budgets was devoted to instruction (60.5%) in 2002–2003, with more than

FIGURE 2
Funding Distribution for Academic Year 2002–2003
Total: $440.3 billion

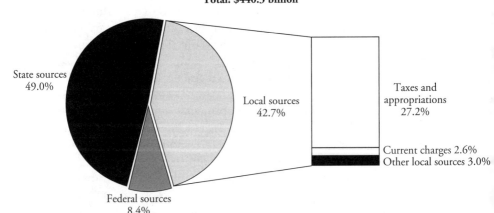

State sources 49.0%

Local sources 42.7%

Federal sources 8.4%

Taxes and appropriations 27.2%

Current charges 2.6%
Other local sources 3.0%

Source: Adapted from: U.S. Census Bureau. (2005). *Public education finances 2003.* Washington, DC: Author.

FIGURE 3
Public Elementary-Secondary Spending by Function: 2002–2003

Total: 389.9 billion

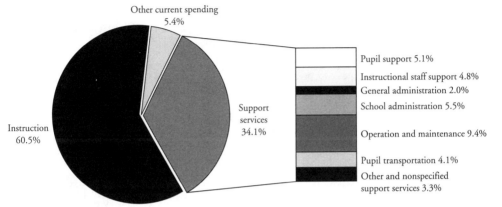

Source: Adapted from: U.S. Census Bureau. (2005). *Public education finances 2003.* Washington, DC: Author.

34% devoted to support services. Support services include pupil transportation (4%), operation and maintenance of schools (9%), general and school-based administration (7.5%), instructional staff support (5%), pupil support (5%), and other support services (3%). These resources translate at the student level to per-pupil expenditures. Per-pupil expenditures are generally calculated using a formula of district operating expenses and the numbers of pupils supported by federal, state, and local monies. Categories of operating expenses included in the per-pupil expenditure figure are as follows, but are not limited to the following:

- Administration
- Athletics
- Attendance
- Fixed charges
- Food
- Health
- Instructional
- Plant maintenance
- Student body activities
- Transportation (Massachusetts Department of Education, 1997)

There is great disparity in per-pupil expenditures between states and between districts within states principally because of local tax bases. The national average per-pupil expenditure for the academic year 2002–2003 was $8,019. However, as you might imagine, some states spent in excess of or far less than that figure per student.

Reflect on the 43% of school budgets that comes from principally local real estate taxes. If a district has a large number of rental properties as opposed to owner-occupied units, is heavily industrialized, or is home to upper-income versus low-income families, you can begin to see the roots of fiscal disparity.

Judicial decisions relative to schooling issues, such as access and desegregation, have historically mandated changes in practice through the interpretation of existing law. The courts at all levels exert their control over schools because they are petitioned to interpret laws. Court decisions are just as political as other venues because judges are either appointed by elected officials or are themselves elected. Cases that come to the courts are the result of social conflicts that were not resolved in other venues, such as the *Brown v. Board of Education* decision of 1954. A verdict may resolve one aspect of discord while creating other forms of social disagreement. The judiciary's influence is not particularly relevant to this discussion and, as such, will not be expanded upon here (Richardson, 2006).

State and Local Educational Governance

Given the power afforded governors, state legislatures, and state boards of education as a function of state constitutions, the most influential bodies relative to schools are found at the state level. Although the specificity of language differs from state to state, the general premise is the same: States have formally assumed the responsibility of providing public K–12 education to their citizens. Additional sections of said constitutions also create enforcement bodies for compulsory attendance and curricula.

Like the federal government, states have three distinct branches: executive, legislative, and judicial. The executive branch is headed by the governor, who appoints his or her cabinet and the directors of various state agencies. In some states, she or he appoints the Secretary of Education or State Superintendent of Public Instruction, and in other states these individuals are elected. With the exception of the state legislature, the most influential body with respect to public education policy tends to be the State Board of Education (or in the case of New York, the Board of Regents), and state constitutions dictate whether these individuals are appointed or elected. Table 1 compares the role of several state-level officials, their terms, and how they ascend to office as an example of how states' educational policymaker configurations can differ.

Governors, like the president, exert influence on schools. Their power is tied to their approval or veto of bills and the appointments they make to policy-making bodies as provided in their state's constitution. The direct or indirect authority they exert is a function of their state constitutions and varies between states. For example, Virginia governors only serve one 4-year term, whereas there are no term limits in New York or Massachusetts and governors appoint individuals to key positions. Governors may or may not possess budget line item power after state legislatures submit state budgets. Depending on this authority, governors may increase or decrease funding for programs or agencies.

The legislative branch of state government consists of the Senate and House of Representatives (or Assembly). In some cases, legislatures only assemble every biennium, as is the case in Oregon. The power of these bodies lies in their joint prerogative to establish and amend state law and to distribute fiscal resources throughout the state. State budget offices control both the collection of funds within states and the disbursal of federal funds earmarked for districts. State legislatures are important because these bodies can mandate practices that redirect resources and constrain or support individual districts' decision-making scope (Richardson, 2006).

As is the case with federal bills, state legislation is submitted either to the Senate or House (sometimes companion bills are submitted to both at the same time). The bills are then referred to standing committees that deliberate the merit of the proposal and determine whether the bill will ever come to a vote on the Senate or House floor. Most bills "die" in committee for various reasons. Bills that survive (that are passed) then cross over to the companion chamber and, if passed, are forwarded to the governor. There are procedures in place for state legislatures to override a veto from the governor should he or she not sign the bill into law similar in protocol to those practiced in Congress (Richardson, 2006).

A similar process ensues for state budgets; however, states determine appropriations on different schedules. For example, some states approve state budgets every 2 years and others annually. Depending upon state constitutional precedent, governors or legislative bodies or both propose a budget, which is remanded to House and Senate finance or appropriation committees to undergo a process similar to that of a legislative bill. In this way, legislative and executive branches of state government distribute fiscal

TABLE 1
Governors and K–12 Educational Policy and Funding

State	Gubernatorial Term Limits	Secretary of Education	Superintendent of Public Instruction	State Board of Education or Equivalent	Governor's Role After Legislature Approves Budget
California	Two terms	Governor appoints	Elected	Eleven members appointed by the governor	Line item veto and funding for an entire program or agency
Virginia	One term	Governor appoints	Appointed by State Board of Education	Nine members appointed by the governor	Line item veto and funding for an entire program or agency
Michigan	No term limits	N/A	Appointed by the State Board of Education	Eight members elected	Line item veto and funding for an entire program or agency
Louisiana	Two-term limit	N/A	Appointed by the Louisiana Board of Elementary & Secondary Education	Eleven members. Eight are elected and three are appointed by the governor	Line item veto and funding for an entire program or agency
New York	No term limits	Appointed by the Board of Regents and the title is Commissioner of Education and President of the New York State University	N/A	Sixteen members of the Board of Regents elected	Line item veto and funding for an entire program or agency
Massachusetts	No term limits	Commissioner of Education appointed by the State Board of Education	N/A	Nine members appointed by the governor	Line item veto and funding for an entire program or agency

Source: Adapted from: Zinth, K. (2005). *What governors need to know: Highlights of state education systems.* Retrieved October 6, 2005, from http://www.ecs.org/html/Document.asp?chouseid = 5845

resources to school districts and determine the parameters of district-level control.

State legislatures have the broad prerogative to pass laws or delegate power to other bodies, such as a state department of education or boards of education. Some convene for several months a year (e.g., in Louisiana and Michigan) whereas others are in session for the calendar year (such as in California). Once in session, they pass education laws that distribute funds, govern state licensure of teachers and administrators, delineate school districts, and prescribe and evaluate curricula.

State boards of education are called upon to implement and enforce the mandates set forth by the state legislature or its designees. As shown in Table 1, differences manifest between just these few states, where some board members are appointed and others are elected. Generally, the offices of State Superintendent of Public Instruction and the Secretary (Commissioner) of Education interact with the State Board and oversee the implementation of state and federal regulations at the local level. In some cases, states fill both offices (such as in California and Virginia) and in other states only one of these offices exists (such as in Michigan, Louisiana, New York, and Massachusetts).

Local school boards and educational agencies interpret the state mandates and manage the operating funds and in some cases the physical capital resources coming from federal, state, and local sources. School districts tend to be headed by a superintendent who serves as a chief executive officer and employee of the school board. Members of school boards are most often elected; however, even within states there is variance. For example, in Michigan, the mayor of Detroit appoints school board members. Schools with their administrators, faculty, and support staff are in turn charged with the implementation of directives from federal, state, and local authoritative bodies.

The No Child Left Behind Act of 2001

No discussion of educational policy and its impact on teachers is complete without some reference to what has been deemed one of the most significant impositions of the federal government into K–12 education (Wright, Wright, & Heath, 2004). The No Child Left Behind Act of 2001, also referred to as NCLB, is actually the reauthorized Elementary and Secondary Education Act (ESEA) (Wright et al., 2004; Yell & Drascow, 2005). The law represents an unprecedented increase in federal mandates complete with punitive consequences for noncompliance. As was the case with its predecessor statutes, NCLB provides funding through appropriations and grants in exchange for accountability standards.

Table 2 provides a synopsis of the 10 titles articulated within the NCLB legislation. Each focuses on different aspects of the educational process. In addition, it is important to note that some of the programs are funded through competitive grants. Technically, more money could be provided under NCLB that is not accessible by all school districts because of the grant submission process. This helps explain how the federal government reports a 25% increase in funding, and states consider NCLB under- or unfunded.

ESEA provided the framework for NCLB relative to the focus of titles. During the reauthorization process the number of titles decreased from 14 to 10. Some retained their names such as Title I, "Helping Disadvantaged Children Meet High Standards," whereas others did not. For example, Title IV was changed from "Safe and Drug-Free Schools and Communities" to "21st Century Schools." Nuances and consolidations aside, the comprehensive goal of NCLB is to increase student achievement by requiring that 100% of students demonstrate proficiency in core subjects by the academic year 2013.

Between 2001 and 2013, schools must achieve what is called "adequate yearly progress" (AYP), which is a school district's predetermined percentage improvement in student performance as defined by the relevant state and submitted to the U.S. Department of Education. NCLB mandates proficiency of virtually all members of student bodies and requires schools close achievement gaps between socioeconomic, racial, and ability groups (Yell & Drascow, 2005). For example, students who are in need of individualized education programs (IEPs) because of emotional, mental, or physical disabilities are expected by the academic year beginning 2013 to demonstrate core subject proficiency at the same levels as "mainstream" students (U.S. Department of Education National Center for Education Statistics, 2004). NCLB also demands "highly qualified" teachers teach all students (Title II), that all youth are to be educated in safe and drug-free schools (Title IV), that children with limited English prowess become proficient in English (Title III), and that all students graduate from high school (Yell & Drascow, 2005).

As per NCLB, states must establish standards that

(a) Describe what students will be able to know and do, (b) include coherent and rigorous content standards, and (c) encourage the teaching of advanced skills. (Yell & Drascow, 2005, p. 21)

TABLE 2
No Child Left Behind Legislative Titles

Title	NCLB
Title I	**Improving the Academic Achievement of the Disadvantaged** Programs include student reading programs; education of migratory children; preventions and intervention for neglected, delinquent, or at-risk children; comprehensive school reform; advanced placement programs; school dropout prevention; Title I assessment and other general provisions.
Title II	**Preparing, Training, and Recruiting High-Quality Teachers and Principals** Programs included a teacher and principal training and recruiting fund; mathematics and science partnerships; innovation for teacher quality (i.e., all teachers must be "highly qualified"); and enhancing education through technology.
Title III	**Language Instruction for LEP and Immigrant Students** Includes the English Language Acquisition Act; designating funding for programs intended to improve language instruction; and several general provisions.
Title IV	**21st-Century Schools** These programs primarily deal with providing safe and drug-free schools and communities, learning centers, and tobacco smoke prevention.
Title V	**Promoting Informed Parental Choice and Innovative Programs** Provides funding for "innovative programs," public charter schools, magnet schools, and general improvement of education.
Title VI	**Flexibility and Accountability** Improving academic achievement and a rural education initiative.
Title VII	**Indian, Native Hawaiian, and Alaska Native Education** Providing for Indian, Native Hawaiian, and Alaska Native education.
Title VIII	**Impact Aid Program** Aid to districts that serve children of employees of the federal government (especially the military).

TABLE 2 (Continued)

Title	NCLB
Title IX	**General Provisions** This section includes definitions, flexibility in the use of funds, coordination of programs, waivers, uniform provisions, and unsafe school choice options.
Title X	**Repeals, Redesignations, and Amendments to Other Statutes** This section includes repeals, designations, homeless education programs, Native American education improvements, the Higher Education Act of 1965, and general education provisions.

Source: Adapted from: Wright, P. W. D., Wright, P. D., & Heath, S. W. (2004). *Wrightslaw: No Child Left Behind.* Deltaville, VA: Harbor House Law Press; and Yell, M. L., & Drascow, E. (2005). *No Child Left Behind: A guide for professionals.* Columbus, OH: Pearson/Prentice Hall.

States must also articulate and define at least three levels of achievement: advanced, proficient, and basic. Statewide assessment systems are to be aligned with state curricula and standards in reading, mathematics, and eventually science in addition to being consistently applied throughout the state. More specifically, AYP is the minimum improvement from year to year that schools must achieve. For the most part, verification that schools have achieved AYP has been a disaggregation of standardized test scores, some of which are idiosyncratic to states and some which are national examinations (e.g., New York Regents versus National Assessment of Educational Progress examinations).

All public schools must participate in the statewide assessments and test at least 95% of students. Beginning in the school year 2005, reading, language arts, and math were to be assessed/tested annually between grades 3 and 8 and once between grades 10 and 12. During the next academic year (2006), science tests were to be applied to the same grades. Additionally, NCLB requires that in alternating years states administer to a random sample of fourth and eighth graders a reading and math test designed by the National Assessment of Educational Progress (NAEP) (Wright et al., 2004; Yell & Drascow, 2005).

Special groups of students may require test environment modifications but must be tested at the same intervals as mainstream or traditional students. One such group is youth with disabilities as defined by IDEA criteria.

Accommodations are defined in each child's individualized education plan (IEP). An IEP is required for every child receiving services under IDEA and is a plan developed in collaboration with teachers, parents, administrators, and other professionals. Its purpose is to improve the educational achievement levels of children who without special consideration might not maximize their educational potential. Districts and schools must then report the percentage of students taking tests with modifications or alternative assessments (Yell & Drascow, 2005).

Students with limited English proficiency must also be included in statewide assessments. Initial accommodations may be extra time when taking a test, small-group administration, and the use of dictionaries or audiotaped instructions in native languages. However, children who have attended school in the United States or Puerto Rico for 3 consecutive years must take all examinations in English without modifications (Yell & Drascow, 2005).

Test scores and other school and district data are compiled and published annually in what is called a school report card, which is also a mandated activity of NCLB (Title V). Test data are to be disaggregated by student subgroups (limited English proficiency, economically disadvantaged, race, and ethnicity, for example) and made available to the general public. There are two levels of report cards that are required under NCLB, state and district. Minimum requirements of state report cards include data such as the most recent 2-year trend in student achievement of students in all grades and subject areas, graduation rates by subgroup, aggregate teacher qualifications (provisionally certified or highly qualified), and the performance of specific districts across the states. District report cards provide information about the specific schools relative to AYP within said districts (Wright et al., 2004; Yell & Drascow, 2005).

Schools that do not achieve AYP face punitive consequences that accrue if AYP is not met in consecutive years. The first year a school fails to meet its AYP a technical assistance plan is to be developed in conjunction with parents and experts. The purpose of the technical assistance plan is to improve academic performance by incorporating research-based strategies and to provide targeted teacher professional development and student learning enhancement activities. If a school fails to meet AYP for 2 years in a row, the state must provide the technical assistance and post in the statewide report card that the school is identified as "needing improvement" (Yell & Drascow, 2005).

By year 3, the school district is obligated to provide technical assistance and to offer school choice. Restated, schools must provide supplemental educational services and funding for parents to send their children, if they so choose, to an alternative school on the respective state-approved list. Educational service providers could be public charter schools, faith-based schools, and nonprofit or for-profit entities. In the fourth year of noncompliance, in addition to providing supplemental education services and offering parents the option of transferring their children to a public school choice, the school is also noted on the statewide and district report card as "needing corrective action." At this point, school staff can be replaced, curricula changed, outside advisors appointed, and the school day or year extended as viable options. If a school fails to make AYP after 5 consecutive years, the states are to take over the school and proceed with a major restructuring (Yell & Drascow, 2005). As in previous versions of ESEA, threats of fiscal withdrawal for noncompliance exist. However, the consequences of noncompliance are articulated more specifically in NCLB and relative to teachers involve job security and professional development.

Part of the political fury surrounding NCLB is the disagreement about whether federal support to states has increased or decreased in light of the expensive and extensive testing and accountability reporting. As per federal government sources, funding under NCLB increased almost 25% from the funding levels of ESEA (Yell & Drascow, 2005). Conversely, some experts note that federal school funding post NCLB only increased 1 percentage point (West & Peterson, 2003). Many states and municipalities would argue that significant reallocations of funds have left states and school districts with budget gaps, yet districts are still required to comply if they are to retain their federal money. Given reported state and district shortfalls, NCLB is commonly referred to as an unfunded mandate requiring additional services and duties without the requisite funds to meet established goals (Baines & Stanley, 2004; Richard & Davis, 2005).

Governors and the National Conference of State Legislatures have decried the pressures of NCLB compliance on state budgets because of spiraling Medicaid and other health care expenses, which deplete funds for public education (Odland, 2005; Richard & Davis, 2005). This is particularly problematic in light of rising costs associated with NCLB accountability standards, that is, significantly higher testing costs (Richard & Davis, 2005). For example, it has been estimated that 5.5–14% of every dollar spent for public schools is now being spent on testing and test administration services (Baines & Stanley, 2004). One of the most important aspects of NCLB is this: School districts and states are preoccupied with meeting the criteria of NCLB because failure to do so places 6–10% of school budgets at risk.

Furthermore, to comply, states and municipalities have to divert funding from other programs that might have been successful to meet NCLB standards.

The teacher is the most important figure insofar as educational reform is concerned. Dewey (1910) advises that there is simply no point in attempting a reform without the active participation of the teacher's abilities, interests, and desires. NCLB, therefore, requires not simply new funding mechanisms but a process of interaction involving reform and teachers. From all accounts, no such interaction exists.

A Day in the Life With NCLB: A Teacher's Tale

I began my teaching career on August 27, 2007, at an elementary school in Crowley, Texas. As with many first-year teachers, it all really began 2 weeks before the start of school at a new staff in-service program where we learned of our districts' and schools' policies on everything from dress codes, attendance, Internet decorum, to how we would manage our classrooms. I soon learned that even though when I had asked my school principal in my interview whether she encouraged "teaching to the test" in the classroom and she had responded, "No," I would be encouraged to do just that in my own classroom. Every day I would need to start my class with a 15-minute math warm-up that was based on the Texas Standards for Academic Achievement, the TAKS (Texas Assessment of Knowledge and Skills) test. The second hint that things would be based around the standardized test came just 2 school days before school was set to begin. Instead of having a self-contained third-grade classroom, we would be doing rotations. This would allow for reading and math to have a set 45 minutes each for lessons. Writing, science, and social studies would also each have 45 minutes, but as such, math and reading should both be integrated regularly into our lessons. So, I began each rotation with a 15-minute TAKS-based science, reading, or math warm-up. At my school, the staff also had to write and turn in weekly lesson plans, which included the TEKS (Texas Essential Knowledge and Skills) content standards that were being taught. We also had to turn in monthly calendars that let the office know what TEKS were being taught which weeks. It was an abundance of unnecessary paperwork to provide the office with documentation if our students were unsuccessful. Nevertheless, this is how I started my first year of teaching.

By November 2007, we began our district-wide benchmarks. At this time, TAKS tests from previous administrations were given to the third-grade students. As teachers, we were required to make the testing conditions as close as possible to an actual standardized testing environment. Posters plastered our school and classroom walls. Exact instructions for the TAKS test were to be read aloud to students. After the students took the tests and the tests were processed, the teachers were given the data for their students. The math and reading teacher from our grade level grew concerned over the struggling students. At the request of a single influential teacher to the principal, our rotation schedule would change. It would change to accommodate 1-hour 30-minute blocks of reading and math. Science and social studies would each have 45 minutes. Writing would be taught in conjunction with reading. The way it worked was that science and social studies subjects were now taught by each student's homeroom teacher in the first hour and a half of the day. Reading then got the next block of time. The students for both the math and reading groups were grouped according to the objectives on which they were struggling. In other words, they were ability grouped. My school's administration and the team lead did this to allow for remedial teaching for those who needed it. On my own and because my students loved science, I still continued to plan science at this time in the year and would pass it on to the other members of my team to complete with their homeroom classes.

It was not long after the new change in schedules that I got a call from a mother of a student who was not in my science class. The mother inquired as to why her child was not receiving science lessons. After speaking with that child's homeroom teacher, I discovered that these teachers, as well as others on my team, had abandoned science except to amass the minimum amount of grades needed for each 6 weeks. Instead, they were using the time to provide more math and reading practice. As the spring semester got under way, my school hosted a TAKS Parents Night, in which the TAKS test was explained to the families of our students. In April, the administration at our school provided two tutors to our grade level. One would tutor our lower math students, the other our lower reading students. These students, to create as few interruptions as possible, would be pulled from science or social studies time.

In Texas, third grade is the first year in which the TAKS test is administered. It is also the first year that NCLB requires schools to begin tracking Adequate Yearly Progress, AYP. The third graders in Texas are allowed to take the Reading TAKS test three times. The Reading TAKS test was administered March 4th, April 30th, and the final chance on July 2nd. All third-grade students, in order to advance, must pass their third-grade Reading TAKS test or meet with a grade placement committee. Unlike the Reading TAKS test, the Math TAKS test for third grade has only one administration date: April 29th. Third-grade students are not required to pass it to move on. Schools are assessed not only according to how the grade level does overall but also in five subcategories, which include different ethnic groups and low-income students. Many of the teachers' class preparation from December until the first administrations included many practice TAKS reading passages and math word problems to prepare students for their first TAKS test.

I was strongly encouraged several times to abandon my teaching practices of allowing hands-on activities in my math class because the students would not have manipulatives on the test. All but 2 of my 20 math students showed growth on every benchmark. When it came to reading, I was encouraged to use more practice tests to ensure that my students would be ready for the tests. I continued to teach reading in a way that focused more on the skills addressed by the TEKS objectives and less on the questions from passages. As such, I encouraged my students with challenging questions from all levels of Bloom's taxonomy, including higher-level-thinking questions often not asked on the TAKS tests. This, however, made many of the TAKS test questions seem too basic or easy for the students in my class. In March 2008, all third-grade students across the state took the first administration of the Reading TAKS test. Of the students who were in my reading class, 18 of the 22 passed the test on the first try. Soon after, we got the results for our grade level, and the teachers of the grade were made to tutor four students for 30 minutes during our math class time. During that time, a teacher's aide would teach our classes. The students we were tutoring were all students who had not passed the first administration of the Reading TAKS test. The school year continued in this fashion until the first administration of the third-grade Math TAKS test on April 29th and the second administration of the Reading TAKS test for those who did not pass the first administration.

My school and the administration were on pins and needles awaiting these results. Only the first two administrations of the reading test count toward a school's statistics for measuring whether that school has made AYP. When the results came back, there was a lot of talk about our school's statistics and what they would mean for the coming year. It was not until these tests were over that the teachers had more flexibility over what and how things were taught. At this time, the teachers were finally able to push for testing of students who had been struggling all year and were showing signs of a learning disability; before this time, it had not been a priority at our school. The teachers were told they needed more documentation. Several of the students who were tested were added to our school's special education program or dyslexia classes for the 2008–2009 school year. I ended my first year finally understanding that, with NCLB, many schools were succumbing to the pressure of national guidelines; it slowly devoured us in so many small ways.

Thoughts on Policy Meeting Practice

Politics and policy as they relate to public education influence more than the decision-making parameters of superintendents and school boards. Policies and politics also can narrow opportunities to accommodate the varied learning styles and needs of children. Whether we consider a legislated heavy reliance on standardized test scores an appropriate accountability measure is beside the point. The more important issue is that the decision-making process should not be permitted to proceed in the absence of input from those charged with implementation. Failure to integrate the experiences and best thinking of teachers diminishes the success of the legislation and the freedom of teachers and districts to meet the idiosyncratic needs of their respective communities. We, as teachers, must shed our political timidity and hold elected and appointed officials as accountable for the policies dictating classroom practice as they hold us.

It would be wonderful to set forth a one-size-fits-all advocacy strategy that could be used by teachers and other school personnel. Unfortunately, it would be difficult to articulate in one chapter because each state's constitution differs. The idiosyncratic nature of state control means that one of the first steps is to become informed about the roles and rules that exercise authority over schools.

What is clear is that if we as educators do not attempt to address the shortcomings of NCLB, political actors will do it for us. Who knows better than a teacher, as illustrated in the preceding teacher's tale, the complex challenges facing children and the professionals doing their best to serve them? How is it fair to judge the contributions of any teacher when so many confounding variables influence the teaching–learning exchange?

There is already movement of the federal government to drill even deeper into schools. In discussions about upcoming reauthorization of NCLB, former Secretary of Education Margaret Spellings indicated one of the changes to be advocated is suspending collective bargaining agreements if schools are being restructured (U.S. Department of Education, 2007). Instead of waiting for a "bad" law to be enacted, teachers should alternatively advocate for appropriate solutions. Perhaps then the power dynamic would shift from top-down decision making to statutes informed by bottom-up and top-down collaborations. Becoming politically savvy is not solely useful as a matter of self-preservation, it is also a critical skill relative to advocating on behalf of the children and communities public educational institutions serve. Stated another way, it behooves educators of all ranks to become informed about public educational policy decision makers and how policy is formulated, implemented, and enforced if we are to influence statutes proactively.

We have functioned under external edicts like NCLB for decades. If we continue to leave advocacy to others, we will continue to get the types of policies we currently are charged to implement. As an alternative, we must hearken to the words of Barbara Jordon:

If you're going to play the game properly, you'd
better know every rule.
   —Barbara Jordan, *The Life 101 Quote Book*

References

Baines, L. A., & Stanley, G. K. (2004). High-stakes hustle: Public schools and the new billion dollar accountability. *Educational Forum, 69*(1), 8–16.

Colmers, J. (2002). Why "government, politics, and law"? *American Journal of Public Health, 92*(8), 1217.

Dewey, J. (1910). *How we think.* Boston, MA: D.C. Heath.

Dunn, W. N. (1994). *Public policy analysis: An introduction.* Upper Saddle River, NJ: Prentice Hall.

Earley, P. M. (2000). Finding the culprit: Federal policy and teacher education. *Educational Policy, 14*(1), 25–36.

Gregorian, V. (2004). No more silver bullets: Let's fix teacher education. In J. Matthews (Ed.), *The last word* (pp. 10–16). San Francisco: Jossey-Bass.

Jones, E. B. (2001). *Cash management: A financial overview for school administrators.* Lanham, MD: Scarecrow Press.

Massachusetts Department of Education. (1997). *School finance: Statistical comparisons: FY95 per pupil expenditures.* Retrieved September 2, 2005, from http://finance1.doe.mass.edu/statistics/pp95.html

McWilliams, P. (1996). *The life 101 quote book.* Los Angeles: Prelude Press.

Moe, T. M. (2003). Politics, control, and the future of school accountability. In P. E. Peterson & M. R. West (Eds.), *No Child Left Behind? The politics and practice of school accountability* (pp. 80–106). Washington, DC: Brookings Institution.

Odland, J. (2005). NCLB—more questions than answers. *Childhood Education, 81*(3), 158b–158c.

Richard, A., & Davis, M. R. (2005). Governors seek help from federal officials on NCLB law, funds. *Education Week, 24*(26), 19.

Richardson, J. W. (2006). *Public K–12 federal educational policy.* Battle Creek, MI: W.K. Kellogg Foundation.

Richardson, J. W. (2007). Building bridges between school-based health clinics and schools. *Journal of School Health, 77*(7), 337–343.

Richardson, J. W. (2008). From risk to resilience: Promoting school-health partnerships for children. *International Journal of Educational Reform, 17*(1), 19–36.

Swanson, C. B. (2008). *Cities in crisis.* Bethesda, MD: Editorial Projects in Education Research Center: Supported by America's Promise Alliance and the Bill & Melinda Gates Foundation.

U.S. Census Bureau. (2005). *Public education finances 2003.* Washington, DC: Author.

U.S. Department of Education. (2007). *Reform, renewal and results.* Retrieved May 2, 2008, from http://www2.ed.gov/policy/elsec/leg/nclb/factsheets/reform.html

U.S. Department of Education National Center for Education Statistics. (2004). *The condition of education 2004 (NCES 2004–077).* Washington, DC: U.S. Government Printing Office.

U.S. Department of Education National Center for Education Statistics. (2006). *The condition of education 2006 (NCES 2006–071).* Washington, DC: U.S. Government Printing Office.

Valente, W. D., & Valente, C. M. (2005). *Law in the schools* (6th ed.). Columbus, OH: Pearson/Prentice Hall.

West, M. R., & Peterson, P. E. (2003). The politics and practice of accountability. In P. E. Peterson & M. R. West (Eds.), *No Child Left Behind? The politics and practice of school accountability* (pp. 1–22). Washington, DC: Brookings Institution.

Wirt, F. M., & Kirst, M. W. (2001). *The political dynamics of American education* (2nd ed.). Richmond, VA: McCutchan.

Wright, P. W. D., Wright, P. D., & Heath, S. W. (2004). *Wrightslaw: No Child Left Behind.* Hartfield, CT: Harbor House Law Press.

Yell, M. L., & Drascow, E. (2005). *No Child Left Behind: A guide for professionals.* Columbus, OH: Pearson/Prentice Hall.

Zinth, K. (2005). *What governors need to know: Highlights of state education systems.* Retrieved October 6, 2005, from http://www.ecs.org/html/Document.asp?chouseid = 5845

9

CONSTRUCTING 21ST-CENTURY
TEACHER EDUCATION

Linda Darling-Hammond

M uch of what teachers need to know to be successful is invisible to lay observers, leading to the view that teaching requires little formal study and frequent disdain for teacher education programs. The weaknesses of traditional program models that are collections of largely unrelated courses reinforce this low regard. This chapter argues that we have learned a great deal about how to create stronger, more effective teacher education programs. Three critical components of such programs include tight coherence and integration among courses and between coursework and clinical work in schools, extensive and intensely supervised clinical work integrated with coursework using pedagogies linking theory and practice, and closer, proactive relationships with schools that serve diverse learners effectively and that develop and model good teaching. Also, schools of education should resist pressures to water down preparation, which ultimately undermine the preparation of entering teachers, the reputation of schools of education, and the strength of the profession.

Teachers should know and be able to do in their work a spectacular array of things, such as understanding how people learn and how to teach effectively, including aspects of pedagogical content knowledge that incorporate language, culture, and community contexts for learning. Teachers also need to understand the person, the spirit of every child and find a way to nurture that spirit. And they need the skills to construct and manage classroom activities efficiently, communicate well, use technology, and reflect on their practice to learn from and improve it continually.

Powerful teaching is increasingly important in contemporary society. Standards for learning are now higher than they have ever been before because citizens and workers need greater knowledge and skill to survive and succeed. Education is increasingly important to the success of both individuals and nations, and growing evidence demonstrates that, among all educational resources, teachers' abilities are especially crucial contributors to students' learning. Furthermore, the demands on teachers are increasing. Teachers must be able to keep order, provide useful information to students, and be increasingly effective in enabling a diverse group of students to learn ever more complex material. In previous decades, teachers were expected to prepare only a small minority for ambitious intellectual work, whereas today they are expected to prepare virtually all students for higher-order thinking and levels of performance once reserved for only a few.

Given this variety of teacher education goals and the realities of 21st-century schooling, this chapter considers what those of us in the field of teacher education might do to support the kinds of learning teachers require to undertake this complex job with some hope of success. I draw on the recently released work of the National Academy of Education Committee on Teacher Education, a group of researchers, teachers, and teacher educators that worked for 4 years to summarize how the learning process in children and adults can inform the curriculum and design of teacher education programs (Darling-Hammond & Bransford, 2005).[1] The National Academy of Education Committee's report begins with this description:

> To a music lover watching a concert from the audience, it would be easy to believe that a conductor has one of the easiest jobs in the world. There he stands, waving his arms in time with the music, and the orchestra produces glorious sounds, to all appearances quite spontaneously. Hidden from the audience—especially from the musical novice—are the conductor's abilities to read and interpret all of the parts at once, to play several instruments and understand the capacities of many more, to organize and coordinate the disparate parts, to motivate and communicate with all of the orchestra members. In the same way that conducting looks like hand-waving to the uninitiated, teaching looks simple from the perspective of students who see a person talking and listening, handing out papers, and giving assignments. Invisible in both of these performances are the many kinds of knowledge, unseen plans, and backstage moves—the skunk works, if you will, that allow a teacher to purposefully move a group of students from one set of understandings and skills to quite another over the space of many months.

On a daily basis, teachers confront complex decisions that require many different kinds of knowledge and judgment and that can involve high-stakes outcomes for students' futures. To make good decisions, teachers must be aware of the many ways in which student learning can unfold in the context of development, learning differences, language and cultural influences, and individual temperaments, interests, and approaches to learning. In addition to foundational knowledge about these areas of learning and performance, teachers need to know how to take the steps necessary to gather additional information that will allow them to make more grounded judgments about what is going on and what strategies may be helpful. Above all, teachers need to keep what is best for the child at the center of their decision making. This sounds like a simple point, but it is a complex matter that has profound implications for what happens to and for many children in school (Darling-Hammond & Bransford, 2005, pp. 1–2).

Contemporary Dilemmas for Teacher Education

To the noninitiated, both the apparent ease of teaching and the range of things teachers really do need to know to be successful with all students—not just students who can learn easily on their own—are relevant to the dilemmas that teacher education programs find themselves in today. On one hand, many lay people and a large share of policymakers hold the view that almost anyone can teach reasonably well, that entering teaching requires, at most, knowing something about a subject and that the rest of the fairly simple "tricks of the trade" can be picked up on the job.

These notions—which derive both from a lack of understanding of what good teachers actually do behind the scenes and from tacit standards for teaching that are far too low—lead to pressures for backdoor routes into teaching that deny teacher candidates access to much of the knowledge base of teaching and the supervised clinical practice that would provide them with models of what good teachers do and how they understand their work. It is tragic that individuals who are likely to be seduced into teaching through pathways that minimize their access to knowledge are those who teach high-need students in low-income urban and rural schools where the most sophisticated understanding of teaching is needed.

On the other hand, the realities of what it takes to teach in U.S. schools such that all children truly have an opportunity to learn are nearly overwhelming. In the classrooms most beginning teachers will enter, at least 25%

of students live in poverty and many of them lack basic food, shelter, and health care; from 10% to 20% have identified learning differences; 15% speak a language other than English as their primary language (many more in urban settings); and about 40% are members of racial/ethnic "minority" groups, many of them recent immigrants from countries with different educational systems and cultural traditions.

Not only is the kind of practice needed to teach students with a wide range of learning needs an extremely complex, knowledge-intense undertaking—demanding of extraordinary personal and professional skills—but also U.S. schools rarely support this kind of practice. In contrast to schools in high-achieving European and Asian countries, American factory model schools offer fewer opportunities for teachers to come to know students well during long periods of time and much less time for teachers to spend working with one another to develop curriculum and plan lessons, observe and discuss teaching strategies, and assess student work in authentic ways. As the National Academy of Education Committee on Teacher Education observes, "Many analysts have noted that there is very little relationship between the organization of the typical American school and the demands of serious teaching and learning" (Darling-Hammond & Bransford, 2005, p. 4).

Thus, schools of education must design programs that help prospective teachers to understand deeply a wide array of things about learning, social and cultural contexts, and teaching and be able to enact these understandings in complex classrooms serving increasingly diverse students. In addition, if prospective teachers are to succeed at this task, schools of education must design programs that transform the kinds of settings in which novices learn to teach and later become teachers. This means that the enterprise of teacher education must venture out further and further from the university and engage ever more closely with schools in a mutual transformation agenda, with all of the struggle and messiness that implies. It also means that teacher educators must take up the charge of educating policymakers and the public about what it actually takes to teach effectively in today's world—both in terms of the knowledge and skills that are needed and in terms of the school contexts that must be created to allow teachers to develop and use what they know on behalf of students (Fullan, 1993).

Strides were made on both of these agendas in the late 1980s when the Holmes Group (1986, 1990) issued the first of its reports, the Carnegie Forum on Education and the Economy Task Force on Teaching as a Profession (1986) outlined a major agenda for professionalizing teaching, and the National Network for Educational Renewal was launched (Goodlad, 1990,

1994). Many important reforms of teacher education that have since taken place owe much of the impetus to these initiatives. These have strengthened both the subject matter and pedagogical preparation teachers receive (and the content pedagogical preparation that joins the two), introduced professional development school (PDS) partnerships that have sometimes changed the nature of schooling along with training for teaching, and created signature pedagogies and more authentic assessments for teacher education that link theory and practice and are beginning to change the ways in which teachers are taught.

However, in recent years, under pressure from opponents of teacher education and with incentives for faster, cheaper alternatives (see, e.g., U.S. Department of Education, 2002), teacher education as an enterprise has probably launched more new weak programs that underprepare teachers, especially for urban schools, than it has further developed the stronger models that demonstrate what intense preparation can accomplish. As a result, beginning teacher attrition has continued to increase (National Commission on Teaching and America's Future, 2003), and the teaching force is becoming increasingly bimodal. Although some teachers are better prepared than they ever were before, a growing number who serve the most vulnerable students enter teaching before they have been prepared to teach and are increasingly ill prepared for what they must accomplish (Darling-Hammond & Sykes, 2003). In addition, teacher educators seem to have lost their voice in arguing for—and helping to shape—the kinds of schools and education that will allow teachers to practice well and children to learn and thrive.

Thus, I argue that teacher educators, as a professional collective, need to work more intently to build on what has been learned about developing stronger models of teacher preparation—including the much stronger relationships with schools that press for mutual transformations of teaching and learning to teach—while resisting the pressures and incentives that lead to the creation of weaker models that ultimately reinforce dissatisfaction with the outcomes of teacher education and undermine the educational system.

Building Strong Models of Preparation

Although reform initiatives have triggered much discussion about the structures of teacher education programs (e.g., 4 year or 5 year, undergraduate or graduate) and the certification categories into which programs presumably fit (e.g., "traditional" or "alternative"), there has been less discussion about what goes on within the black box of the program—inside the courses and clinical experiences that candidates encounter—and about how the experiences programs design for candidates cumulatively add up to a set of knowledge, skills, and dispositions that determine what teachers actually do in the classroom.

Knowledge for Teaching: The "What" of Teacher Education

There are many ways of configuring the knowledge that teachers may need. In articulating the core concepts and skills that should be represented in a common curriculum for teacher education, the National Academy of Education Committee on Teacher Education adopted a framework that is organized on three intersecting areas of knowledge found in many statements of standards for teaching (see Figure 1):

- Knowledge of learners and how they learn and develop within social contexts, including knowledge of language development
- Understanding of curriculum content and goals, including the subject matter and skills to be taught in light of disciplinary demands, student needs, and the social purposes of education
- Understanding of and skills for teaching, including content pedagogical knowledge and knowledge for teaching diverse learners because these are informed by an understanding of assessment and of how to construct and manage a productive classroom

These interactions between learners, content, and teaching are framed by two important conditions for practice: First is the fact that teaching is a profession with certain moral and technical expectations—especially the expectation that teachers, working collaboratively, will acquire, use, and continue to develop shared knowledge on behalf of students. Second is the fact that, in the United States, education must serve the purposes of a democracy. This latter condition means that teachers assume the purpose of enabling young people to participate fully in political, civic, and economic life in our society. It also means that education—including teaching—is intended to support equitable access to what that society has to offer.

The implications of this framework for teacher education are several: First, like the work of other professions, teaching is in the service of students, which creates the expectation that teachers will be able to come to understand how students learn and what various students need if they are to learn more effectively and that they will incorporate this into their teaching and

FIGURE 1
A Framework for Understanding Teaching and Learning

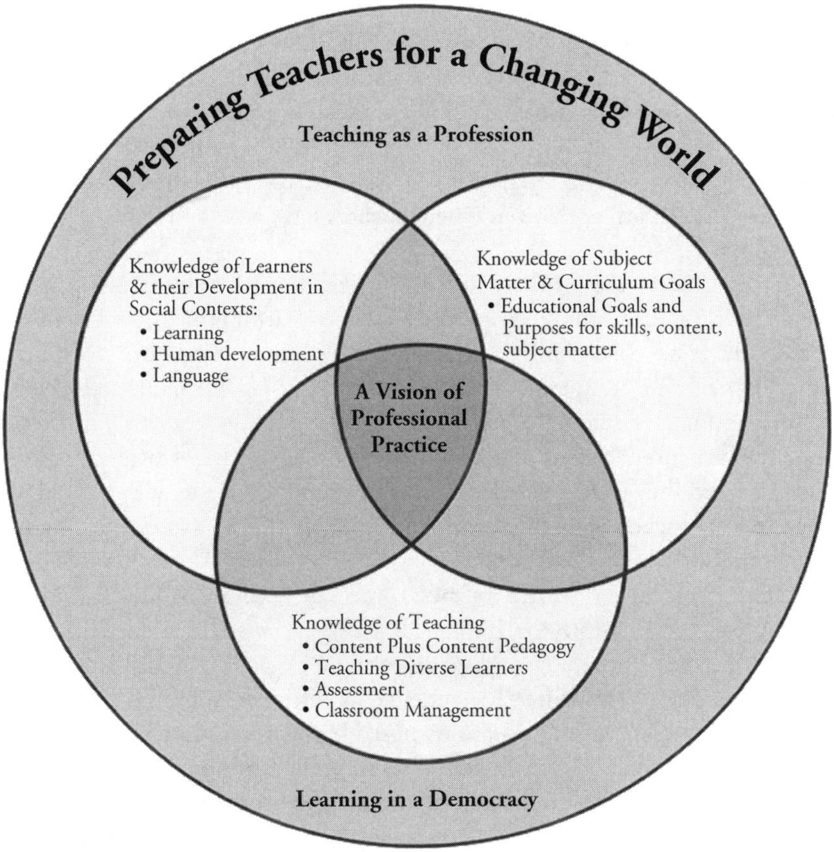

Preparing Teachers for a Changing World

Teaching as a Profession

Knowledge of Learners
& their Development in
Social Contexts:
• Learning
• Human development
• Language

Knowledge of Subject
Matter & Curriculum Goals
• Educational Goals and
  Purposes for skills, content,
  subject matter

A Vision of
Professional
Practice

Knowledge of Teaching
• Content Plus Content Pedagogy
• Teaching Diverse Learners
• Assessment
• Classroom Management

Learning in a Democracy

Source: Darling-Hammond & Bransford (2005, p. 11).

curriculum construction. Deep understanding of learning and learning differences as the basis of constructing curriculum has not historically been a
central part of teacher education. These domains were typically reserved for
psychologists and curriculum developers who were expected to use this
knowledge to develop tests and texts, whereas teachers learned teaching strategies to implement curriculum that was presumably designed by others. In
some ways, this approach to training teachers was rather like training doctors
in the techniques of surgery without giving them a thorough knowledge of

anatomy and physiology. Without knowing deeply how people learn, and how different people learn differently, teachers lack the foundation that can help them figure out what to do when a given technique or text is not effective with all students. And teachers cannot achieve ambitious goals by barreling from one lesson to the next without understanding how to construct a purposeful curriculum. This requires incorporating subject matter goals, knowledge of learning, and an appreciation for children's development and needs. Connecting what is to be learned to the learners themselves requires curriculum work, even when teachers have access to a range of texts and materials.

Furthermore, the work of teaching, like that of other professions, is viewed as nonroutine and reciprocally related to learning; that is, what teachers do must be continually evaluated and reshaped based on whether it advances learning, rather than carried out largely by curriculum packages, scripts, and pacing schedules as many districts currently require. This means that teachers need highly refined knowledge and skills for assessing pupil learning, and they need a wide repertoire of practice—along with the knowledge to know when to use different strategies for different purposes. Rather than being subject to the pendulum swings of polarized teaching policies that rest on simplistic ideas of best practice—"whole language" versus "phonics," for example, or inquiry learning versus direct instruction—teachers need to know how and when to use a range of practices to accomplish their goals with different students in different contexts. And given the wide range of learning situations posed by contemporary students, who represent many distinct language, cultural, and learning approaches, more than ever before teachers need a much deeper knowledge base about teaching diverse learners and more highly developed diagnostic abilities to guide their decisions.

Finally, teachers must be able continually to learn to address the problems of practice they encounter and to meet the unpredictable learning needs of all of their students—and they must take responsibility for contributing what they learn not only to their own practice but also that of their colleagues. This means that programs must help teachers develop the disposition to continue to seek answers to difficult problems of teaching and learning and the skills to learn from practice (and from their colleagues) as well as to learn for practice.

These expectations for teacher knowledge mean that programs need to provide teachers access to more knowledge, considered more deeply, and help teachers learn how to continually access knowledge and inquire into their work. The skills of classroom inquiry include careful observation and reasoned analysis, as well as dispositions toward an open and searching mind and a sense of responsibility and commitment to children's learning (Zeichner & Liston, 1996). Preparing teachers as classroom researchers and expert collaborators who can learn from one another is essential when the range of knowledge for teaching has grown so expansive that it cannot be mastered by any individual and when students' infinitely diverse ways of learning are recognized as requiring continual adaptations in teaching.

Program Designs and Pedagogies: The "How" of Teacher Education

Although it is important to have well-chosen courses that include core knowledge for teaching, it is equally important to organize prospective teachers' experiences so that they can integrate and use their knowledge in skillful ways in the classroom. This is probably the most difficult aspect of constructing a teacher education program. Teacher educators must worry about not only what to teach but also how so that knowledge for teaching actually shapes teachers' practice and enables them to become adaptive experts who can continue to learn.

Accomplishing this requires addressing some special—and perennial—challenges in learning to teach. Three in particular stand out. First, learning to teach requires that new teachers come to understand teaching in ways quite different from their own experience as students. Dan Lortie (1975) calls this problem "the apprenticeship of observation," referring to the learning that takes place by virtue of being a student for 12 or more years in traditional classroom settings. Second, learning to teach also requires that new teachers learn to "think like a teacher" and "act as a teacher"—what Mary Kennedy (1999) terms "the problem of enactment." Teachers need to understand and do a wide variety of things, many of them simultaneously. Finally, learning to teach requires that new teachers be able to understand and respond to the dense and multifaceted nature of the classroom, juggling multiple academic and social goals requiring trade-offs from moment to moment and day to day (Jackson, 1974). They must learn to deal with "the problem of complexity" that is made more intense by the constantly changing nature of teaching and learning in groups.

How can programs of teacher preparation confront these and other problems of learning to teach? A study examining seven exemplary teacher education programs, public and private, undergraduate and graduate, large and small, that produce graduates who are extraordinarily well prepared from their first days in the classroom finds that despite outward differences, the programs had common features, including the following:

- A common, clear vision of good teaching that permeates all coursework and clinical experiences, creating a coherent set of learning experiences
- Well-defined standards of professional practice and performance that are used to guide and evaluate coursework and clinical work
- A strong core curriculum taught in the context of practice and grounded in knowledge of child and adolescent development and learning, an understanding of social and cultural contexts, curriculum, assessment, and subject matter pedagogy
- Extended clinical experiences—at least 30 weeks of supervised practicum and student teaching opportunities in each program—that are carefully chosen to support the ideas presented in simultaneous, closely interwoven coursework
- Extensive use of case methods, teacher research, performance assessments, and portfolio evaluation that apply learning to real problems of practice
- Explicit strategies to help students confront their own deep-seated beliefs and assumptions about learning and students and to learn about the experiences of people different from themselves
- Strong relationships, common knowledge, and shared beliefs among school- and university-based faculty jointly engaged in transforming teaching, schooling, and teacher education (Darling-Hammond, in press)

These features confront many of the core dilemmas of teacher education: the strong influence of the apprenticeship of observation candidates bring with them from their years as students in elementary and secondary schools, the presumed divide between theory and practice, the limited personal and cultural perspectives all individuals bring to the task of teaching, and the difficult process of helping people learn to enact their intentions in complex settings. They help produce novice teachers who are able, from their first days in the classroom, to practice like many seasoned veterans, productively organizing classrooms that teach challenging content to very diverse learners with levels of skill many teachers never attain.

In addition to the deeper knowledge base I have described, such power-ful teacher education, I believe, rests on certain critically important pedagog-ical cornerstones that have been difficult to attain in many programs since teacher education moved from normal schools into universities in the 1950s. I highlight three of these here because I think they are essential to achieving radically different outcomes from preparation programs.

Coherence and Integration

The first cornerstone is a tight coherence and integration among courses and between coursework and clinical work in schools that challenges traditional program organizations, staffing, and modes of operation. The extremely strong coherence extraordinary programs have achieved creates an almost seamless experience of learning to teach. In contrast to the many critiques that have highlighted the structural and conceptual fragmentation of tradi-tional undergraduate teacher education programs (see, e.g., Goodlad, Soder, & Sirotnik, 1990; Howey & Zimpher, 1989; Zeichner & Gore, 1990), coursework in highly successful programs is carefully sequenced based on a strong theory of learning to teach; courses are designed to intersect with each other, are aggregated into a well-understood landscape of learning, and are tightly interwoven with the advisement process and students' work in schools. Subject matter learning is brought together with content pedagogy through courses that treat them together; program sequences also create cross-course links. Faculty plan together and syllabi are shared across univer-sity divisions as well as within departments. Virtually all of the closely inter-related courses involve applications in classrooms where observations or student teaching occur. These classrooms, in turn, are selected because they model the kind of practice that is discussed in courses and advisement. In some particularly powerful programs, faculty who teach courses also super-vise and advise teacher candidates and sometimes even teach children and teachers in placement schools, bringing together these disparate program elements through an integration of roles.

In such intensely coherent programs, core ideas are reiterated across courses and the theoretical frameworks animating courses and assignments are consistent across the program. These frameworks "explicate, justify, and build consensus on such fundamental conceptions as the role of the teacher, the nature of teaching and learning, and the mission of the school in this democracy," enabling "shared faculty leadership by underscoring collective roles as well as individual course responsibilities" (Howey & Zimpher, 1989, p. 242).

Programs that are largely a collection of unrelated courses without a common conception of teaching and learning have been found to be relatively feeble change agents for affecting practice among new teachers (Zeichner & Gore, 1990). Cognitive science affirms that people learn more effectively when ideas are reinforced and connected both in theory and in practice. Although this seems obvious, creating coherence has been difficult in teacher education because of departmental divides, individualistic norms, and the hiring of part-time adjunct instructors in some institutions that have used teacher education as a "cash cow" rather than an investment in our nation's future. Fortunately, a number of studies of teacher education reform document how programs have overcome the centrifugal forces that leave candidates on their own to make sense of disparate, unconnected experiences (Howey & Zimpher, 1989; Patterson, Michelli, & Pacheco, 1999; Tatto, 1996; Wideen, Mayer-Smith, & Moon, 1998).

Extensive, Well-Supervised Clinical Experience Linked to Coursework Using Pedagogies That Link Theory and Practice

The second critically important feature that requires a wrenching change from traditional models of teacher education is the importance of extensive and intensely supervised clinical work—tightly integrated with coursework—that allows candidates to learn from expert practice in schools that serve diverse students. All of the adjectives in the previous sentence matter: *Extensive* clinical work, *intensive* supervision, *expert* modeling of practice, and *diverse* students are critical to allowing candidates to learn to practice in practice with students who call for serious teaching skills (Ball & Cohen, 1999). Securing these features will take radical overhaul of the status quo. Furthermore, to be most powerful, this work needs to incorporate newly emerging pedagogies such as close analyses of learning and teaching, case methods, performance assessments, and action research that link theory and practice in ways that theorize practice and make formal learning practical.

One of the perennial dilemmas of teacher education is how to integrate theoretically based knowledge that has traditionally been taught in university classrooms with the experience-based knowledge that has traditionally been located in the practice of teachers and the realities of classrooms and schools. Traditional versions of teacher education have often had students taking batches of front-loaded coursework in isolation from practice and then adding a short dollop of student teaching near the end of the program, often in classrooms that did not model the practices that had previously been described in abstraction. By contrast, the most powerful programs require students to spend extensive time in the field throughout the entire program, examining and applying the concepts and strategies they are simultaneously learning about in their courses alongside teachers who can show them how to teach in ways that are responsive to learners.

Such programs typically require at least a full academic year of student teaching under the direct supervision of one or more teachers who model expert practice with students who have a wide range of learning needs, with the candidate gradually assuming more independent responsibility for teaching. This allows prospective teachers to grow "roots" on their practice, which is especially important if they are going to learn to teach in learner-centered ways that require diagnosis, intensive assessment and planning to adapt to learners' needs, and a complex repertoire of practices judiciously applied.

Many teacher educators have argued that novices who have experience in classrooms are more prepared to make sense of the ideas that are addressed in their academic work and that student teachers see and understand both theory and practice differently if they are taking coursework concurrently with fieldwork. A growing body of research confirms this belief, finding that teachers-in-training who participate in fieldwork with coursework are better able to understand theory, to apply concepts they are learning in their coursework, and to support student learning (Baumgartner, Koerner, & Rust, 2002; Denton, 1982; Henry, 1983; Ross, Hughes, & Hill, 1981; Sunal, 1980).

It is not just the availability of classroom experience that enables teachers to apply what they are learning, however. Recent studies of learning to teach suggest that immersing teachers in the materials of practice and working on particular concepts using these materials can be particularly powerful for teachers' learning. Analyzing samples of student work, teachers' plans and assignments, videotapes of teachers and students in action, and cases of teaching and learning can help teachers draw connections between generalized principles and specific instances of teaching and learning (Ball & Cohen, 1999; Hammerness, Darling-Hammond, & Shulman, 2002; Lampert & Ball, 1998).

It is worth noting that many professions, including law, medicine, psychology, and business, help candidates bridge the gap between theory and practice—and develop skills of reflection and close analysis—by engaging them in the reading and writing of cases. Many highly successful teacher education programs require candidates to develop case studies on students, on aspects of schools and teaching, and on families or communities by observing, interviewing, examining student work, and analyzing data they have collected. Proponents argue that cases support both systematic learning from particular contexts as well as from more generalized theory about teaching and learning. Shulman (1996) suggests that cases are powerful tools for professional learning because they require professionals in training to

> move up and down, back and forth, between the memorable particularities of cases and the powerful generalizations and simplifications of principles and theories. Principles are powerful but cases are memorable. Only in the continued interaction between principles and cases can practitioners and their mentors avoid the inherent limitations of theory-without-practice or the equally serious restrictions of vivid practice without the mirror of principle. (p. 201)

These benefits of connecting profession-wide knowledge to unique contexts can also be gained by the skillful use of tools such as portfolios, teachers' classroom inquiries and research, and analyses of specific classrooms, teachers, or teaching situations when teacher educators provide thoughtful readings, guidance, and feedback.

Although it is helpful to experience classrooms and analyze the materials and practices of teaching, it is quite another thing to put ideals into action. Often, the clinical side of teacher education has been fairly haphazard, depending on the idiosyncrasies of loosely selected placements with little guidance about what happens in them and little connection to university work. And university work has often been "too theoretical"—meaning abstract and general—in ways that leave teachers bereft of specific tools to use in the classroom. The theoretically grounded tools teachers need are many, ranging from knowledge of curriculum materials and assessment strategies to techniques for organizing group work and planning student inquiries, and teachers need opportunities to practice with these tools systematically (Grossman, Smagorinsky, & Valencia, 1999).

Powerful teacher education programs have a clinical curriculum as well as a didactic curriculum. They teach candidates to turn analysis into action by applying what they are learning in curriculum plans, teaching applications, and other performance assessments that are organized on professional teaching standards. These attempts are especially educative when they are followed by systematic reflection on student learning in relation to teaching and receive detailed feedback, with opportunities to retry and improve. Furthermore, recent research suggests that to be most productive, these opportunities for analysis, application, and reflection should derive from and connect to both the subject matter and the students candidates teach (Ball & Bass, 2000; Grossman & Stodolsky, 1995; Shulman, 1987). In this way, prospective teachers learn the fine-grained stuff of practice in connection to the practical theories that will allow them to adapt their practice in a well-grounded fashion, innovating and improvising to meet the specific classroom contexts they later encounter.

New Relationships With Schools

Finally, these kinds of strategies for connecting theory and practice cannot succeed without a major overhaul of the relationships between universities and schools that ultimately produces changes in the content of schooling as well as teacher training. It is impossible to teach people how to teach powerfully by asking them to imagine what they have never seen or to suggest they "do the opposite" of what they have observed in the classroom. No amount of coursework can, by itself, counteract the powerful experiential lessons that shape what teachers actually do. It is impractical to expect to prepare teachers for schools as they should be if teachers are constrained to learn in settings that typify the problems of schools as they have been—where isolated teachers provide examples of idiosyncratic, usually theoretically based practice that rarely exhibits a diagnostic, assessment-oriented approach and infrequently offers access to carefully selected strategies designed to teach a wide range of learners well.

These settings simply do not exist in large numbers, and where individual teachers have created classroom oases, there have been few long-lasting reforms to leverage transformations in whole schools. Some very effective partnerships, however, have helped to create school environments for teaching and teacher training through PDSs, lab schools, and school reform networks that are such strong models of practice and collaboration that the environment itself serves as a learning experience for teachers (Darling-Hammond, in press; Trachtman, 1996). In such schools, teachers are immersed in strong and widely shared cultural norms and practices and can leverage them for greater effect through professional studies offering research, theory, and information about other practices and models. Such schools also support advances in knowledge by serving as sites where practice-based and practice-sensitive research can be carried out collaboratively by teachers, teacher educators, and researchers.

In highly developed PDS models, curriculum reforms and other improvement initiatives are supported by the school and often the district; school teams involving both university and school educators work on such tasks as curriculum development, school reform, and action research; university faculty are typically involved in teaching courses and organizing professional development at the school site and may also be involved in teaching children; and school-based faculty often teach in the teacher education program. Most classrooms are sites for practica and student teaching placements, and cooperating teachers are trained to become teacher educators, often holding meetings regularly to develop their mentoring skills. Candidates learn in all parts of the school, not just individual classrooms; they receive more frequent and sustained supervision and feedback and participate in more collective planning and decision making among teachers at the school (Abdal-Haqq, 1998, pp. 13–14; Darling-Hammond, 2005; Trachtman, 1996).

Some universities have sought to create PDS relationships in schools that are working explicitly on an equity agenda, either in new schools designed to provide more equitable access to high-quality curriculum for diverse learners or in schools where faculty are actively confronting issues of tracking, poor teaching, inadequate or fragmented curriculum, and unresponsive systems (see, e.g., Darling-Hammond, in press; Guadarrama, Ramsey, & Nath, 2002). In these schools, student teachers or interns are encouraged to participate in all aspects of school functioning, ranging from special education and support services for students to parent meetings, home visits, and community outreach to faculty discussions and projects aimed at ongoing improvement. This kind of participation helps prospective teachers understand the broader institutional context for teaching and learning and begin to develop the skills needed for effective participation in collegial work concerning school improvement throughout their careers.

Developing sites where state-of-the-art practice is the norm is a critical element of strong teacher education, and it has been one of most difficult. Quite often, if novices are to see and emulate high-quality practice, especially in schools serving the neediest students, it is necessary not only to seek out individual cooperating teachers but also to develop the quality of the schools so that prospective teachers can learn productively. Such school development is also needed to create settings where advances in knowledge and practice can occur. Seeking diversity by placing candidates in schools serving low-income students or students of color that suffer from the typical shortcomings many such schools face can actually be counterproductive. As Gallego (2001) notes,

Though teacher education students may be placed in schools with large, culturally diverse student populations, many of these schools . . . do not provide the kind of contact with communities needed to overcome negative attitudes toward culturally different students and their families and communities. . . . Indeed, without connections between the classroom, school, and local communities, classroom field experiences may work to strengthen pre-service teachers' stereotypes of children, rather than stimulate their examination . . . , and ultimately compromise teachers' effectiveness in the classroom. . . . (p. 314)

Thus, working to create PDSs that construct state-of-the-art practice in communities where students are typically underserved by schools helps transform the eventual teaching pool for such schools and students. In this way, PDSs develop school practice as well as the individual practice of new teacher candidates. Such PDSs simultaneously restructure school programs and teacher education programs, redefining teaching and learning for all members of the profession and the school community.

Although not all of the more than 1000 school partnerships (Abdal-Haqq, 1998) created in the name of PDS work have been successful, there is growing evidence of the power of this approach. Studies of highly developed PDSs suggest that teachers who graduate from such programs feel more knowledgeable and prepared to teach and are rated by employers, supervisors, and researchers as better prepared than other new teachers. Veteran teachers working in highly developed PDSs describe changes in their own practice and improvements at the classroom and school levels as a result of the professional development, action research, and mentoring that are part of the PDS. Some studies document gains in student performance tied to curriculum and teaching interventions resulting from PDS initiatives (for a summary, see Darling-Hammond & Bransford, 2005, pp. 415–416).

Although research has also demonstrated how difficult these partnerships are to enact, many schools of education are moving toward preparing all of their prospective teachers in such settings both because they can more systematically prepare prospective teachers to learn to teach in professional learning communities and because such work is a key to changing schools so that they become more productive environments for the learning of all students and teachers.

Resisting Pressures to Water Down Preparation

Although heroic work is going on to transform teacher education and a growing number of powerful programs are being created, more than 30 states continue to allow teachers to enter teaching on emergency permits or waivers with little or no teacher education at all. In addition, more than 40 states have created alternative pathways to teaching—some of which are high-quality post-baccalaureate routes and others of which are truncated programs that short-circuit essential elements of teacher learning. Many candidates who enter through emergency or alternative routes do not meet even minimal standards when they start teaching, and researchers have found that pressures to get them certified in states where thousands are hired annually can undermine the quality of preparation they ultimately receive. In some states, such as California and Texas, unlicensed entrants have numbered in the tens of thousands annually, hired to teach to the least advantaged students in low-income and minority schools. Even when these candidates are required to make some progress toward a license each year by taking courses for teaching while they teach, the quality of preparation they receive is undermined (Shields et al., 2001).

Institutions that train these emergency hires cannot offer the kinds of tightly integrated programs described here in which candidates study concepts and implement them with guidance in supported clinical settings. They are forced to offer fragmented courses on nights and weekends to candidates who may never have seen good teaching and who have little support in the schools where they work. The part-time instructors who are often hired to teach these courses are not part of a faculty-wide conversation about preparation, and neither do they have a sense of a coherent program into which their efforts might fit.

When these candidates work full-time, colleges often water down their training to minimize readings and homework and focus on survival needs such as classroom discipline rather than curriculum and teaching methods. Candidates often demand attention to classroom management, without realizing that their lack of knowledge of curriculum and instruction cause many of the classroom difficulties they face (Shields et al., 2001). When they skip student teaching, colleges cannot weave good models of teaching into courses that would connect theory and practice, and candidates can only imagine what successful practice might look like.

Studies observe that both recruits and employers typically find the outcomes of this kind of training less satisfactory than those of a more coherent experience that includes supervised clinical training along with more thoughtfully organized coursework (California State University, 2002; Shields et al., 2001), and many programs that try to train candidates while they teach have had extremely high attrition rates (Darling-Hammond,

2001). If medical schools were asked to develop programs for already practicing doctors or nurses that would eliminate or truncate some courses and skip clinical rotations and the internship entirely, they would refuse to do so. However, universities participate in this kind of training for teachers for many reasons:

- They feel an obligation to help teachers who have found their way into the classroom without proper training.
- They are required to do so by laws governing state-funded programs or encouraged to do so by federal, state, or local incentives to construct alternative pathways that train teachers while they teach.
- They believe, like many policymakers, that this is the only way to meet persistent supply problems, especially in poor urban and rural districts.
- Such recruits are a source of money and may absorb little in the way of services for the tuition they pay.

In states where large numbers of individuals enter teaching in this way, most programs are pressured to bend to this mode of entry, gradually eroding the quality of stronger programs that have been developed. Programs experience pressures to reduce the amount of time devoted to preparing teachers, to admit candidates on emergency licenses who then require a fragmented program without student teaching, and to short-circuit clinical requirements that would allow candidates to learn to practice under supervision.

The irony is that when institutions are complicit in cobbling together weak programs, even when they do so for the most helpful reasons—and when they do not speak out against emergency hiring—the teacher education enterprise as a whole is blamed for any and all teachers who are ill prepared, including those who entered teaching without preparation.

Few realize that rapidly producing poorly prepared teachers for this system is a major part of the problem rather than a solution. The current practice is like pouring water into a bucket with a gaping hole at the bottom. Aside from true shortage fields such as mathematics and physical science, the nation actually produces more newly credentialed teachers each year than it hires. Most of the real problems that appear as shortages have to do with teacher distribution and retention, not production. In addition to unequal funding and salary schedules that hamper poor urban and rural districts, many districts that hire underprepared teachers have cumbersome and dysfunctional hiring systems or prioritize the hiring of unqualified teachers because such teachers cost less than qualified teachers who have applied (Darling-Hammond & Sykes, 2003).

In these districts, teacher turnover is even higher than the already high rate elsewhere. Nationally, about one third of beginning teachers leave within 5 years, and the proportions are higher for teachers who enter with less preparation. For example, teachers who receive student teaching are twice as likely to stay in teaching after a year, and those who receive the kinds of preparation that include learning theory and child development are even more likely to stay in teaching (Henke, Chen, & Geis, 2000; Luczak, 2004; National Commission on Teaching and America's Future, 2003). The costs of this teacher attrition are enormous. One recent study estimates that depending on the cost model used, districts spend between US$8,000 and US$48,000 in costs for hiring, placement, induction, separation, and replacement for each beginning teacher who leaves (Benner, 2000). On a national scale, it is clear that teacher attrition costs billions annually that could more productively be spent on preparing teachers and supporting them in the classroom.

A number of states and districts have filled all of their classrooms with qualified teachers by streamlining hiring, investing in stronger teacher preparation and induction, and equalizing salaries (Darling-Hammond & Sykes, 2003). They have ended the practice of hiring unqualified teachers by increasing incentives to teach rather than lowering standards. As Gideonse (1993) notes in an analysis of teacher education policy:

> As long as school systems are permitted to hire under-prepared teachers through the mechanism of emergency certificates and their equivalent, teacher preparation institutions and the faculty in them will have reduced incentives to maintain standards by preventing the advancement of the marginally qualified to licensure. All the hype in the world about raised standards and performance-based licensure is meaningless absent a real incentive working on school districts to recruit the qualified through salary and improved conditions of practice, rather than being allowed to redefine the available as qualified. (p. 404)

Whereas many countries fully subsidize an extensive program of teacher education for all candidates, the amount of preparation secured by teachers in the United States is left substantially to what they can individually afford and what programs are willing and able to offer given the resources of their respective institutions. Although many U.S. institutions are intensifying their programs to prepare more effective teachers, they lack the systemic policy supports for candidate subsidies and programmatic funding that their counterparts in other countries enjoy. And in states that have not developed induction supports, programs are continually called on to increase the production of new recruits who are then squandered when they land in an unsupportive system that treats them as utterly dispensable.

In every occupation that has become a profession during the 20th century, the strengthening of preparation was tied to a resolve to end the practice of allowing untrained individuals to practice. Teaching is currently where medicine was in 1910, when doctors could be trained in programs ranging from 3 weeks of training featuring memorizing lists of symptoms and cures to Johns Hopkins University graduate school preparation in the sciences of medicine and in clinical practice in the newly invented teaching hospital.

In his introduction to the Flexner Report, Henry Pritchett (Flexner & Pritchett, 1910), president of the Carnegie Foundation for the Advancement of Teaching, noted that although there was a growing science of medicine, most doctors did not gain access to this knowledge because of the great unevenness in the medical training they received. Pritchett observed that

> very seldom, under existing conditions, does a patient receive the best aid which it is possible to give him in the present state of medicine, . . . [because] a vast army of men is admitted to the practice of medicine who are untrained in sciences fundamental to the profession and quite without a sufficient experience with disease. (p. x)

He attributes this problem to the failure of many universities to incorporate advances in medical education into their curricula.

As in teaching today, there were those who argued against the professionalization of medicine and who felt that medical practice could best be learned by following another doctor around in a buggy. Medical education was transformed as the stronger programs Flexner (Flexner & Pritchett, 1910) identified became the model incorporated by accrediting bodies and as all candidates were required to complete such programs to practice. In a similar manner, improving teaching and teacher education in the United States depends on strengthening individual programs and addressing the policies needed to strengthen the teacher education enterprise as a whole.

Although teacher education is only one component of what is needed to enable high-quality teaching, it is essential to the success of all the other reforms urged on schools. To advance knowledge about teaching, to spread good practice, and to enhance equity for children, thus it is essential that teacher educators and policymakers seek strong preparation for teachers that is universally available rather than a rare occurrence that is available only to a lucky few.

Notes

1. The National Academy of Education Committee members included James Banks, Joan Baratz-Snowden, David Berliner, John Bransford, Marilyn Cochran-Smith, James Comer, Linda Darling- Hammond, Sharon Derry, Emily Feistritzer, Edmund Gordon, Pamela Grossman, Cris Gutierrez, Frances Degan Horowitz, Evelyn Jenkins-Gunn, Carol Lee, Lucy Matos, Luis Moll, Arturo Pacheco, Anna Richert, Kathy Rosebrock, Frances Rust, Alan Schoenfeld, Lorrie Shepard, Lee Shulman, Catherine Snow, Guadalupe Valdes, and Kenneth Zeichner.

References

Abdal-Haqq, I. (1998). *Professional development schools: Weighing the evidence.* Thousand Oaks, CA: Corwin Press.

Ball, D. L., & Bass, H. (2000). Interweaving content and pedagogy in teaching and learning to teach: Knowing and using mathematics. In J. Boaler (Ed.), *Multiple perspectives on the teaching and learning of mathematics* (pp. 83–104). Westport, CT: Ablex.

Ball, D. L., & Cohen, D. C. (1999). Development practice, developing practitioners: Toward a practice-based theory of professional education. In L. Darling-Hammond & G. Sykes (Eds.), *Teaching as the learning profession: Handbook of policy and practice* (pp. 3–32). San Francisco: Jossey-Bass.

Baumgartner, F., Koerner, M., & Rust, F. (2002). Exploring roles in student teaching placements. *Teacher Education Quarterly, 29,* 35–58.

Benner, A. D. (2000). *The cost of teacher turnover.* Austin: Texas Center for Educational Research.

California State University. (2002). *First system wide evaluation of teacher education programs in the California State University: Summary report.* Long Beach, CA: Office of the Chancellor.

Carnegie Forum on Education and the Economy Task Force on Teaching as a Profession. (1986). *A nation prepared: Teachers for the 21st century.* New York: Carnegie Foundation.

Darling-Hammond, L. (2001). The challenge of staffing our schools. *Educational Leadership, 58*(8), 12–17.

Darling-Hammond, L. (Ed.). (2005). *Professional development schools: Schools for developing a profession* (2nd ed.). New York: Teachers College Press.

Darling-Hammond, L. (in press). *Powerful teacher education: Lessons from exemplary programs.* San Francisco: Jossey-Bass.

Darling-Hammond, L., & Bransford, J. (with LePage, P., Hammerness, K., & Duffy, H.). (2005). *Preparing teachers for a changing world: What teachers should learn and be able to do.* San Francisco: Jossey-Bass.

Darling-Hammond, L., & Sykes, G. (2003). Wanted: A national teacher supply policy for education: The right way to meet the "highly qualified teacher" challenge. *Educational Policy Analysis Archives, 11*(33). Retrieved from http://epaa .asu.edu/epaa/v11n33/

Denton, J. J. (1982). Early field experience influence on performance in subsequent coursework. *Journal of Teacher Education, 33*(2), 19–23.

Flexner, A., & Pritchett, H. S. (1910). *Medical education in the United States and Canada: A report to the Carnegie Foundation for the Advancement of Teaching.* New York: Carnegie Foundation for the Advance of Teaching.

Fullan, M. (1993). Why teachers must become change agents. *Educational Leadership, 50*(6), 12–17.

Gallego, M. A. (2001). Is experience the best teacher? The potential of coupling classroom and community-based field experiences. *Journal of Teacher Education, 52*(4), 312–325.

Gideonse, H. (1993). The governance of teacher education and systemic reform. *Educational Policy, 7*(4), 395–426.

Goodlad, J. I. (1990). *Teachers for our nation's schools.* San Francisco: Jossey-Bass.

Goodlad, J. I. (1994). *Educational renewal: Better teachers, better schools.* San Francisco: Jossey-Bass.

Goodlad, J. I., Soder, R., & Sirotnik, K. A. (1990). *Places where teachers are taught.* San Francisco: Jossey-Bass.

Grossman, P. L., Smagorinsky, P., & Valencia, S. (1999). Appropriating tools for teaching English: A theoretical framework for research on learning to teach. *American Journal of Education, 108*(1), 1–29.

Grossman, P. L., & Stodolsky, S. S. (1995). Content as context: The role of school subjects in secondary school teaching. *Educational Researcher, 24*(8), 5–11, 23.

Guadarrama, I. N., Ramsey, J., & Nath, J. L. (Eds.). (2002). *Forging alliances in community and thought: Research in professional development schools.* Greenwich, CT: Information Age.

Hammerness, K., Darling-Hammond, L., & Shulman, L. (2002). Toward expert thinking: How case-writing contributes to the development of theory-based professional knowledge in student-teachers. *Teaching Education, 13*(2), 221–245.

Henke, R., Chen, X., & Geis, S. (2000). *Progress through the teacher pipeline: 1992–93 college graduates and elementary/secondary school teaching as of 1997.* Washington, DC: U.S. Department of Education, National Center for Education Statistics.

Henry, M. (1983). The effect of increased exploratory field experiences upon the perceptions and performance of student teachers. *Action in Teacher Education, 5*(1–2), 66–70.

Holmes Group. (1986). *Tomorrow's teachers: A report of the Holmes Group.* East Lansing, MI: Author.

Holmes Group. (1990). *Tomorrow's schools: Principles for the design of professional development schools: Executive summary.* East Lansing, MI: Author.

Howey, K. R., & Zimpher, N. L. (1989). *Profiles of preservice teacher education: Inquiry into the nature of programs.* Albany: State University of New York Press.

Jackson, P. W. (1974). *Life in classrooms.* New York: Holt, Rinehart & Winston.

Kennedy, M. (1999). The role of preservice teacher education. In L. Darling-Hammond & G. Sykes (Eds.), *Teaching as the learning profession: Handbook of policy and practice* (pp. 54–85). San Francisco: Jossey-Bass.

Lampert, M., & Ball, D. L. (1998). *Teaching, multimedia, and mathematics: Investigations of real practice.* New York: Teachers College Press.

Lortie, D. C. (1975). *Schoolteacher: A sociological study.* Chicago: University of Chicago Press.

Luczak, J. (2004). *Who will teach in the 21st century? Beginning teacher training experiences and attrition rates.* Unpublished doctoral dissertation, Stanford University, Stanford, CA.

National Commission on Teaching and America's Future. (2003). *No dream denied: A pledge to America's children.* Washington, DC: Author.

Patterson, R. S., Michelli, N. M., & Pacheco, A. (1999). *Centers of pedagogy: New structures for educational renewal.* San Francisco: Jossey-Bass.

Ross, S. M., Hughes, T. M., & Hill, R. E. (1981). Field experiences as meaningful contexts for learning about learning. *Journal of Educational Research, 75*(2), 103–107.

Shields, P. M., Humphrey, D. C., Wechsler, M. E., Riel, L. M., Tiffany-Morales, J., & Woodworth, K. et al. (2001). *The status of the teaching profession 2001.* Santa Cruz, CA: Center for the Future of Teaching and Learning.

Shulman, L. S. (1987). Knowledge and teaching: Foundations of the new reform. *Harvard Educational Review, 57*(1), 1–22.

Shulman, L. S. (1996). Just in case: Reflections on learning from experience. In K. T. J. Colbert, P. Desberg, & K. Trimble (Eds.), *The case for education: Contemporary approaches for using case methods* (pp. 197–217). Boston: Allyn & Bacon.

Sunal, D. W. (1980). Effect of field experience during elementary methods courses on preservice teacher behavior. *Journal of Research in Science Teaching, 17*(1), 17–23.

Tatto, M. T. (1996). Examining values and beliefs about teaching diverse students: Understanding the challenges for teacher education. *Educational Evaluation and Policy Analysis, 18*(2), 155–180.

Trachtman, R. (1996). *The NCATE professional development school study: A survey of 28 PDS sites.* Washington, DC: National Council for Accreditation of Teacher Education.

U.S. Department of Education. (2002, June). *Meeting the highly qualified teachers challenge: The secretary's annual report on teacher quality.* Washington, DC: Office of Postsecondary Education.

Wideen, M., Mayer-Smith, J., & Moon, B. (1998). A critical analysis of the research on learning to teach: Making the case for an ecological perspective on inquiry. *Review of Educational Research, 68*(2), 130–178.

Zeichner, K. M., & Gore, J. (1990). Teacher socialization. In W. R. Houston, M. Haberman, J. P. Sikula, & Association of Teacher Educators (Eds.), *Handbook of research on teacher education* (pp. 329–348). New York: Macmillan.

Zeichner, K. M., & Liston, D. P. (1996). *Reflective teaching: An introduction.* Mahwah, NJ: Lawrence Erlbaum.

THIS IS OUR MOMENT

Contemplating the Urgency of Now
for the Future of Teacher Education

Chance W. Lewis and Valerie Hill-Jackson

As the editors of this highly anticipated book, we are grateful that you have taken the time to utilize this resource to facilitate a new way of thinking about teacher education, which must be (re)envisioned, critically implemented, held accountable, and reconstructed to meet the needs of K–12 educators in the 21st-century classroom. As an addendum, we provide a few closing thoughts so that you can have a clearer understanding of the overarching thesis and importance of this book. To do so, we outline four significant historical moments in teacher education and liken them to the life cycle of a butterfly.

The First Moment of Teacher Education: 1872–Late 1940s

In the first stage of its life cycle, a butterfly actually starts out as an *egg*; like all new life, this is a period of enormous vulnerability. You may ask, "How does this align with teacher education?" Teacher education began amid a similar frailness of conception with the first teacher education program of 1872 to the new building of American institutions post World War II. This first stage is what we term the *invention* moment of teacher education when the infancy of teacher education was responsible for conceptualizing current ideologies and teacher practices.

Although the founders of teacher education had high hopes for the field, we must not forget that teacher education at its formation was visionless and was created on the foundation of sexism and intolerance in the new nation.

More specifically, teacher education began with a major emphasis on preparing teachers to educate children of the wealthy and social elite and was erected within a religious framework and situated in an agrarian school calendar. Teacher education was seen as a female profession where low salaries were the custom at the outset. Female teachers were paid very low wages for their labor and they had to stay on the land of their wealthy employers. If teachers were deemed "acceptable" over a certain time period, they could earn property rights on their jobs (tenure) to continue living on the land. However, these property rights were only earned at the pleasure of the employer if the teacher was "socially acceptable." Within this atmosphere of *invention*, the status quo ideology ensured that teacher education would maintain and reproduce such societal norms as individualism, capitalism, and efficiency.

If we examine the current status of teacher education, the impact of the *invention* stage is still evident. Today, teaching as a profession has not moved beyond this invented status of the undervalued, professional female babysitter. At the same time, children of color were never factored into the new post slavery / Jim Crow American educational system, so their educational fate would forever suffer from overt, then covert, neglect. The subsequent moment in teacher education would seal its flawed inception and purposes.

The Second Moment of Teacher Education: 1950–2000

Phase 2 of the life cycle of a butterfly is called the *larva* stage. Here, the larva (caterpillar) hatches from an egg and eats leaves or flowers almost constantly. The caterpillar molts (loses its old skin) many times as it grows. This is commonly known as a ravenous stage of the larva. The parallel to this stage in the field of teacher education is the time period of 1950 through the cusp of the 21st century, a voracious stage for the field of teacher education, outlined in the prologue as a moment of *change-ism* that was characterized by unfettered reform and research.

From 1950 through 2000, the field of teacher education underwent rapid changes resulting from post–World War II social change efforts, the Cold War, *Sputnik*, the civil rights movement, and the infamous *A Nation at Risk* report. All of these monumental events generated a period of *change-ism* that, in many ways, propelled the field of teacher education to reinforce its initially weak and socially defenseless goals and objectives. For example, *Sputnik* was a catalyst for the race into space and intellectual dominance.

Given this change in national priorities, teacher education suffered dramatic shifts (a political agenda emphasizing quantitative accountability results) that forced teacher education to shed its old skin many times as it continued to recycle ineffective change agendas. However, the *change-ism* moment never helped K–12 educators or underserved children experience full democracy in schools but forever influenced the future of teacher education initiatives in the United States.

The Third Moment of Teacher Education: 2001–Present

In the third stage of development, the caterpillar turns into a *pupa* (chrysalis). More specifically, this is the resting stage before the butterfly emerges. Inside the pupa, a staggering mutation occurs. Although the pupa appears to be lifeless, there is tremendous change occurring inside as the caterpillar is literally liquefied and then reassembled as a butterfly. Before emerging from its cocoon, the pupa dangles from a leaf in a state of suspended animation. As mere mortals, we find it hard to understand this process of metamorphosis; but suffice it to say, it is one of nature's miracles. For the field of teacher education, this era of quiet *reflection* takes place from 2001 to the present writing of this book. This juncture represents an age of serious innovation and introspection about old habits in teacher education that have impeded our transformation, but there is a looming critical silence in the field.

Not a coincidence, this volume signifies a contemplative and restorative moment in teacher education: the nexus of old ideologies and reconceptualized ways in the art and science of teacher education. Analogous to the resting stage of a pupa, the *reflection* moment is a time of articulation in teacher education. We must liquefy or dissolve old formulas in teacher education so that we might surface anew and authentically improve the way we prepare teachers for the future. The question then becomes, Do we have the courage and scholarly fortitude to undergo metamorphosis during this defining moment so that we can take the decisive and transformative next steps for the future of teacher education?

The Fourth Moment of Teacher Education: The Transformed Future

The fourth and final stage in the life cycle of the butterfly is to become an adult. At this stage, a beautiful, fully formed, and mature butterfly breaks free of its shelter. The butterfly is truly magnificent because it represents triumph, completion, and imagination. So, what does this mean for teacher education? In the spirit of reinvention, a fulfilled and didactic metamorphosis is our ultimate goal for the *transformation* of teacher education. We envision successful, far-reaching, and productive teacher preparation programs that have a trickle-down effect: Powerful programs engender quality teachers, who affect underserved children. The moment of transformation, although it represents a promising future, is a place of comprehensiveness in teacher education—the product of an educational metamorphosis that mere mortals, with the audacity to lead, can create.

Contemplating Transformative Possibilities

As a profession, we know what we are currently doing is not working for the most important stakeholders: teachers and students in our nation's schools. This book is a wake-up call for our field to use this moment in history to reinvent ourselves. We have endeavored to produce a blueprint for transformative teacher education that attends to the underserved, the canaries in the educational mineshaft. If we focus on the least among our learners, we can effectively serve all of America's learners; truly this is teacher education *for* the 21st century. The authors of the various chapters in this edited work have shown us the way.

The four historical moments we share in this epilogue explore the lineage of teacher education, including *invention, change-ism, reflection,* and *transformation.* In support of 21st-century teachers and underserved learners, let us forge boldly ahead proclaiming, *"This Is Our Moment!"* The future of teacher education depends on now, this moment of *reflection,* a watershed for transformative possibilities.

CONTRIBUTORS

Valerie Hill-Jackson is a clinical associate professor in the Department of Teaching, Learning, and Culture at Texas A&M University (TAMU) in College Station, Texas, where she teaches critical multicultural education, community education, and curriculum studies. Dr. Hill-Jackson's research interests are passionately located in improving educational experiences for all of America's children through transformative adult and community education. Prior to arriving at TAMU, Dr. Hill-Jackson worked as a principal investigator and director of a TRIO program, curriculum designer, department chair, and science teacher in two urban school districts.

Dr. Hill-Jackson's educational philosophy is *every child, every opportunity*. She believes that the institution of education should never compromise when it comes to educating its most vulnerable citizens. As the 11th child of 12, the first and only child in the family to go to college, with parents who were illiterate migrant workers, she has discovered that education is the great equalizer. She is committed to education because she knows that few school districts have provided meaningful learning experiences in underserved communities—for learners and their families.

Dr. Hill-Jackson is a 2001–2002 AERA/Spencer fellow and received the national LEAD (poisoning) STAR award for her research on parents and childhood lead poisoning in urban communities. She is also a Geraldine R. Dodge fellow for outstanding teaching. Additionally, Dr. Hill-Jackson received the C.O.E *Distinguished Educator of the Year* award; the 2007 Time Inc./People Magazine/Maybelline *Women Who Empower Through Education* award; the TAMU 2008 ASF Award for Distinguished Teaching; and 2010 TAMU Teacher Excellence Award. She is on the editorial review board of two national journals and is a member of the Association of Teacher Education's (ATE) Commission for Diverse Communities, and she has several journal articles and book chapters to her credit. Dr. Hill-Jackson completed part of her undergraduate studies in London, England, at Kingston University, received her B.S. in Biology and Environmental Studies from Rutgers University, earned an M.A. in Conservation and Environmental Education from Rowan University, and completed her doctorate in Interdisciplinary

Educational Leadership at St. Joseph's University. Dr. Hill-Jackson is also a national and international speaker, has presented papers at various professional meetings and conferences, and provides consulting to educational and nonprofit agencies. She can be reached by e-mail at vhjackson@tamu.edu or on the web at www.thenexusgroup.info.

Chance W. Lewis is the Houston Endowment, Inc., Endowed Chair in urban education and an associate professor of urban education in the Department of Teaching, Learning, and Culture in the College of Education at Texas A&M University. Additionally, he is the co-chair of the urban education graduate program and co-director of the Center for Urban School Partnerships at Texas A&M University. Also, Dr. Lewis is the deputy director for research at the Center for African American Research and Policy at the University of Wisconsin–Madison. Dr. Lewis is the co-editor of the nationally acclaimed book and DVD entitled *White Teachers/Diverse Classrooms: A Guide for Building Inclusive Schools, Promoting High Expectations, and Eliminating Racism* (Stylus, 2006). He has also co-authored the book entitled *The Dilemmas of Being an African American Male in the New Millennium: Solutions for Life Transformation* (Infinity, 2008). Additionally, he recently completed the single-authored book entitled *An Educator's Guide to Working with African American Students: Strategies for Promoting Academic Success* (Infinity, 2009). Dr. Lewis has received more than $2 million in external research funding and has published more than 75 publications. Dr. Lewis received his B.S. and M.Ed. in business education and education administration/supervision from Southern University and his Ph.D. in Educational Leadership/Teacher Education from Colorado State University. At Texas A&M University, Dr. Lewis teaches courses in the field of urban education. Dr. Lewis can be reached by e-mail at chance.lewis@tamu.edu or on the web at http://www.chancewlewis.com.

Linda Darling-Hammond is Charles E. Ducommun Professor of Education at Stanford University, where she has launched the Stanford Center for Opportunity Policy in Education and the School Redesign Network and served as faculty sponsor for the Stanford Teacher Education Program. She is a former president of the American Educational Research Association and member of the National Academy of Education. Her research, teaching, and policy work focus on issues of school restructuring, teacher quality, and educational equity. From 1994 to 2001, she served as executive director of the National Commission on Teaching and America's Future, a blue-ribbon panel whose 1996 report, *What Matters Most: Teaching for America's Future*, led to sweeping policy changes affecting teaching and teacher education. In 2006, this report was named one of the most influential affecting U.S. education and Darling-Hammond was named one of the nation's 10 most influential people affecting educational policy over the last decade. She recently served as the leader of President Barack Obama's education policy transition team.

Among Darling-Hammond's more than 300 publications are *Preparing Teachers for a Changing World: What Teachers Should Learn and Be Able to Do* (with John Bransford, for the National Academy of Education, winner of the Pomeroy Award from AACTE), *Powerful Teacher Education: Lessons From Exemplary Programs* (Jossey-Bass, 2006); *Teaching as the Learning Profession* (Jossey-Bass, 1999) (co-edited with Gary Sykes), which received the National Staff Development Council's Outstanding Book Award for 2000, and *The Right to Learn*, recipient of the American Educational Research Association's Outstanding Book Award for 1998.

Martin Haberman is a distinguished professor, emeritus, at the of University Wisconsin–Milwaukee and the 2009 winner of the American Education Research Association Legacy Award. AERA is the most prestigious research association in the United States. Over the past 50 years Dr. Haberman has developed more teacher education programs that have prepared more teachers for children in poverty than anyone in the history of American education. The most widely known of his programs is the National Teacher Corps, which is based on his intern program in Milwaukee. He is an advisor for alternative certification programs around the country and has developed effective ways of bringing more minorities into teaching. His interviews for selection of teachers who will be successful with children in poverty are used in 260 cities throughout the country. His principal selection interview is currently used in 25 cities. Both interviews have online pre-screeners that can be accessed nationally to assist school districts' use of research-based tools for selection of educators. Star Principal and Star Teacher Selection Interview trainings are based on his research and book publications, which are now available from the Haberman Educational Foundation in Houston. Currently, his developmental efforts focus on helping to resolve the crises in urban schools serving 7 million at-risk students by helping these school districts "grow their own" carefully selected teachers and principals.

In addition to an extremely long list of publications (8 books, 50 chapters, 200 articles and papers) and numerous research studies, Professor

Haberman served 6 years as the editor of the *Journal of Teacher Education* and 11 years as dean in the University of Wisconsin, trying to apply the successes of extension in rural America to the problems of life in urban areas. Professor Haberman has served on 11 editorial boards. He holds several awards for his writing, a Standard Oil Award for Excellence in Teaching, a special award from the Corporation for Public Broadcasting, and American Association of Colleges for Teacher Education (AACTE) medals for offering a Hunt Lecture as well as the Pomeroy Award. He is a distinguished member of the Association of Teacher Educators (ATE) and a laureate of Kappa Delta Pi. The University of Wisconsin Board of Regents has named him a distinguished professor. In November 2004, Dr. Haberman was awarded the Distinguished Alumni Award in Education at Columbia University. In March 2005, the Haberman Educational Foundation published his latest book: *Star Teachers: The Ideology and Best Practice of Effective Teachers of Diverse Children and Youth in Poverty.* January 2009 marks the second printing of this publication. Contact the Haberman Educational Foundation at http://www.habermanfoundation.org.

Nathalia E. Jaramillo is an assistant professor in the department of Education Studies, Cultural Foundations at Purdue University. She is author and co-author of numerous articles and essays on the topic of critical pedagogy, feminism, and education politics and policy. Most recently, she co-authored the book entitled *Pedagogy and Praxis in the Age of Empire: Towards a New Humanism.* She is affiliated with the Centro Internacional Miranda in Caracas, Venezuela, and is currently involved in research that examines the Bolivarian education model.

Peter McLaren is a professor in the Division of Urban Schooling, the Graduate School of Education and Information Studies, University of California–Los Angeles. He is the author and editor of 45 books and hundreds of scholarly articles and chapters. Professor McLaren's writings have been translated into 20 languages. Four of his books have won the Critic's Choice Award of the American Educational Studies Association. In 2004, one of his books, (Pearson/Allyn & Bacon, 5th edition, 2007) *Life in Schools*, was chosen by an international panel of experts organized by the Moscow School of Social and Economic Sciences and by the Ministry of Education of the Russian Federation as one of the 12 most significant education books in existence worldwide. McLaren was the inaugural recipient of the Paulo Freire Social Justice Award presented by Chapman University, California. The charter for

La Fundacion McLaren de Pedagogia Critica was signed at the University of Tijuana in July 2004. La Catedra Peter McLaren was inaugurated in Venezuela on September 15, 2006, as part of a joint effort between El Centro Internacional Miranda and La Universidad Bolivariana de Venezuela. Professor McLaren left his native Canada in 1985 to work in the United States, where he continues to be active in the struggle for socialism. A Marxist humanist, he lectures widely in Latin America, North America, Asia, and Europe. His most recent book (co-authored with Nathalia Jaramillo) is *Pedagogy and Praxis in the Age of Empire* (Sense Publishers, 2009). With Steve Best and Anthony Nocella, he has co-edited a forthcoming book, *Academic Repression: Reflections From the Academic Industrial Complex* (AK Press, in press) . Professor McLaren's work has been the subject of two recent books: *Teaching Peter McLaren: Paths of Dissent*, edited by Marc Pruyn and Luis M. Huerta-Charles (Peter Lang Publications, 2005) (translated into Spanish as *De La Pedagogia Critica a la pedagogia de la Revolucion: Ensayos Para Comprender a Peter McLaren*, Siglo Veintiuno Editores) and *Peter McLaren, Education, and the Struggle for Liberation*, edited by Mustafa Eryaman (Hampton Press, 2008).

Jennifer Milam is an assistant professor of Elementary and Middle Grades Curriculum at the University of Akron in the Department of Curriculum and Instructional Studies. Her primary areas of interest and research are curriculum and cultural studies, specifically the intersections of race and ethnicity in education and teaching. Jennifer serves as an assistant editor of the *Journal of Curriculum and Pedagogy* as well as an external reviewer for the *International Journal of Qualitative Studies in Education* and the *Journal of Curriculum Theorizing*. Current projects include a qualitative exploration of *currere* and its uses in educational research, curriculum theory, and teacher education and theorizing the complexities, contradictions, and complications of being scholar/woman/mother/feminist.

Jennifer King Rice is associate professor in the Department of Education Policy Studies at the University of Maryland. She earned her M.S. and Ph.D. degrees from Cornell University. Prior to joining the faculty at the University of Maryland, she was a researcher at Mathematica Policy Research in Washington, D.C. Dr. Rice's research draws on the discipline of economics to explore education policy questions concerning the efficiency, equity, and adequacy of U.S. public education. Her current work focuses on teachers as a critical resource in the education process, and she is working on several projects focused on the policies and resources needed to hire and retain qualified teachers in difficult-to-staff schools. Her research has been published in numerous scholarly journals and edited volumes. She serves on the editorial boards of *Educational Evaluation and Policy Analysis, Education Finance and Policy,* and *Policy and Leadership in Schools.* She is co-editor (with Chris Roellke) of *Fiscal Policy in Urban Education* and is author of *Teacher Quality: Understanding the Effectiveness of Teacher Attributes,* winner of the 2005 American Association of Colleges for Teacher Education writing award. Dr. Rice has consulted with numerous state and federal agencies and policy research organizations and was recognized with a National Academy of Education/Spencer Foundation postdoctoral fellowship in 2002–2003. She has served two terms on the board of directors and is currently president of the American Education Finance Association.

Jeanita W. Richardson is an associate professor in the Department of Public Health Sciences at the University of Virginia and is concurrently the president of the Turpeau Consulting Group, an organization supporting the creation of health and educational policy collaborations. Her research expertise has been garnered from senior-level policy positions in state government, and as an educator in public and postsecondary institutions. Her University of Virginia graduate degrees include a Ph.D. in Educational Policy and a master's degree (M.Ed.) in Curriculum and Instruction, and her bachelor of science in Biology Education was awarded from Temple University. Her scholarship highlights the divergent needs of dispossessed children and youth particularly as they pertain to the nexus between the health and learning readiness of children and has been featured in numerous publications and national and international conferences.

Kris Sloan is an assistant professor in the School of Education at St. Edward's University in Austin, Texas. In the summers, he teaches at the Massachusetts College of Liberal Arts in the Leadership Academy. Dr. Sloan has worked as a curriculum designer and has taught in the United States and abroad. He is the author of numerous journal articles and book chapters on the ways accountability-related curriculum policies influence the classroom practices of teachers and learning experiences of children, in particular children of color. His most recent book, *Holding Schools Accountable: A Handbook for Educators and Parents,* offers parents and teachers straightforward information about current accountability policies and clear advice on ways to demand accountability policies that lead to genuine improvements in educational quality and equity.

F. Blake Tenore, Alfred C. Dunn, Judson C. Laughter, and H. Richard Milner IV   **F. Blake Tenore**, doctoral student in Language, Literacy, and Culture at Vanderbilt University, is interested in the preparation of teachers for culturally and linguistically diverse students. He has presented on the topic at National Association for Gifted Children (NAGC), National Council of Teachers of English (NCTE), American Association of Colleges for Teacher Education (AACTE), and American Educational Research Association (AERA) and has co-authored multiple publications dealing with teacher education for diverse students. He has experience teaching in urban public schools and at the university level. **Alfred C. Dunn II** is currently a third-year doctoral student in the Department of Education Leadership and Policy and a member of the Experimental Education Research Training Program (ExPert), which is supported by the Institute for Education Sciences (IES) at Vanderbilt University. His research interests are teacher quality, teacher induction and mentoring, schools as organization, teacher job satisfaction, and teacher turnover. **Judson C. Laughter** is a clinical assistant professor of English education at the University of Tennessee, Knoxville. Dr. Laughter earned his Ph.D. from Peabody College of Vanderbilt University in 2009. His research and teaching interests include critical multicultural teacher education and the preparation of teachers for the diverse classroom. His current projects include the development of teacher education curricula for the preparation of White female pre-service teachers as change agents through dialogue and counter-narrative. **H. Richard Milner IV** is associate professor of Education in the Department of Teaching and Learning at Peabody College of Vanderbilt University. His research, policy, and teaching interests are urban education, race and equity in society and education, and teacher education. In 2006, Dr. Milner was awarded the SCE Early Career Award of the American Educational Research Association. Professor Milner has written more than 50 journal articles and book chapters and has edited or co-edited 3 books including: *Culture, Curriculum, and Identity in Education* (Palgrave Macmillan, 2010), *Diversity and Education: Teachers, Teaching, and Teacher Education* (Charles C. Thomas, 2009), and *Race, Ethnicity, and Education: The Influences of Racial and Ethnic Identity in Education,* with E. W. Ross (Praeger Publishers, 2006). He consults with school districts across the country regarding issues of diversity, equity, popular culture, teaching, and learning. He can be reached at rich.milner@vanderbilt.edu.

INDEX

Note: The letter *t* indicates a table; *n* indicates a footnote reference.

Also available from Stylus

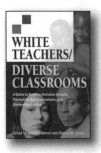

White Teachers / Diverse Classrooms
*A Guide to Building Inclusive Schools, Promoting High Expectations,
and Eliminating Racism*
Edited by Julie Landsman, Chance W. Lewis

"This book offers practical advice for teachers and administrators on ways to improve the education of students of color. Topics include recognizing white privilege, reforming multicultural education, confronting institutional racism, addressing the challenges of educating minority students in predominantly white schools, and forging alliances with students' parents and communities.

The contributors stress that white teachers must avoid assuming that children of color do not possess the necessary skills, knowledge or desire to learn, emphasizing that low expectations are the worst form of racism."—***Education Week***

"This is a very good book for teachers to put on their shelves; I recommend its use at the university level as a teaching tool as well."—***Multicultural Review***

White Teachers / Diverse Classrooms DVD
*Teachers and Students of Color Talk Candidly about Connecting with
Black Students and Transforming Educational Outcomes*
Edited by Julie Landsman, Chance W. Lewis

Interviews with Black students and experienced educators provide guidance on how to teach successfully in multicultural classes. The feature 33-minute track is enhanced by a further 83 minutes of footage that presents more extensive interviews with many of the participants, to add depth to pedagogical approaches they advocate.

- Insights and ideas to promote observation, reflection, and effective classroom practice
- Ideal for initiating constructive discussion in pre-service courses, and for professional development
- Defines the seven characteristics of successful multicultural teaching

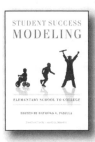

Student Success Modeling
Elementary School to College
Edited by Raymond V. Padilla
Foreword by Sarita E. Brown

"Focusing on the reasons for success in student performance rather than failure, Padilla presents a framework for understanding student success and how it can be improved and replicated. He presents a general model and one for specific, local situations and how they have been applied in a minority high school, community college, and Hispanic-Serving University, and to compare high-performing and non- high-performing elementary schools. Chapters address the characteristics of students, teachers, and the school, its resources, and barriers to success."—***Book News***

22883 Quicksilver Drive
Sterling, VA 20166-2102

Subscribe to our e-mail alerts: www.Styluspub.com